WORSHIP!

Your Tool to Departure
As The World's Economy
System Changes

THERESA B MUMFORD

Contents

WORSHIP!

Your Tool to Departure as the World's
Economy System Changes

~

Zimbabwe, Britain & the Christian
Church in Perspective

Theresa Babazile (Mhlabi) Mumford

Introduction

In February 2008 I had a vision. Since that time God has been speaking and revealing many other visions and dreams to me and as I pondered over them, I felt His Spirit leading me to put them down in writing as a matter of urgency. I cannot afford to sit on these revelations any longer, as doing so would not only be letting the Lord Jesus Christ down, but I would be living in disobedience to God as these revelations are not just for me, they are for the benefit of His people, the Body of Christ and all who are yet to receive Him as their Lord and Saviour.

It is a one-day-at-a-time kind of book, because I rely totally on God's guidance and direction. I had a few eye-opening experiences from the people He allowed into my life and those He led me to. Some experiences were good, some were not, but they were also part of my education, my journey of discovery. Surely the Lord God will do nothing, but He revealeth His secret unto His servants the prophets (Amos 3: 7). It is written that no weapon that is formed against thee shall prosper; and every tongue that shall rise against thee in judgment thou shall condemn. This is the heritage of the servants of the Lord, and their righteousness is of me, saith the Lord (Isaiah 54: 17).

The reader might find some of the issues raised in this book very sensitive. The names of certain people may be mentioned but some may not be revealed. I was not sure if I should write some of the revelations, but God emphasised the Gospel Truth and that He only rewards courage! He wants His people to be aware of the time and the season. He wants His people to be able to humble themselves and repent of all their rebellious and evil ways. He wants His people to prepare for the coming of His Son to the earth for His Church. Jesus is coming sooner than we realise!

The unreachable must be reached; the untouchable must be touched. Jesus did not die for a small fraction of people, He died for all nations on this earth. Therefore the Body of Christ cannot silently monopolise the gospel truth at the expense of the lost souls and the poor. We cannot allow fear to hold us back. Believe in the Lord thy God, so shall you be established: Believe in His prophets, so shall ye prosper (2 Chronicles 20:20). He is a loving God and a fearful God. Therefore I will not fear what men can do to me. I only fear God. God's promises are yea and amen!

I hope and pray that this book will encourage us all as we read it to focus on our purpose here on earth and to refuse to be observers, but to take our positions and be active participants in what God is orchestrating on the earth today for the establishment of His kingdom. I also hope that this book will challenge some readers and help them from their slumber.

I surrender this book back to God, as He is the one who enabled me to write it. Therefore may this book give Him the Glory! I thank Him for Divine Guidance and Direction throughout the writing of this book and for the revelations He gave me in the process. He is amazing! I also thank God for those He used to preach messages that woke me up from my slumber and gave me hope again. I am grateful for God's redeeming Grace, the forgiveness of my sins and being reconciled back to Him through Jesus Christ, my Redeemer and my Saviour.

I thank the Lord Jesus for the sacrifice He made on the cross of Calvary for me. I thank Him for the new identity I have in Him (1 Peter 2: 9 - But ye are a chosen generation, a royal priesthood, a holy nation, a peculiar people; that ye should shew forth the praises of Him who hath called you out of darkness into His marvellous light.) I also thank the Lord for His faithfulness at all times in my life and that His faithfulness makes guidance always available to me even in my darkest moments; His faithfulness will cause Him to finish that which He has begun in my life and I confess I'm fully persuaded that what He has promised, He is surely able to fulfil. For He promised and it is written: My grace is sufficient for thee: for my strength is made perfect in weakness (2 Corinthians 12:9). Therefore I am confident to say I can do all things through Christ, which strengtheneth me (Phil. 4:13); not because of who I am, but because of *whose* I am!

CHAPTER 1

The Silence of the Christian Church

In the beginning God created the heaven and the earth. And the earth was without form, and void; and darkness was upon the face of the deep. And the Spirit of God moved upon the face of the waters. And God said, Let there be light: and there was light.

Genesis 1:1–3

In the beginning was the Word, and the Word was with God, and the Word was God. The same was in the beginning with God. All things were made by Him; and without Him was not anything made that was made.

John 1:1–2

If the world began with God, why has His voice been shut out of the affairs of this world? Who gave the politicians the upper hand in decisions that have affected so many? When did the politicians become more important than God, the Creator of heaven and earth?

I once heard a great preacher confess, "I am not a politician." But this was a great man of God with amazing ideas and solutions that are vital for the current state of the world. He, and others I have heard, have the answers the whole world needs. God has put these great ideas in their hearts for such a time as this, but I do not know how they are hoping the politicians will know these ideas unless the politicians can hear them. How will the politicians know what is right to do if the Church is not speaking out concerning the biblical consequences of their rebellious behaviour to God?

For decades, most politicians have worked hard and have succeeded in kicking the Word of God out of their vicinity. Why has the Christian Church been silent about it?

God knows the names of the politicians and He knows the positions they have been put in and the reason they have been put in those positions. The fact is, most of them do not know God. They have no clue that He watches their performance. God never goes to sleep! "Behold He that keepeth Israel shall neither slumber nor sleep" (Psalms 121: 4).

If politicians involved God in all their decisions, they would be wiser and successful in all their accomplishments. The Holy Bible gives us an account of past clear examples of God's involvement in the affairs of the nations that feared Him and those that did not fear Him. These can be traced throughout the Old Testament in the books of Exodus, Kings and Chronicles and the struggles faced by God's Prophets, Moses, Joshua, Samuel, Elijah, Elisha, Isaiah, Jeremiah, Ezekiel, Daniel all the way down to Malachi. After Adam and Eve's fall, God always looked for upright men to use, men like Abraham, Noah and His prophets, men and women. He uses rich and poor, slave and master, child and adult, queens and kings, homeless and orphans. God is no respecter of persons (Acts 10:34).

If the Servants of God, who have been empowered by the Holy Ghost to move mountains and bring change in the lives of the poor and the suffering today, are using the excuse that "we are not politicians", what good is that? What good is it if God's Saints also suffer the consequences of the policies that are created, passed and legalised by unwise and unholy heathens in parliament? I say unwise, because wisdom only comes from God and the Holy Bible clearly states that the wisdom of this world is foolishness to God. What good is it that even the unborn child is already affected by the unholy policies that have been created by people who do not even know God?

For example, the Western Christian Church is silent on the oppression of asylum seekers. There is no repentance and therefore no compassion in the Western Christian Church as far as the plight of black Africans seeking asylum is concerned. Most of them are in prison awaiting the hearing of their cases. Some of those in prison actually left little children back in Zimbabwe. Those children are now homeless and they do not understand what happened to their mothers.

Others are professionally qualified doctors, teachers, artisans and so on, but they are not offered any jobs that relate to their positions. There are African doctors and lawyers working as cleaners, in McDonald's and in nursing homes as care workers. These are people who came to the West to find refuge. They have to work to survive because they cannot claim any kind of Social Security benefit while their immigration cases are still pending.

All former white Rhodesians are able to get the jobs they want and decent accommodation in the UK. If they were not white skinned, they could be in the same predicament as the black Zimbabweans.

Furthermore, every normal person desires to be loved, whether young or old. Love is something that young immigrants cannot put on hold while the Home Office is considering their asylum applications. Most young Zimbabweans desire marriage as opposed to cohabiting, yet when they approach local churches in the UK for help, they get shunned. Even though a church wedding is the first preference of most Zimbabweans, they have no option but to end up marrying in a Registry Office. I have been asked in the past few years to bless the marriages of my own relatives who were married in civil ceremonies after being turned down by their local churches. Just because our young people are awaiting asylum approval does not mean they have no desire to have an education or to marry and start families.

My own research shows me that the Church of England has always had the upper hand and the stronger voice in the affairs of the world. Why has the Church of England been silent about the postcolonial indebtedness of Africa to the West, or the instability and devastation of human life in Sub-Saharan Africa as a result of rigged elections and sponsored banditry. The Archbishop of York, Dr John Sentamu, a black man from Uganda, has been strongly campaigning against the injustices done to poor Third World states by politicians, but his efforts have been ignored, especially in Britain. The voice of the Anglo-Catholic Church has in the main been very subtle on issues of injustice. Could it be that it has been the main oppressor? That is food for thought for the body of Christ. "Ye shall know the truth and the truth shall make you free" (John 8:32).

CHAPTER 2

Christianity's Contribution to Third World Oppression

T he Railway Mission in Southern Africa and the building of the railway line from Cape to the North was very much the work of the Anglo-Catholic Church, also known as the Church of England, my own father's employer and oppressor.

Cecil John Rhodes and others are celebrated in the West as famous pioneers. However, they also brought harm to the people of Southern Africa, and those of Zimbabwe's Matabeleland in particular, in their quest for power and wealth (the Gold of Ophir from King Solomon's mines).

My father's detailed struggles and those of other black Anglican Priests in Rhodesia are highlighted in a book written by John Roden: *Northward from Cape Town: The Anglican Church Railway Mission in Southern Africa 1885–1980* (Sacram Publishing, 1999). Roden states (1999: 93) that in its final period the Railway Mission became involved with another "African school", that of Mbizi, in Zimbabwe, founded by one of the few African Railway Mission priests, Rev. John Mhlabi (my father).

At the Annual Festival of the Railway Mission, in September 1966, Harold Crane, the Missioner/Secretary, reported:

> *The two Railway Missioners who have the longest service with the mission are Rev. Noel Borerwe and the Rev. William Sigeca, our African Chaplains in Mashonaland and Matabeleland respectively. These two priests are veritable dynamos. They are as active and enthusiastic, zealous and diligent as they were when they joined the mission some six years ago. They are truly a blessing to the people and a wonderful example to all of us on the staff.*

After serving eight years with the Railway Mission William Sigeca was, in 1967, asked by Bishop Kenneth Skelton to go to St Athanasius's Mission at Ngamba, Ngai. His work was taken over by two priests, the Rev. John Mhlabi as Railway Missioner for Matabeleland, and the Rev. Matthius Damasane as priest-in-charge of the church of Christ the King, Sizinda (Roden, 1999: 245). Roden states:

> *If Fr. Borerwe is to be known as "The Church builder", then Fr. Mhlabi ought to be known as "The Letter writer". It is beyond the scope of this work to detail all the correspondence he entered into, particularly over his project of a "railway school" at Mbizi. Few people or organisations, whether they were the Executive Committee of the Railway Mission (Bulawayo), the London Committee, the World Council of Churches, the Rhodesia Railways, the bishops, or the government, plus various individuals, were spared his constant pleas for help. Even in retirement, letters still cross the world to would be supporters, including the writer [John Roden] soliciting help for his orphanage and other projects.*

Parts of my father's letter to the USPG in London (October 1972) illustrates the school project and his enthusiastic pleading:

> *I am an African Anglican Priest employed by the Diocese of Matabeleland along the Railway Lines in Matabeleland from Bulawayo to Victoria Falls, Bulawayo to Vila Salazar, P E A boarder to Beitbridge border and Bulawayo to Gwelo, finally Bulawayo to West Nicholson – Bulawayo into Botswana. I have done the Rhodesia Railways Mission work since 1968 up to now. Christianity is of a small beginning scale along the Rail lines everywhere in Rhodesia. My personal problem especially to the Eastern Lowveld areas to P.E.A border is poverty, shortage of food and shortage of Primary Schools for our African Education in these remote areas. Our Government accepts your cheques for charity.*
>
> *Here at Mbizi, there are over 170 little children who need a school... My bishop helped me in persuading the General Manager of the R.*

Railways to grant a Ground for the pupils ranging from 7 years old to even 13 to 14 without any pre-schooling knowledge at all.

The R. Railways have a ground for school facilities but they have no materials and money to grant towards the building of this new Pre-school class at all. As the school manager I appeal for money towards R.R. Mbizi African Village School which is very urgent indeed. [Details of rooms, costs, fees, facilities etc., follow along with details of other projects.]

Roden reports that USPG forwarded the letter to the London Committee of the Railway Mission. Although the Committee was sympathetic towards the appeal, they were obliged to refer it back to the Committee in Rhodesia, especially as they were unsure of the project's viability. The chief problem was that the Mbizi School project involved permissions and decisions from the Railway Mission, the Rhodesia Railways, the Ministry of Finance, the Rural Council and the Ministry of Education. No single authority would or could take overall responsibility. This is shown in a Minute of the Executive Committee of the Railway Mission in April 1973:

The report submitted by the Secretary on his investigations into the feasibility of establishing an African School at Mbizi, was discussed together with the findings of Fr. R. Woods on his "on-the-spot" investigations.

It was accepted that the proposed site at Mbizi was totally unsuitable and that future plans must be directed towards the site offered under certain conditions by Nuanetsi Estates. This location is situated three miles from Mbizi and had its own borehole.

The various responsibilities of the Mission and the Railway Administration in this matter were again discussed. The Chairman [bishop of Matabeleland] stated that whilst he appreciated the Mission lacked the means and the Railway Administration had no function in regard to the education he did feel it was the Mission's duty to officially bring the Railway's attention to the lack of educational facilities at Mbizi for he saw it as part of their duty to their employees. The bishop added that he did not consider the provision of these facilities would be setting a precedent.

In reply Mr. Wright stated that he appreciated the Chairman's point of view but was restricted both by legislation and resources as to what he could do. The Railway Administration saw quite clearly that, particularly in areas away from the main centres of population, it was their responsibility to provide housing, services and welfare facilities but schooling was never taken to be a Railway function. Under the present Railways Act he was not allowed to make any financial grant to an educational institution without the permission of the Minister of Finance. Indeed, since direct Government control of the Railway finances was instituted the Mission had become the sole recipient of annual donations.

It appears to me here that it was my father's oppressor, the Bishop of Matabeleland, who made my father's work difficult. If the Mission had the money as the sole recipient of annual donations, could the Bishop not help my father build reasonable facilities for the poor railway workers and their families, claiming reimbursement from the Railway Administration? The Bishop of Matabeleland clearly did not care about my father's challenges in the rural area; he was very comfortable in his Bulawayo city home in the suburb. How was my father supposed to ignore the needs of the people he was sent to evangelise to? It is obvious here that the building of the railway line was more important to the Bishop of Matabeleland than the needs of the poor black workforce.

Roden confirms that no further action was taken on Mbizi school. My father's letter to him of March 1995 gives the end of the story:

Re: Mbizi School (1971–73)
I brought in a female teacher in 1971 and another one in 1972 and in 1973; a male teacher was in as well to teach the boys carpentry and woodwork, while lady teachers did cookery, basketry and washing utensils and yard cleaning and sweeping, whilst boys did agriculture and vegetable gardening and caring for cottage-fruit trees in the cottage for parents.

I used to say Mass at 6pm to 7pm, the church music teaching for 45 minutes, and then give Ndebele, Shona and Lozwi pamphlets for their

own interest in the [anglo-]Catholic faith. During the morning time I used
to say Mass and then group children and teach them stories in the Bible.
Their parents used to group with their children as well.

(i)   *The school was just a tent of Railway sail to cover the roof of sticks and*
      wood from wind and rain.

(ii)   *Music players used to visit Mbizi School to organise concerts.*

(iii) *The money collected paid the schoolteachers and paid for their food*
      rations. The food stuff, soap, candles, utensils, exercise books, ballpoints
      and reading books were cheap [at] that time, and people liked the children's
      education, because it was free.

(iv)   *The huge sail classroom was along the back yard of the cottage. Some*
      children who were in Standard V and VI did go to Dadaya Secondary
      School, Zvishavane.

(v)   *I was given the site of sails by the Station Master, including huge bundles*
      of sails, poles that were not being used. The Cottage Bossboy agreed with
      the Station Master to choose a free site for a Primary School.

The terrorists came in and the Railway Station Master and the Bossboy
were removed to Bulawayo. There was danger in their lives. In 1973 the
Railway Mission was discontinued between 1973 to 1974 because of
Terrorists and all black priests worked in Bulawayo until 1980 onwards.

Railway Mbizi Station employees whose children were at school, were
paying Levy for the Teachers who were not trained.

My questions here include, did my father have a proper facility to hold
church services or did he use the same site as the school? Where did he
cook his meals or sleep in rural Mbizi? What did the Bishop think about
all this? I cannot ask my father such questions now as he forgets and gets
very agitated. His mind needs God's healing hand and I believe that God
will restore his memory and that he will live to see his dreams fulfilled
in Jesus' mighty name.

Roden comments, "This was clearly not the noblest episode in the
Railway Mission's history, although it is difficult to know what more
the Mission could have done, given the intransigence of the various
authorities."

My father remained on the Mission for a further two years. When he left, the Railway General Manager, Trevor Wright, said:

Fr. Mhlabi had [become] a worthy member of that conscientious band of Anglican clergy who have, since the early days of the Railways in Southern Africa, brought spiritual comfort to the people of all races and creeds along the line of rail. But the rigors of almost continual travelling, mainly on goods trains, with attendant trips on bicycle and on foot became a strain for him, and the executive committee decided that he had earned a respite from this arduous life. He was transferred to Luveve.

This was a very sarcastic statement to be written in the railway newspaper about my father when all his efforts to help his fellow African people, the manpower on the railway line and their suffering wives and children, had been totally ignored. He never got a response to any of his letters because he was not respected or regarded as anyone important. Meanwhile there was a good school for the white railway Missioners' children and proper church facilities for them.

However, I am grateful that God always has faithful, dedicated, compassionate and uncommon people like the author John Roden. Without his book, I would never have had a full picture of my father's struggles outside his home. My father never told us anything about his struggles. Roden's book gives an honest and detailed account of the experiences of the Railway Missioners, black or white, from the Cape to Rhodesia, now Zimbabwe.

The missionary life

Prior to being transferred to the Railway Mission in 1968, my father had other severe mission field experiences, such as his sudden transfer from St Mark's Mission in Lower Gwelo to the jungle of Gokwe, where daily encounters with wild animals and poisonous snakes became a way of life for us, whether indoors or outdoors. Our first long, dangerous journey was during the heavy rainfall season, travelling on a huge lorry that carried all our belongings and us on the back of it with the furniture. Being faced with life-threatening tsetse flies, mosquitoes and wildlife without any protection was a great challenge for our family.

Our neighbours, the Tonga people, still walked along in a line with their bows and poisoned arrows, dressed in their traditional attire with barely any clothes on their bodies. Funerals were the order of the day as they perished from malaria. There was always a wailing cry among the Tonga people after the death of a loved one and I never forgot that until sickness hit me too. I remember my mother holding me as I walked, my chest feeling like a solid rock. My mother's hot soup was all I could eat and it would come out gushing after that.

One day I was left sitting in one of the huts when a rainbow-coloured snake crawled in. I depended on people moving me around; if they forgot about me I would silently remain there until they remembered me. In desperation, I made my first call for my mother after a long period of not speaking. To have been able to move my lips and project my voice was the greatest miracle. However, the snake left me alone very quickly at the sound of my deep, slow cry for mama. God must have allowed it to creep into that hut just to force me to talk again.

It was in Gokwe that I learnt how to speak, read and write the Shona language at the age of 6. I started school at the age of 4 as I refused to remain at home. I accompanied my older siblings every morning to school, which was only around the corner. Teachers had to accept me in their classrooms because my father was the Mission Priest. I never thought of myself as a child, I always saw myself as a grown-up person.

There was no borehole water in the Gokwe mission. As children we collected water from the huge, dry bed of a river we called Rwizi, which we had to climb down the cliff to reach. All you saw was sand, but as you dug the dry sand clean water appeared and filled the hole. We scooped it into our buckets very quickly before the hyenas caught up with us. My sister and I had to quickly learn the different cries of a hyena: we knew from the cry when the hyena was too close so we could run for our lives. We had to learn to jump over poisonous snakes as we ran back home too. It was a life of adventure.

We left Gokwe when my father caught malaria and had to go to Silobela to recuperate in the care of my maternal grandmother's brother and his son in law, who were rich businessmen. The family still runs the bakery in Bulawayo and have endured a great deal of suffering at the hands of Robert Mugabe's looters. When my father recovered and went back to his duties as an Anglican priest, he was transferred to Tshabalala in Bulawayo, where he became a Railway Missioner.

In Bulawayo our family life was not easy because my father was often very frustrated; there were often periods of hardship due to his unmet endeavours, as it was him who saw at first hand the needs of the railway workers and their families, hence the burden on him to minister to them.

All we knew of my father as children was that he had a nickname my mother and her sisters, our aunties, had given him: *usvunguzane*, the whirlwind. This described his arrival home from his Mission trips. There were two sides to my father. Our home was a place where he did not pretend to be the goody-goody priest to anyone but could be his real self. If you were caught in the way of the whirlwind, all his frustrations would be vented on you. To be able to assess him properly, we ran into the house like mice as soon as we heard the sound of his motorcycle.

As a result of the tough way in which we were raised, for years no physical pain could move me enough to cause tears to come out of my eyes. But we all still loved our father because he was our father and we respected him. He tried hard to educate us, feed us and protect us from the outside world. We were not allowed to play with the neighbourhood children, but we sneaked out to play during his absence. The Ndebele people say, *Imamba yalukile, ubuchakide buchelesile*: there is freedom among the little birds when the black mamba is absent.

Ten children were not easy to handle, but we were content with what we had. We never envied other people. To this day, there is no envy in my heart. I thank God for the father He gave us, who taught us how to pray on our knees and to be grateful to God for every meal. Salvation was not part of the Anglican Church's theological concept at the time, we were simply a religious family.

However, we never slept on a hungry stomach. My father hated hunger and I cannot bear the thought of orphaned children on the streets of Zimbabwe today, going without food or digging up garbage for food. This is a curse on our nation that came with Robert Mugabe's independence. Even the thugs who walked the streets in those days had proper homes. They were wild and mischievous young men who robbed people as a bad habit because they had not made it in school, therefore they vented their frustrations on others. Most would not work for a white man and therefore they chose an easy lifestyle.

The true home of every black family was in the rural area. Cities were mainly for workers and their families, because cities came with British colonialism. Otherwise most black people preferred life in the countryside, where they kept their livestock and grew their own food crops for their livelihood. However, as a child I observed a lot of poverty and suffering among the families of Anglican priests.

A black Anglican priest's life was not his own because of having to be moved from one region to the other. No furniture or any financial subsidy was provided for the move, yet they obediently took the Bishop's orders without any protest. My parents had to rely on the community's kind gestures in most cases for provision. Relying on the community's kind gestures was very dangerous for my family. A few neighbours tried to wipe us all out by bringing cooked food to my parents. On one occasion it was a large container of home-made cottage cheese which in Ndebele we call *amasi*. In St Mark's or at St Patrick's in Lower Gwelo, we never ate any of the food that was brought to our Mission home by the neighbours. We had a family dog, Puza (named after Joshua Nkomo's political party, ZAPU, that was banned by Ian Smith at the time). Puza had just had a lot of puppies. As a child, I loved to go round and have a look at the puppies, but I was very disappointed when my late uncle Solomon, who lived with us at the time, gave them the cottage cheese. However, the day they were given the cottage cheese from the neighbour, they all died. I never forgot how they looked when I found them; they had all died with very swollen throats from the cottage cheese. That's how we were all supposed to have died. The second occasion was when some *inkobe*, a cooked pot of a mixed salad of nuts, maize, brown peas and beans, was brought for us. Again, my uncle Solomon gave it to our chickens; they all died. All that my poor parents were being threatened for was their large family of beautiful daughters. We were all very pretty as children, I must admit.

My brother once ate from a relative's home and he sustained a swollen belly. He looked like those round African frogs with tiny legs that we call *unanane bosele-sele* in Ndebele. They move very slowly and they bury themselves under the soil. If you poke their backside it produces a milky sweat. Parents had to force my brother to drink plenty of milk to flush the poison out. However, my younger brother was not so lucky: at the age of 2 he came back home with meningitis after vising a relative with my older siblings, he lost his hearing and ended up deaf and dumb.

Owning livestock was the normal way of life for an average black family, but if my parents had to acquire livestock, where would they have kept that and who would have looked after the goats, sheep, cows and donkeys? If the Anglo-Catholic church had really cared for black priests, they would have made proper provision for them besides the little income they paid them. All they cared for was the building of the railway line and for our fathers to teach humility and submission to the workforce.

While Dr. Joshua Nkomo, in his capacity as the leader of the PF ZAPU party, struggled for democracy and equality as a so-called terrorist leader, my father also struggled for equality as a native Anglo-Catholic priest. The Railway Mission line in Southern Rhodesia would not have been a success without the manpower contribution of those poor hungry "natives", as confirmed in John Roden's book.

As a native Anglican priest, my father was left to deal with the consequences of oppression. He saw at first hand the pain and suffering of the families of the natives who worked on building the railway line; yet he had an obligation to introduce to the native railway workers and their hungry families the gospel of the white missionary, their very oppressor. "And ye shall know the truth and the truth shall make you free" (John 8: 32).

The black Anglican priests were the ones who did the missionary work of evangelising the country's rural areas on foot, as hungry as they were.

In most cases my father would use his own income to help the people, despite his own large family needs. We simply lived beyond poverty, as my father came back home with hardly any money left. In Bulawayo my mother had to find a job, first as a maid for a white family and later in the textile industry. Even though my paternal grandfather was a prominent businessman, he never did much to educate my mother and her sisters because he had many women in his life, like King Solomon, his ancestor. My mother and her sisters actually worked in their father's businesses. It was my father who encouraged my mother to study.

In the suburbs, the Chairman of the Railway Mission and my father's boss were living very comfortably. I know because I visited his house twice when there were functions in Rhodesia: for me it was like being in heaven!

In Rhodesia, our black fathers were always regarded as boys. They cleaned the offices, ran with the tea trolley from office to office, hand-delivered external mail around the local offices and did the banking. So how did they handle being treated like innocent and naïve children by their oppressive bosses and then switch to being fathers and husbands in their own homes? I have observed over the years that even riches and education have failed to eliminate the emotional damage and racial inferiority complex of most African black men. This is worsened by the fact that those who oppressed them never repented, because the African oppression never stopped.

In 1960, when Rhodesia was still a British colony, my father had a £1000 winning lottery ticket. However his boss, the Bishop of Matabeleland, gave my father an ultimatum to hand over his winning ticket or risk being struck off the register as an Anglican Priest, since priests were not allowed to play the lottery. My father handed the ticket to the Bishop and chose to continue as a poor, struggling priest. It is not for me to judge whether or not it was justified under the circumstances for the Bishop to relieve my father of his winnings when my father was not paid enough to support his seven children (the family later grew to 10 children) as well as his own widowed mother, my grandmother, "MaDhlamini".

When my father came to Britain in 1998, he hoped to find sponsorship for completion of the building work at his orphanage and old people's home in Matabeleland. My husband helped him with the information he required to apply. However, he was turned down for the reason that funding is only available to local charities. But when I did some further research, I found out that most of the local charities also help charities abroad, in poor parts of Europe and Russia mainly but hardly in Africa. I then researched where the funding for local charities actually comes from; to my surprise I found that the British Government for this very reason set up the UK Lottery Fund. How ironic.

CHAPTER 3

We Are Still Being Ignored

In 2008, after I read about the campaign of the Archbishop of York, Dr John Sentamu, in support of the plight of Zimbabwean refugees in the UK and against the cruel government of Robert Mugabe, I phoned the Office of the Archbishop of York to find out how I could get hold of him by letter or by email. His assistant advised me to send my email and attachments to her address and she would pass it on to him.

Below is the email I sent to the Archbishop of York, which unfortunately went unanswered.

Subject: For the attention of Archbishop Dr John Sentamu: Please help my father accomplish his vision for the orphans and the homeless

Dear Man of God,

I have been following your burden for the suffering people of Zimbabwe and the world in general. I would like to say to you, even though you might not have received any "thank you cards or roses" the people of Zimbabwe very much appreciate your voice and your efforts will never go unnoticed by God Himself. May God continue to strengthen you as you press on towards the mark of the high calling. Saint Paul in 1 Cor. 16: 9 stated that "For a great door and effectual is opened unto me, and there are many adversaries." Adversaries are a sign that you are disturbing the plans of Satan and his agents, the workers of iniquity. God be with you.

However, to introduce myself, I am 49 years of age and the 7th born of the ten children of the retired Rev. John Mhlabi. I met my English husband back in Zimbabwe where we got married and came to live here in April 1994. My husband was seconded by British Rail to train the Botswana Rail Staff in computing in 1988. I met him through my cousin he worked with in Botswana Railways. His contract finished in 1990 and he had to come back to Britain. He then came back to Zimbabwe to marry me in March 1994; this is when I moved to Britain as well. My father was able to visit Britain in 1998, which he enjoyed very much. He visited most of the cathedrals here including St Paul's in London. He actually took communion in St Paul's Cathedral. We have photographs of my father on that wonderful occasion.

All my father's friends of around his age or younger, the former Anglican priests of Rhodesia now Zimbabwe, have since died and my father is kept alive by the hope that his orphanage home will one day be sponsored and the building completed.

The building of Siyabonga (We are grateful) Orphanage Home began back in 1992/3 after a struggle. My father's only surviving brother, Moses, is the builder, but his efforts have been crushed by lack of funding and most of the rooms are still half built to this day. My uncle Moses still lives out there. The home is near a farm owned by a white farmer and I understand he helped with food provision sometimes in that they bought from him. My father has not been able to visit his orphanage home in a long time due to economic hardship causing transport problems for him, poverty and now his old age. When he visited us in 1998, his mind was more on getting funding for his orphanage home and he never rested from it. He then asked my husband and me to take over and finish off the orphanage, but I did not answer him, as I did not have much interest in it as his vision was not my vision at the time, but now it is my vision and my burden too. I had seen him suffer for funding just for the home to reach where it is today. He used to get financial help from the casino owners and runners there who played and then donated funds to him sometimes. This has not happened for him in a long time. However, his efforts to appeal for funding when he visited here were all turned down. I have a letter written to him by the Grants Administrator of Charities Aid Foundation (CAF), the organisation that funds charities here and internationally, which my father appealed to in 1998. He was, however, turned down for the reason that his request fell outside their Trustees' current policy.

My father is now too old to visit me. He spends all his time in his bedroom there in Zimbabwe, reading the newspapers and his Bible. I wonder if the young priests of Zimbabwe remember to take the Holy Communion to him. My mother is quite old as well. Unless those with cars offer them a lift to church, they remain at home. He is simply a forgotten man. Telephoning home has been a problem as there are a lot of power cuts and poor network or reception.

My father's poverty was not necessary. As a young priest, the Anglican Bishops in Rhodesia always moved him around the rural and remote parts of the country, where he was always expected to evangelise from scratch. As a result we survived a lot of danger from the communities where we lived. They would bring food to my father and my father never allowed us to touch the food, he would give it to the chickens and they would all die. At one time they brought milk and my father gave it to the puppies. The puppies all died with swollen throats. I was only about three years or four years old, but I remember all these incidents. My father never had an opportunity to establish himself anywhere in Rhodesia as we were always on the move. While other families had cattle and goats etc., my father owned none. He did many years of missionary work, developing many parts of rural Rhodesia and building churches from scratch and schools in different remote areas such as Gokwe, where our lives were always at risk from wild animals, as the house we lived in was not well secured. Snakes always crept in; the area was full of tsetse flies and mosquitoes that almost took my life and my father's life. As my maternal grandmother lived in Silobela at the time, we all moved to live with her there. This is where my father recuperated from malaria. Afterwards, my father was eventually moved to settle in the city of Bulawayo where he was assigned by the Bishop of Matabeleland, to work for the Railway Mission. We never spent a week with him. My mother missed her husband as they hardly spent time together.

My father's struggles as a Railway Mission Anglican priest are highlighted in the book I have in my possession, Northward From Cape Town written by Senior Chaplain, Selby Coalfield Industrial Chaplaincy and part-time priest-in-charge of a small parish near York. Dr David Hope endorsed the Foreword of this book in 1999, the then Archbishop of York. Pages 93, 245, 250–4, and 294 highlight these struggles. All my father's friends who are mentioned there are now dead. Like I said beforehand, *the only thing keeping my father alive is the vision that God gave him, to build an orphanage and old people's home. "Where there is no vision, people perish" (Prov. 29: 18).*

In the early 1960s my father won a lottery of £1000 but the Bishop of Matabeleland took it away from him because my father was not supposed to have played the lottery as a priest. I disagree totally with this action by the Bishop. My father was thinking of the welfare of his huge poor family. Proverbs 13: 22 states that "A good man leaves an inheritance for his children's children: and the wealth of the sinner is laid up for the just." My father is a good man but he doesn't have any inheritance to leave his children's children, our children. Haggai 2: 8 states: "The silver is mine, and the gold is mine, saith the Lord of hosts." Ps 24: 1 states: "The earth is the Lord's, and the fullness thereof; the world, and they that dwell therein." Needless to say that without money, we cannot reach the world for Jesus Christ. So, what I do not understand is that if purchasing a lottery ticket was sinful, why then is the Lottery Fund expected to go towards good causes? Isn't this a contrast in beliefs? Is it not hypocrisy then if charities are to receive funds from the Lottery Fund?

However, I was only a year or less old when this happened in 1960, but long after it happened, I always heard this thing being spoken about and other late priests, my father's friends, were not amused by this move by the Bishop then.

My question is: what then did Bishop – do with my father's lottery ticket? I keep thinking about this, whether he threw it into the bin or he gave it back to the Lottery Fund, or did he keep it for his family, or did he use it to meet the needs of the church? Only God knows the truth and what I like about God is that He is no respecter of persons, He is a God of justice. I believe with all my heart that my father would not have been this poor if the Bishop had not forced him to hand over his ticket. One thing I know about my father is that he always obeyed his superiors. He ran like a child at the order of his superiors. I never forgot this. My father was a faithful man.

All I'm asking you to do is help my forgotten father. He is now looking shameful to other pastors of other churches. Rev. – of the Assemblies of

God Church used to live next door but one when he started the Assemblies of God Church in Bulawayo. I recently asked him to visit my father just to ensure that he is in the right standing with God. He then asked me if he is being looked after by the church at all. I told him that he receives a small amount of pension, which does not even buy bread. He only gets it every six months or so and it reaches him after a long delay. It comes from South Africa.

Looking after my parents is our burden, and it is very hard. I wish I could have my father here so that I could cook him nice food. My father never wanted to see hungry people, yet he has suffered hunger right there in Zimbabwe. When I think of my father I'm very tearful. I care for my first daughter who is disabled from birth due to brain damage. Otherwise, I wish my father and mother could be here with me to eat bread in their last days. The Anglican Church they served so faithfully all their lives does not remember them any longer.

I love my father and I miss him very much. I only want justice for him and his orphanage home. I will also send to you my father and mother's recent photos taken by my sister's husband during my father's birthday celebration in May. He is now very old. He still keeps his white priesthood collar on!

Even though I had no reply, I followed this up with a subsequent email:

Further to my last email about my father, I forgot to mention that after he was relieved of the Railway Mission work, he was put in charge of the Holy Cross Church in Luveve, Bulawayo from 1974 to 1976. He was again moved back to the rural area. This time he was sent to Tsholotsho in 1976 to 1983/4 where he was the priest-in-charge of the Anglican Church that served the community there. In Tsholotsho, my father lived alone because my mother could not leave her job as her income was much needed to sustain the family, and hence the accessibility of schools in Bulawayo for our education. However, my father enjoyed helping the poor community he served in Tsholotsho. He grew vegetables of every kind in his church garden and freely gave them to his congregation. He *also distributed food and blankets to the poor there. People used to come there for food and blankets, as a result of which Mugabe's Fifth Brigade or Gukurahundi threatened his life when they accused him of being a traitor, feeding dissidents, and thoroughly beat him for it and left him for almost dead, but my father still survived. This resulted in his transfer back to Bulawayo where he remained as a part-time priest up to the time of his retirement.*

I thought I should also mention this to you as part of my father's struggles as a priest. After his retirement he became passionate about helping the orphans. He put all his energy in pursuing his vision for the orphanage and old people's home. He managed to acquire land about 100 miles from Bulawayo. The orphanage home still needs completion as a lot of work was already accomplished.

To this day I have received no reply.

For decades the Christian Church, which represents the Body of Christ, has failed to set a heavenly example of harmony and unity, but has taken the upper hand in instigating racial hatred, division and oppression. Even Jesus washed the feet of His disciples, so how could we be better than our Master? We continue to undermine others and to do good only to our kind, those who are close to us.

The black African man, because of racial oppression, has therefore believed the lie of the devil that Jesus is for white people only. This lie has for decades been embraced by many oppressed black African people and others. It has not done much good except bring more misery and poverty to those who reject Christ based on their oppression. "My people are destroyed for lack of knowledge: because thou has rejected knowledge, I will also reject thee, that thou shalt be no priest to me: seeing thou hast forgotten the law of thy God, I will also forget thy children" (Hosea 5: 6).

CHAPTER 4

The Damaged Identity of the Black Man

Jesus came to the earth for all people, He was God the Son. The Word became flesh and dwelt among us. "Believe in the Lord your God, so shall ye be established; believe His prophets, so shall ye prosper" (2 Chronicles 20: 20).

The oppressor hid the gospel truth from the oppressed black people, the black slave. In Southern Africa the gospel truth was only made available to the upper class, not the slaves. This was the oppressor's ideology. The oppressed black people were all pushed into the Islamic religion, to worship Allah. This is the reason for the consequences we see today. This was not what God instructed the missionary, to use the gospel to oppress His black people. This was a further betrayal of the Lord Jesus. His suffering was not in vain; Jesus did not suffer for the gospel to be treated as a lottery.

For He knew who should betray Him; therefore said he, Ye are not all clean.

John 13:11

So after He had washed their feet, and had taken His garments, and was set down again, he said unto them, Know ye what I have done to you? Ye call me Master and Lord: and ye say well for so I am. If I then, your Lord and Master, have washed your feet; ye also ought to wash one another's feet. For I have given you an example, that ye should do as I have done to you. Verily, verily, I say unto you, The servant is not greater than his lord; neither he that is sent greater than he that sent him. If ye know these things, happy are ye if you do them.

John 13: 12–17

Only God can restore the damaged identity of the black man. This damage can be corrected, because the sacrifice was already made for all humanity. Jesus paid the price for the restoration of our lost identity. His body was broken for this purpose. His blood was shed for this purpose.

> *Surely he hath borne our griefs, and carried our sorrows: yet we did esteem him stricken, smitten of God, and afflicted. But he was wounded for our transgressions, he was bruised for our iniquities: the chastisement of our peace was upon him; and with his stripes we are healed.*
>
> *Isaiah 53: 4–5*

God wants justice for the oppressed. He wants to hear the powerful voice of worship rising from those who are oppressed. It is time for restoration. Worship will ensure our healing and restoration as black Africans. We have to rise up and find our place in the Holy Bible. There is no more time for excuses.

If the black man can accept and embrace that Jesus suffered for all people, then the black man will find his true identity; there will be nothing broken and nothing missing. Then, the black man will be able to worship God in honesty and in truth. As we worship God, He heals us and restores us from within, because He is a healer (Exodus 15: 26) and He is a restorer (Joel 2: 25). As we worship God, He fills us with His love because He is love (1 John 4: 7-8). His love in us will cause us to forgive those who oppressed us and to love them. Jesus forgave those who whipped and nailed Him on the cross. "Then said Jesus, Father, forgive them, for they know not what they do" (Luke 23: 34a). It is entirely up to the black man to embrace this truth to end the legacy of hatred and division.

> *If ye be willing and obedient, ye shall eat the good of the land: But if ye refuse and rebel, ye shall be devoured with the sword: for the mouth of the Lord hath spoken it.*
>
> *Isaiah 1: 19–20*

Dr Joshua Nkomo, like my father and his colleagues, was a good person. They had certain things in common: they hated poverty and injustice. That is the reason I believe that Joshua Nkomo kept it a secret that God forewarned him and his friends "not to fight the white settlers" when he resolved to fight. I am not condoning his disobedience to the voice of God, I am simply highlighting the frustrations experienced by people like him and my father, given the attitudes of the British settlers and the unfair treatment they gave them. As the first black office clerk Joshua Nkomo states that he was the only one at work with a diploma; none of the whites was educated. The white settlers held their positions through the colour of their skin. This was the reason African people resolved to go into battle.

As one born in Rhodesia, the revolutionary war against minority rule, racial segregation and oppression that took place from the 1950s to the end of 1980 robbed many of us of our childhood and our youth. We were born in racial oppression and our parents were in the struggle against segregation. The history of our nation that we were taught at school was limited and the facts were hidden from us as black students. We were only taught European history in detail and all history examinations were based on European history. We had to study and know everything about the involvement of European countries in the First World War and the events leading to the First and Second World Wars. We did not know much about the struggles of our own African people against the policies that controlled us as black people.

We were not taught why we were not allowed to walk in the city centre as black people. In Rhodesia there were "no go" areas in the city where only white people walked. In banks there were white-only, coloured-only and black-only queues and not all banks allowed black people in. There were banks for black people, right at the end of the city towards the commuter bus rank for the buses to the black townships, where we lived.

In 1978, after my high school years while I was still looking at doing a college course, the war became intense between the black revolutionary fighters (the so-called terrorists) and Ian Douglas Smith's RF, Rhodesia Front security forces. At the same time the negotiations for peace at Lancaster House were going on between the African leaders and the

British and Ian Smith's delegates. This was hopeful for us, as we were all tired of the loss of life during the struggle.

During this time, Ian Smith did something very painful and also foolish. In desperation, his government forced all the black young men of my age, my former schoolmates and those in employment from the age of 18 upwards, into military training. This was utter chaos. My brother had been one of the first young men to work as an air traffic assistant for Air Rhodesia. In 1978 he and his peers trained to fight against their own relatives who had left the country to fight against racial segregation and oppression. I used to visit the barracks at the weekend and it was not pleasant to see all the young educated black men marching back to the barracks saluting their white commanders. The punishments and torture they received from the white officers during their training were very severe. It was not every black man's desire to hold a gun and to kill, but in its frustration and anger, Ian Smith's regime forced every black male into the army, even those who were born-again believers in Christ.

Dr Joshua Nkomo says that he could not reconcile Christianity and nationalism after the manner in which Christianity was introduced in Southern Africa. He rebelled against Christianity for this very reason, that the religion of the white settlers was also economically oppressive to his people. (However, it is important that I alert the reader here that in his last days, Joshua Nkomo was visited with the gospel and he accepted Christ as his Lord and Saviour before he died.)

Jesus was not white

Books and pictures portray Jesus as white and very good looking. Even *The Passion of the Christ* features Jesus as a white man, yet He was not. Jesus was dark skinned and His appearance was not handsome, but he was attractive because of the Wisdom in Him. The Word of God tells us:

Who hath believed our report? and to whom is the arm of the Lord revealed? For he shall grow up before him as a tender plant, and as a

root out of a dry ground; he hath no form nor comeliness; and when
we shall see him, there is no beauty that we should desire him. He is
despised and rejected of men; a man of sorrows, and acquainted with
grief: and we hid as it were our faces from him; he was despised, and
we esteemed him not.

Isaiah 53: 1–3

I never went to Bible School or Seminary School, as they call it in the West. However, to me the above scripture does not sound like the description of Jesus after the Roman soldiers had beat and bruised him; it describes a growing child, whose country, physical appearance and life are not as glamorous as Hollywood portrays them in the movies. The above scripture is very clear; there is nothing complicated about it except the people who interpret it.

I wonder how many physical-beauty-inspired people would have accepted Jesus' message if they had lived on this earth at the same time as Him? Listening to the British National Party leader describing himself as a Christian and yet firmly believing that British citizens should only be white skinned is proof of the ignorance of the above scripture.

Jesus has appeared to many people in visions or in near-death experiences as resembling different ethnic groups. He may appear looking white or Chinese or black or Asian – so what? He is God. He chooses how he should appear to suit the situation. To portray Him as having been white when He walked this earth is to encourage racial bias and to deprive those like the black Jews of Matabeleland and other oppressed nations, who still deny Jesus based on their oppression by white Christian settlers, believing that He was white from the way He was always portrayed by the oppressor in pictures and movies. I have seen Him with dark, brushed-back short hair and an olive Mediterranean skin and I have seen Him as a black man with blue eyes and blond hair!

Even King Solomon wrote prophetically in Song of Solomon 1: 5–6:

I am black but comely, O ye daughters of Jerusalem, as the tents of Kedar,
as the curtains of Solomon.

Look not upon me, because I am black, because the sun hath looked upon me: my mother's children were angry with me; they made me the keeper of the vineyards; but my own vineyard have I not kept.

Jesus was black but comely, meaning He was attractive. He attracted crowds of people to Him. He was attractive in speech and in His actions. People found comfort and hope in his teachings. He healed the sick and He delivered the oppressed. This biblical truth has to be clarified to the nations of this world.

As I had received the Lord Jesus on 7th October 1979, during the period of intense fighting and just before independence, my salvation helped my maturity at the time and I was able to cope with a lot of racism that I had not been exposed to before. Being in Christ gave me patience and a higher level of understanding, especially when, as the first black female employee, my white colleagues protested against sharing the toilet with me. Black people only mixed with white people after 1980, so I believed that they needed to be allowed time to get used to mingling with us, their former servants. Even though our parents are the ones who suffered terrible racial segregation and oppression, they protected us from knowing too much about it, as was naturally their responsibility as parents.

Segregation in education was to our advantage, in that we grew up as confident children even though we were in a racially oppressed nation. What the devil meant for harm, God turned around for our good. If our schools had been integrated with whites, coloureds (as Smith called them) and Asian children, we would have felt the pain of racism. Our confidence would have been crushed from an early age. Ian Smith provided great schools for us compared to the black South Africans who were more deprived by the Boers who oppressed them. To this day, black South Africans have not quite earned their freedom even under a black president. They cannot even secure a ticket to enter the football ground to watch the World Cup.

Therefore most young people of my age never experienced racism until we came to employment in the early 1980s. This is why in the 1970s, many young people left the country to join the struggle. They realised that the education they had received would not help them much as long as racial segregation and oppression were legalised in our Constitution. At the time, it did not look like there was any hope for black people in Rhodesia. We refused to be servants and cleaners to white families like our parents had been.

I tried to join my cousins in 1976, but they secretly left in the early hours to cross the border without me. Crossing the border for military training seemed to be the only hope for change for black people. Those were hard times, because people we loved and cherished had to leave the country. There was great loneliness in most black families, as there is now under Mugabe's regime. I miss Zimbabwe so badly because it is my home, but Mugabe's armed criminals (the military) are in charge of the country. I am stuck in the diaspora. When I met my English husband and married him, I felt saddened to leave my friends behind in Zimbabwe. I did not know that in Matabeleland we were assigned for extermination, and that all the people would soon be following me to seek asylum where I am.

CHAPTER 5

The Hidden History of the Black Jews of Matabeleland

As the Jews of Matabeleland, our Jewish descent and heritage were kept secret from us. There was no mention of it in the history books. I call it the hidden history because Ian Smith never revealed our true history to us in school. We were taught lies. All our focus was directed towards European history, which we had no use for, as we never even thought that one day we could actually live in Europe.

The following is an extract from Henry Rider Haggard's notes on *King Solomon's Mines*:

When I was a lad in Africa I met many men, the pioneer of settlement and exploration – those who had first become acquainted with some of the great savage races of the interior ... [T]he country which is now Rhodesia ... must have become engrained in my mind that it had once been occupied by an ancient people. How I came to conclude that this people was Phoenician I have no idea. Nor to the best of my memory did I hear of the Great Ruins of Zimbabwe, or that an ancient civilisation had carried on a vast gold mining enterprise in the part of Africa where it stands ... All of these ... were the fruit of imagination, conceived I suppose from chance words spoken long ago that lay dormant in the mind ... But of the Matabele, who, in the tale, are named Kukuanas, I did know something. Indeed I went near to knowing too much, for when, in 1877 my friends Captain Patterson and Mr J Serjeant were sent by Sir Bartle Frere on an embassy to their King, Lobengula, I asked leave to go with them. It was refused as I could not be spared from the office. Had I gone my fate would have been theirs, for Lobengula murdered them both, and my two servants whom I had lent them. These two, Khiva, the bastard

Zulu, and Ventvogel, the Hottentot, I have tried to preserve in King Solomon's Mines, for they were such men as I have described.

After the Thatcher administration decided to give power to Robert Mugabe soon after the December 1979 Lancaster Agreement was signed, the people of Matabeleland began their long journey of suffering at the hands of Robert Mugabe's government. The Ndebele people were gang-raped and massacred under Mugabe's instructions, a man with a longstanding grudge against the Ndebele people. With a foreign father and mother who were both from Muslim backgrounds, had escaped from a slave train headed south from Congo/Zaire and were given asylum by a Chief in Mashonaland, Robert Mugabe adopted Shona as his own tribe and language. His father later assumed a Ndebele surname, married a Ndebele woman and had children by her. Robert Mugabe had a grudge against his father for abandoning them and for not educating them. He was educated by the Catholic Church. Robert Mugabe, like his siblings, can speak fluent Ndebele but is never heard doing so. While in Zambia in the mid-1950s, he met a beautiful, young Ndebele woman, whom he impregnated and denied the pregnancy. After being hunted down and forced to admit to impregnating the young woman, he was denied marriage to her as his Ndebele tribal background could not be traced by her family.

It was taboo in the Ndebele/Zulu culture to introduce a Shona girl or boy to the family. The elders would gather together to enquire into the family roots of the prospective bride or groom. If they failed to identify the family roots presented to them, they would never permit the marriage regardless of the education or wealth of the person and the family they came from. This is more evidence of the Jewish heritage of the Ndebele people, that they did not take intermarrying with different nations very lightly.

Mugabe's grudge cost the people of Matabeleland well over 50,000 lives after the declaration of independence in April 1980 and many more still perish to this day. There are mass graves everywhere. Many people were left homeless and terrified, their loved ones either burnt alive or forced to dig their own graves by Mugabe's North Korea-trained 5 Brigade, also known in Matabeleland as the Red Berets. It is reported that people in some villages are still being tormented by the shallow graves around their communities. People are still angry in Matabeleland; they are refusing to hear the gospel of Jesus Christ. What is more painful for them is that the oppression continues by the same people. The perpetrators are in top political and military positions; they are still laughing.

Peter Stiff, in his book *Cry Zimbabwe* (2002, Galago), highlights the mass graves as well as the case of Colonel Perence Shiri, known as the "Butcher of Bhalagwe" and commander of the 5 Brigade, who is currently Air Marshall of the Air Force of Zimbabwe. He was an honoured guest of British Aerospace at the Farnborough Air Show in 2000. He and all his friends who perpetrated the Matabeleland massacres are still in positions of power in Zimbabwe.

Britain owes an overdue apology to the Ndebele people of Matabeleland. There are hungry orphans, homeless and widows suffering at the hands of President Robert Mugabe. There are also thousands of young women who were raped by the ZANLA forces and left with fatherless children. Thesewomenwerenevercompensated. The 5 Brigade continues to rape and to kill under the banner of "War Veterans".

This issue has been avoided for too long now and Robert Mugabe knows very well that no one can remove him from power, because he has said many times that only God will remove him from power. I strongly believe that this act of injustice on the people of Zimbabwe would have been corrected long ago if the Church of England was pure in its representation of Christ.

CHAPTER 6

How It All Began

Not many Zimbabweans have read *Nkomo: The Story of My Life* (Joshua Nkomo, Methuen, 1984). Robert Mugabe banned the book in Zimbabwe where it was originally published and printed, obviously for fear of the revelations that are highlighted in it, such as his character and his coup attempts for party leadership while they were all still imprisoned by Ian Smith at the Gonakudzingwa Prison.

Joshua Nkomo shared the same burden for the poor as my father. The poor lifestyle of the Railway Mission employees drove him to war. He was a people's person. He dwelt among the people and as a result, according to his book, the African railway workforce requested him to represent their union in delivering their grievances to management. The details of his struggles as a railway employee before he resorted to fighting can be read in his book.

Robert Mugabe's dream of leading a political party was suddenly realised in 1976, after the suspicious accident that killed Josiah Tongogara, the original leader of the ZANLA forces, in Mozambique. Joshua Nkomo states in his book that Tongogara died for his forgiving nature and that those who killed him were against the fact that he wanted a peaceful settlement for the future of Zimbabwe. Mugabe managed to win the support of those who were bloodthirsty for revenge, like him.

The war that was fought in Rhodesia was not meant to bring further discrimination by colour, class or tribal background, it was a war against inequality in every area that affects a human being, emotionally, socially, physically or spiritually. Joshua Nkomo's strategy aimed at the holistic transformation of human life. He had observed and seen that life can be better for everybody. He hated the poverty his people had been driven into. Putting everything behind us, forgiving one another and rebuilding the country were all part of Nkomo's transition strategy. It was not meant to bring revenge on anybody.

In Rhodesia 1979 was a period of intense fighting. Our African leaders were in London where the peace negotiation talks were being held. All were dying, black or white.

Nkomo made it clear that the land was the main resource required to upgrade our nation's economy. He recognised that a unity of purpose among all political parties was vital for the rebuilding of the nation. Therefore his campaign was totally against tribal division among black people, because he had seen its futility in the other nations of Africa that had won their independence earlier on. There was chaos everywhere in Africa, deliberately created by the colonisers in order to keep Africa dependent on the West, a divide and rule policy.

According to former Prime Minister of Rhodesia Ian Smith's book *The Great Betrayal* (Blake, 1997), a cartoon by Cummings during Ian Smith's visit to London in 1965 was captioned: "We are doing our best to help the Rhodesian Africans get a nice dictator like General Amin instead of the wicked Mr Smith". This confirms what I heard in 1997 at an African-Caribbean event, that it was Margaret Thatcher and Lord Carrington who gave Robert Mugabe power in a secret location in Tanzania with Julius Nyerere, the then President of Tanzania, as a witness. Did Thatcher and Carrington really think Nyerere would keep it quiet? Did they really think Nyerere was Mugabe's friend?

In his book, Nkomo speaks very suspiciously about the day in 1979 when the talks ended at Lancaster House. He states:

> At Lancaster House our relationships with the white delegates from the Rhodesian Front party were dominated by the knowledge that we were still at war, that as we talked people were fighting and dying. There was no friendship between us; there could not be. Lord Carrington as Chairman arranged the conference as far as possible so as to avoid direct confrontations between the two sides. Before each plenary session he would organise separate meetings, first with the other side and then with the Patriotic Front. This meant that we would find ourselves confronted

with some deal worked out between Carrington and Muzorewa, and
when we argued against it we would be told that altering the terms would
mean the conference breaking down. By dealing with each side separately,
Lord Carrington put himself at the centre of the spider's web, of which he
alone could pull the strings.

The British and the Rhodesians had many common interests, which
they used the conference to preserve. Even after the fifteen years of illegal
independence, British companies still had as large a stake in the country
as the local whites, not just in mines, manufacturing and service business,
but also in land, which was the great point of argument.

Of course the new constitution was not satisfactory. It was the result
of muddle and compromise, reached in haste to stop the bloodshed. It was
dangerous to reserve twenty of one hundred seats in parliament for white
members elected by a whites-only electorate. It was foolish to provide for
a president with no power. But at least the so-called "entrenched clauses"
in the constitution were watered down. A constitution that cannot be
changed if the people want change is not a democratic constitution, and
democracy was what Zimbabwe needed. That was what I thought we
had won when I signed the formal agreement on 21 December 1979.
(Nkomo, 1984: 201)

He had an appointment the next day with Mugabe to finalise the
procedure for the elections, but Mugabe could not be found at his flat.
Nkomo reports:

As agreed, on the morning after the signing of the Lancaster House
agreement, I went to Robert Mugabe's flat for our first talk. Nobody
answered; the place was empty. I waited, with my good friend and
colleague Ariston Chambati, who had kept a detailed account of all
the proceedings at Lancaster House. After a while one of the junior
Zanu people arrived. "Where is Mr Mugabe?" I asked, "Oh, he left
this morning for Dar es Salaam," came the reply. That was the end of
our agreement to talk, broken not by me but by Robert Mugabe and the
leadership of Zanu. Next morning I heard on the radio that Robert, on

arrival in Dar, had announced that he and Zanu would be fighting the elections on their own. The smiles of Lancaster House were left behind in London. The national campaign of reconciliation that I had dreamed of remained a dream. I, and the fighters and followers of Zapu, had been deceived. (Nkomo, 1984: 204–6

During the 1980 presidential elections, Mugabe and his ZANLA forces resolved to ensure that by way of intimidation, none of the political parties would campaign in the Eastern parts of Zimbabwe, not even Ian Smith whose home was there in Selukwe, now Shurugwi. While Joshua Nkomo's ZIPRA forces waited in their assembly points, the ZANLA forces were let loose. What did those monitoring the fairness of the elections do about it? Only Judgment Day will reveal the truth.

In his book, Nkomo stated that he thought Lord Soames, the British Governor who was monitoring the freedom and fairness of the elections in Zimbabwe, was the one who failed him. Even though he reported to Nkomo that there was too much intimidation on the people of the Eastern parts of the country by Mugabe's ZANLA forces, Lord Soames failed to challenge Mugabe to discipline his forces. Nkomo asked Mugabe about it, but Mugabe did not answer him. Nkomo's ZIPRA forces then made direct enquiries with their fellow ZANLA forces, but the ZANLA forces said that whatever was happening had nothing to do with the leadership, thus coming to Mugabe's defence.

This means that the three days we spent queuing to vote in Zimbabwe were a total waste of time. Mugabe's campaign of intimidation ensured total control of all the seats in the eastern part of the country. The people in the area were terrorised; as well as being politically indoctrinated they were compelled to shout the slogan "Down with Nkomo".

CHAPTER 7

The Betrayal of the Zimbabwean People

T he African-Caribbean meeting I attended in 1997 highlighted that the main culprits behind this situation were Britain's Lord Carrington and then Prime Minister Margaret Thatcher. The Western policy was aimed at dividing the Africans against each other by rigging their elections.

Echoing this belief in his book *The Great Betrayal*, Ian Smith believes that the British policy towards their former African colonies led to dictatorship, with the resulting chaos of denial of freedom and justice. He reflects on the events following the independence of Ghana in 1957, Nigeria in 1960, Belgian Congo in 1960, then in very quick succession Tanzania, Zanzibar, Uganda, Kenya and Zambia in 1964. He comments:

> *As I have stated on so many occasions, when the British solutions for Africa went wrong – and this has happened in every case – the British were looking in the opposite direction, disassociating themselves from the resultant disaster.*

Britain has failed to challenge Robert Mugabe's government of intimidation since 1980, because they fear he might expose to the world that they gave him power as the president of Zimbabwe in advance, in 1979 soon after the signing of the Lancaster Agreement, and that they further supported his intimidation of the communities in the Eastern part of the country in 1980 that won him all the seats in parliament. Even when Mugabe's militiamen tormented the white Zimbabwean farmers, he still could not be challenged. Lady Thatcher and Lord Carrington are both responsible for the current situation in Zimbabwe.

If Saddam Hussein was killed for his wicked human rights policy in Iraq, how different has Robert Mugabe's policy been and why has he not been challenged all these years? Is it fair that the people in Matabeleland perished at the hands of 5 Brigade because of a man who did not win the elections in the first place except by intimidation? They were deprived of their fair vote.

Soon after being given power by the British Government, Mugabe began his campaign of terror, first on the Ndebele people in Matabeleland, then on the white farmers. He soon forgot the democracy he had fought for as his real self emerged.

The British Parliament should seriously consider the legacy left by Britain in Zimbabwe. The Anglo-Catholic Church has been a big part of this legacy, in that there was silence as the people of Matabeleland perished. Given that Peter Stiff, a British-born former Rhodesian policeman, has written such a detailed account of the atrocities in Matabeleland and around Zimbabwe in his book *Cry Zimbabwe*, there must have been a level of awareness, especially in Britain, of the holocaust that was taking place in Matabeleland in the early 1980s. Stiff has even given an account by British journalists who found evidence of the extermination, but the Church of England and the British Government chose to remain silent on the matter because they knew the truth.

Many Christian television channels have been in recent months showing the documentary *Lest We Forget*, which highlights the stories of survivors of the atrocities committed on the white Jews by Hitler. Therefore it is only fair and just that someone highlights the atrocities suffered by the black Jews of Matabeleland – and as they are my own people, God chose me to do this job. Therefore, I will write what I can on behalf of my people, including my own experiences at the hands of the perpetrators. To this effect, I sought the permission of Peter Stiff to use extracts from his book, which he granted.

Stiff (2002: 94–7) states that Mugabe's strategy for the holocaust of his enemies had already been settled long before independence, in 1979 (a year prior to the presidential elections) when he produced a red booklet for his ZANU party declaring his strategy to exterminate his enemies.

The North Koreans were secretly appointed to train Mugabe's new force especially for the implementation of this strategy, which he named the 5 Brigade, Gukurahundi/Year of the People's Storm. The 5 Brigade began its scheduled assignment in 1982 with the Matabeleland massacres of the Zulu/Ndebele people.

Bear in mind that this was two years after independence and two years after Joshua Nkomo's ZIPRA forces had been stripped of all power and given two options, to join the National Army or to go back to civilian life and find jobs, by the former Rhodesian, Brigadier Mike Shute of the Zimbabwe National Army and Great Britain's Commonwealth Monitoring Force Commander, Major-General John Acland, both in support of Robert Mugabe's new government. Therefore the ZIPRA forces who were forced to join the United Zimbabwean Army were secretly picked out and eliminated one by one by the same 5 Brigade and the brutal CIOs who operated under Emmerson Munangagwa, the Minister of State for Security in the Prime Minister's Office, currently the Defence Minister in Zimbabwe and a major hand in the holocaust.

Stiff highlights the details of this in his book. Nkomo and his ZIPRA were first stripped of all their ammunition and completely weakened prior to Robert Mugabe's government subjecting them to endless public humiliation, torture and unrest. For unsuspecting and ever-trusting Nkomo and his people of Matabeleland, it was the beginning of another, worse struggle under his own black people and an unanticipated tribal-based extermination. Mugabe knew very well that Nkomo had always hated tribal divisions and had emphasised fighting the war in unity as black people. His knowledge was based on the problems he had seen in other former Western colonies in North Africa, where there was no peace from Western-sponsored bandits who wanted Africa to remain forever dependent on the West for help with ammunition. The West always capitalised on the tribal division of those countries in order to continue blackmailing Africa for its raw materials in exchange for ammunition. Mugabe knew when he divided the people of Zimbabwe that he had got Nkomo where it hurt the most.

Future generations in Africa and the third world are faced with the legacy of division and corruption and hence the poverty of the masses. But God's eyes are on the vulnerable and helpless, the poor nobodies who perish in the Gukurahundi mass graves without a trace or record.

My own first experience of Mugabe's 5 Brigade's campaign of terror occurred one morning on my way to work in 1983. I had an encounter with Colonel Perence Shiri, who I still recognise from the photograph in Peter Stiff's book, also known as the Butcher/or Beast of Bhalagwe and currently Air Marshall in the Zimbabwe Air Force. That morning, 5 Brigade had deliberately created a roadblock as people commuted to work. Shiri stopped our bus and ordered everyone out. When he set eyes on me, he ordered me to remove my hands from my pockets. His words to me in his own (Shona) language were, "Who does she think she is, an air hostess or the Queen of England?" I was only a civilian. I had not been trained to take orders from a soldier.

In the city of Bulawayo we had no clue what was happening and why we were suffering like that. We referred to 5 Brigade as the "Red Berets". They were deployed in the black community townships (the high-density areas where only black people lived) at any time without notice. At the time I worked for a legal firm with another black man, who was a clerk there. We both arrived very late for work most mornings because of the intimidation we experienced.

We did not know at the time that those in the rural areas were worse off than us because they could all suddenly be confined in a curfew system that was designed to stop them moving further from their homes. The curfew was also designed to stop any food supplies reaching the Matabeleland rural communities.

Stiff (2002: 181) states that on 8th September 1982 Defence Minister Sydney Sekeramayi announced that the setting up of 5 Brigade had been completed. Prime Minister Robert Mugabe and President Canaan Banana attended the 5 Brigade passing out parade, which took place in December 1982; and Prime Minister Mugabe personally presented Colonel Shiri with the Brigade's colours, a flag emblazoned with the word

"Gukurahundi". Mugabe ordered 5 Brigade to "plough and reconstruct". This order obviously carried a deeper meaning.

The North Korean heads of state visited Zimbabwe in the course of 2009. Mugabe also sent his own cabinet minister on a secret mission to North Korea the same year. The 5 Brigade are not young any more, and therefore it would not be a surprise if Mugabe intends using the North Koreans to train the next generation of militants for more massacres in order to discourage and silence opposition parties.

According to Stiff, Mugabe's January 1979 party strategy highlighted his plans to maintain the strength of his political army, 5 Brigade. Clause 11 on page 28 of the red booklet for his ZANU party states: "Our ZANLA forces must continue to increase considerably in number while the quality of their training continues to improve." Stiff further states that when Nkomo asked Mugabe why the brigade had been formed if not for the possible imposition of a one-party state, when Zimbabwe already had efficient forces of law, including the civil police, to handle any internal problems, Mugabe, in a delayed response two years later in 1983, stated: "the 5 Brigade were trained by the North Koreans because I wanted one arm of the army to have a political orientation which stems from our philosophy as ZANU-PF" (2002: 93–6).

The God of Abraham, Isaac and Jacob will intervene this time. He has heard the cry of His people. "Ye shall know the truth and the truth shall make you free" (John 8: 32).

Whatever Robert Mugabe's reasons for exterminating his enemies, he sowed seeds for himself. We reap what we sow. Those with the fear of God in their hearts know that vengeance belongs to God. Taking vengeance into our own hands has serious consequences. Being in a position of power does not give one the green light to abuse their power. God is still God in heaven and in the earth. God is no respecter of persons.

People who fought in the war in Zimbabwe have been let down so much that they do not want to hear about politics. Too many lives were lost during the war against Ian Smith's forces who gunned down all the women and children at the Refugee Camps in Zambia and in Mozambique. When the people thought the war was over, they lost more lives as President Mugabe's 5 Brigade exterminated Matabeleland families. Some of those massacred were thrown down the derelict mine shafts that were left exposed by the British colonial miners of gold and other minerals, while others were buried alive in mass graves.

The people of Matabeleland who survived the holocaust still need emotional healing and restoration, because they have lost loved ones and some have lost everything. This has been made difficult by the fact that those who perpetrated the holocaust are still in positions of power in Zimbabwe. How can healing and restoration come unless this issue is addressed? Zimbabweans in the diaspora are professionally redundant and unhappy and also feel trapped because they miss their homeland while Mugabe and his henchmen are enjoying it. He has illegally ruled Zimbabwe since 1980. The British continue with their own lives as if nothing ever happened. The Christian Church remains silent on the matter.

> *And, behold, I come quickly; and my reward is with me, to give every man according as his work shall be. I am Alpha and Omega, the beginning and the end, the first and the last.*
>
> *Revelations 22: 12–13*

> *Blessed are they that do His commandments, that they may have right to the tree of life, and may enter in through the gates into the city. For without are dogs, and sorcerers, and whoremongers, and murderers, and idolaters, and whosoever loveth and maketh a lie.*
>
> *Revelations 22: 14–15*

> *I Jesus have sent mine angel to testify unto you these things in the churches. I am the root and the offspring of David, and the bright and morning star.*
>
> *Revelations 22: 16*

So, to be put in a position of authority and take revenge on your enemies by massacring innocent children and unarmed and defenceless civilians would be a great shame and a waste of one's time on earth, because how does it benefit one at the end? One of my forefathers, King Solomon, wrote in the Book of Ecclesiastes:

> *If thou seest the oppression of the poor, and violent perverting of judgment and justice in a province, marvel not at the matter: for He that is higher than the highest regardeth; and there be higher than they. Moreover the profit of the earth is for all: the king himself is served by the field.*
>
> *Ecclesiastes 5: 8–9*

God watches what those in positions of political authority here on earth are up to.

Peter Stiff gives the story of one foreign journalist who witnessed a massacre (2002: 218–20):

> *Peter Godwin, the foreign correspondent for the London Sunday Times, wrote that truckloads of bodies had been dumped down a disused shaft (at the Antelope Mine, Kezi) "every night for many weeks as part of a cleanup operation". "The soldiers gathered all the people of the area together," he was told. They "made us shout government slogans and they beat many people with rifle butts, screaming at us the whole time: 'Where are the dissidents?' Then they selected three men at random, including my father, and took them behind the hill. We heard three shots and the soldiers returned alone."*
>
> *To get his story – published under the headline "Mass Murder in Matabeleland" – Godwin posed as a monk to infiltrate the affected areas. The dusk-to-dawn curfew was still in force in Matabeleland South and many areas had been sealed off by troops. Civilian visitors, private traffic and journalists were banned from entering. After getting his story, Godwin left in the nick of time, hearing afterwards that the CIO had been tipped off he was in the area and together with 5 Brigade had begun to hunt him. Donald Trelford, the editor of the Observer, followed Peter Godwin to Matabeleland to conduct his own investigations. According to Godwin, the late Tiny Rowland, who owned the Observer, had despatched Trelford to "rubbish" his story at the request of "senior Zimbabwe Ministers".*

Trelford, instead of rubbishing it, reported finding "first hand evidence of widespread killings and torture" carried out by soldiers. "The evidence included a handwritten account by a man who dug a mass grave and watched his neighbours shot down by an officer who leaned against a tree and turned on his radio cassette to cover the noise."

Rowland, in a move designed to protect his Zimbabwean commercial interests, grovelled to Prime Minister Mugabe and humbly apologised, saying that Trelford's story was sensational and based on "unsubstantiated material". Donald Trelford, who had edited the Observer since 1975, replied with dignity that he stood by every word: "The story was solidly based on the evidence of victims whom I interviewed myself."

Joshua Nkomo, in London to launch his memoirs, ignored Rowland and urged the British government to accept Trelford's report as the truth.

Faced by a worldwide storm of protests, the Zimbabwean Government reluctantly agreed to conduct foreign correspondents on a tour of the areas where it was alleged atrocities had taken place. Missionaries and other people soon began to report that troops from 5 Brigade and the Police Support Unit were busily engaged in erasing evidence of atrocities in preparation for the visit.

The long-awaited and long-delayed tour comprising 30 foreign correspondents and 10 local journalists, and conducted by senior government officials and army officers, including Army Commander, Lieutenant-General Rex Nhongo, finally took place in mid May. [Rex Nhongo changed his name later on to Rex Mujuru, by which he is currently known.] It was a highly sanitised event and journalist were refused permission to visit many of the sites where atrocities had allegedly occurred. Yet despite protracted attempts to erase the evidence, the authorities had not succeeded.

Several villagers awaited the little convoy at a Kezi mission. They told how soldiers had murdered six young men on February 1984 and pointed out two sites where the bodies were buried. In an obvious intimidatory move, CIO cameramen filmed the witnesses during the interviews.

John Tsimba, the Director of Information, commented that the "graves" were nothing more than mounds of earth, which made the allegations "very suspicious".

A victim's brother retorted that soldiers had exhumed and cremated the bodies on 12 April 1984. They took two days to burn, following which the ashes were removed. He pointed out as evidence the scorched leaves of bushes demarcating the area.

John Tsimba airily dismissed it as a "setup". Journalists asked a drunken Lieutenant-General Rex Nhongo if he would order an inquiry. "No," he replied, "they are liars." He blamed Peter Godwin for being the cause of his troubles. "Lead the way, you swine," he had said to him. "If you fall, I will get somebody to hit you, you bastard." He also threatened to shoot him. Journalists interviewed an American missionary doctor who told them of a woman whose buttocks were so badly beaten that it necessitated skin grafts. She also knew of 15 young girls soldiers had raped.

"To you that's really atrocities, but to us it is not atrocities," John Tsimba scoffed. Addressing journalists at the end of the tour, Tsimba said, "You have found no evidence of genocide in this whole region, no mass killings, no mass graves. So if from now on you people write stories of mass graves, genocide, we can only interpret that to mean you have a vendetta against the government and the people of Zimbabwe."

The Secretary for Information accused Peter Godwin of being an ex-Selous Scout – he had actually been a National Service policeman during the Bush War. This prompted an editorial in the state-controlled Herald indignantly asking why people who should be in prison in Harare should be allowed to get away with smearing Zimbabwe's good name in London. A second editorial demanded Godwin get "the hangman's rope" for war crimes. A friendly CIO officer tipped off Godwin that his arrest and detention in Chikurubi Maximum Security as a South African agent was imminent, so he took the hint and skipped the country in a hurry. This doubtless suited the Zimbabwe Government because detaining him would have created a political storm in London. To prevent his return the regime declared him an Enemy of the State and he became persona non grata in the land of his birth.

The above report and that of the Catholic bishops are clear proof that Margaret Thatcher and Lord Carrington had enough evidence of what their chosen leader for the Zimbabwean people was up to, yet to this day Britain, for fear of having its secret with Robert Mugabe exposed, has chosen to ignore the cries of the people of Matabeleland and now of the rest of Zimbabwe. But the blood of the black Jews of Matabeleland who perished and those who continue to perish is still speaking in the ground. Margaret Thatcher's term in office lasted throughout the 1983-90 period of the massacres. Even though the rigging of the elections could not have been reversed, if she had cared enough for the people of Matabeleland, could her government not have done something to intervene for the perishing masses? What about the Anglican Church of England, my father's employer, what was its contribution?

I cannot write in detail all that Peter Stiff highlights in his book regarding the genocide and crimes against humanity carried out by 5 Brigade throughout the province of Matabeleland North, South and the Midlands, as most of it is beyond what I could take, especially the sexual crimes committed on little schoolgirls in front of their parents. There were over 30,000 who perished without a record. I will only quote from a few of the victims' witnesses, the survivors.

A woman living near Tsholotsho told what happened to her at the end of January 1983: "The uniformed 5 Brigade soldiers arrived and ordered my husband to carry all the chairs, a table, beds, blankets and clothes and put them in one room. They also took all our cash – we had Z$1,500 saved to buy a scotch cart. They then set fire to our hut and burnt all our property. They accused my husband of having a gun, which he did not have. They shot at him. The first two times they missed him, but the third time they shot him in the stomach and killed him. Then they beat me very hard, even though I was pregnant. I told them I was pregnant and they told me not to have children for the whole of Zimbabwe. My mother-in-law tried to plead with them, but they shouted insults at her. They hit me in the stomach with the butt of the gun. The unborn child broke into pieces in my stomach. It was God's grace that I did not die, too. The child was born afterwards, piece by piece. A head alone, then a leg, an arm, the body – piece by piece."

The largest massacre occurred when 62 villagers were rounded up, marched to the banks of Cewale River in the Lupane area and shot. Seven, all suffering from gunshot wounds, feigned death and survived. A young girl told her story to investigators: "On 5 March 1983, four people were taken from our home. The youngest was myself, then a girl of 15. 5 Brigade took us – there were more than a 100 of them. We were asleep when they came, but they woke us up and accused the four of us – me and my three brothers – of being dissidents. They then marched us at gun-point for about three hours until they reached a camp. We were lined up and had to give our names, before they took us to a building where there were 62 people. They took us out one by one and beat us. They beat me with a stick about 10 inches [45cm] long all over the body. We were beaten until about 3.00 a.m. The 5 Brigade marched us to the Cewale River, a few hundred metres away. All 62 of us were lined up and shot by 5 Brigade. One of my brothers was killed instantly from a bullet through his stomach. By some chance seven of us survived with gunshot wounds. I was shot in the left thigh. 5 Brigade finished off some of the others who had survived, but my two brothers and I pretended to be dead. After some time we managed to get home. 5 Brigade came looking for survivors of this incident at home – they found my brother R who was badly injured, but they left him. My brother had a gunshot wound in the chest and arm, and later had to have him amputated first at the elbow, and then, later at the shoulder. My [other] brother had to have his foot amputated because of a bullet wound." (Stiff, 2002: 188)

A surgeon at Bulawayo's Mpilo Hospital was alarmed by the sudden influx of black civilians with gunshot wounds and assault-related injuries suffered at the hands of 5 Brigade. Some had been so savagely beaten that they died from renal failure while undergoing treatment. His colleagues agreed this should be reported to the Minister of Health. The surgeon detailed the names and the injuries and supported this with photographs and details of the treatment the affected patients had received and sent his report to the Minister. There was no delay on the part of the Minister who promptly demanded the negatives. The surgeon sent them but took the

*precaution of retaining a duplicate set of prints together with a duplicate
set of the patients' medical records. These are now on file with NOVIB,
a non-governmental organisation in the Netherlands. Needless to say
nothing further was heard from the Minister.*

Stiff further states that the massacres on 6 February 1983 were carried
out by 15 Chishona-speaking well-armed "soldiers" wearing 5 Brigade
red berets at Silwane village near Lupane. "They divided 52 villagers into
small groups and announced that 'they had come to kill everybody.' They
shot them next to their homes. The Catholic Commission for Justice
and Peace recorded more than two dozen accounts of this massacre from
survivors" (2002: 188).

Again, Stiff reports:

*On 1 April 1984, Father John Gough, an outspoken critic of the former
Rhodesian Front Government, spoke about 5 Brigade atrocities during a
sermon at Harare's Roman Catholic Cathedral. "You must be prepared
to hear things that make one cold, wish one had never breathed, never
been alive in this country," he told a hushed congregation. "To think of
babies being dropped in boiling water, people buried to necks and shot.
A great tragedy is occurring in this country, which is simply to the point,
murder – murder is being committed in the name of law and order in this
state. Murder is taking place in Matabeleland to a degree that we have
never seen before." He said he was preparing them for a statement by the
Catholic Bishops that would "surprise, shock and horrify". (2002: 218)*

*A four-month-old infant was axed three times and the mother was forced
to eat the flesh of her dead child. An 18-year-old girl was raped by six
soldiers, and then murdered. Molten plastic was dripped on the private
parts of an 1 -year-old child and she was then shot. Infant twins were
buried alive. A group of elderly men were severely beaten for several days
as a punishment for eating a meal at 1 .00 – one died. Electric shocks
were administered to the private parts of a ZAPU district chairman
and his collarbone was broken. His wife was beaten and tortured*

leaving her with partial paralysis in one leg. A woman was beaten into disablement because she could not speak Chishona. A woman sharing tea with neighbours was struck on the head, disabling and blinding her. Eight people were forced to dig their own graves and then shot to death. Thirteen people, including three primary school teachers, were beaten, thrown down a well and grenades tossed in after them to finish them off.

The mass grave in Silobela in the Midlands where I grew up as a child is a wake-up call to me as to why God preserved my life. My own bones could have been in it if I had still lived in the rural area of Silobela. Many people had no homes in the cities, which is why it was easy for Mugabe's curfew to confine them in the rural area, where they were all easily rounded up like cattle and slaughtered. The nearest town to Silobela would have been Kwekwe, the home of the Gukurahundi to this day.

Only God knows what the people of Matabeleland went through. Therefore, where much is given, much is required. I cannot be silent on this because God saw their tears as they all perished at the hands of the 5 Brigade. He preserved my life to write this book and He chose me, I did not choose myself. Even for those who perished justice should happen at the end. God in His capacity as the Creator of all is the ultimate Judge! None can escape His judgment. He is El-Eloyn, the Most High God who is the first cause of everything.

Even though my father, as the priest-in-charge of an Anglican Church parish in Tsholotsho, was visited by 5 Brigade and was beaten by these young men, he did not give us the detailed account of his suffering as he seemed too overwhelmed to talk about it. Given the evil actions highlighted in Stiff's book, it is a miracle that my father survived the beatings and that they did not bayonet or the CIOs "drown him", as they often did.

The CIOs were known for drowning, according to the statements I used to type as a legal secretary at the time. People were bringing their stories to the lawyers I worked for. Our respectable elder and gospel singer, a celebrity in Bulawayo, was dragged behind a lorry from his farm in Matabeleland South. His wife, a nurse and nursing lecturer in

Bulawayo, stormed into our typing pool in great anger. Even though she had a big position at the hospital herself, the CIO did not allow her to visit her husband's hospital bed, they kept police guards at his bed. This was obviously a "clean-up" targeted at all the elders and rich people of Matabeleland.

My maternal grandfather had been a businessman since the time of Rhodesia. He was an entrepreneur in Matabeleland South, where he owned a grocery store and a separate clothes shop. He also had a mill and a bottle store. He had served the rural people for decades. He had many commuter buses between Bulawayo and the rural area. He became a "clean-up" target and all his shops were burnt to the ground, full of stock. Some of his commuter buses were destroyed, but some survived because they were at the bus rank in Bulawayo. My grandfather ran for his life and bought a farm on the Bulawayo–Falls road, but still maintained his township house in Bulawayo, where he stayed. Squatters frustrated my grandfather, stealing from him and refusing to leave the farm. My grandfather was still managing his own affairs and driving his van at 96 years of age when he died of a stroke. I arrived on the day of the funeral in June 2000 and found an incident where a lorry had gone into the farm and removed the water pump. Whoever did it knew very well that a funeral was taking place in Mpopoma, Bulawayo where his home was. The workers were sworn to silence. The police never showed up, even though my cousin's husband reported the matter. Needless to say my grandfather was a black farmer, not a white farmer, and he had worked hard for his riches. The farm invasions are a disorganised criminal plot by those who want everything for nothing.

There are many like this in the Church today, who want every good thing to happen for them for nothing. They hate pastors who preach about tithing and sowing or giving. They want to be prayed for, but they do not want to read the Holy Bible for themselves. They are simply rebellious gossipers and stumbling blocks to those who are growing in the Lord. I am not a pastor of a church, but I hear them all the time, criticising the people of God; but when tragedy hits, they are the same people who are quick to question God's whereabouts.

I was once among the women forced from our homes into the police van to the Stops Camp in Bulawayo. A red-eyed CIO was determined to torture me, but when they found out that I was a legal secretary in a reputable legal firm that was actually dealing with all such matters related to the atrocities that were current then, they feared exposure and they let go of me. This was on a Saturday morning. Even though they had seen that I was advanced in my pregnancy when they picked me up and I had been on my way to a doctor's appointment, the two CIOs did not care. One of my neighbours, a young nurse, was a new mother with a tiny baby a few days' old in her arms. I was worried for her, but I did not know that she was probably safer than I was because she was not a Ndebele like me; she was Shona. (We never spoke about the incident as neighbours afterwards, as we all got on with our lives.) When we reached Stops Camp, the walls in one open cell were full of blood and a group of miserable black young Ndebele boys were detained there. While we all sat on the ground waiting, I kept thinking of ways of escape. The security fence was very high and the guards were armed. I spoke to God while I was in there, wondering at the fate of all those young men starring at us helplessly and all quiet, with the bloodstained walls behind them. It was through the mercy of God that they let us go. I spoke to God a lot; I do not remember what I said exactly, but I was determined that politics was not the reason I should die. I was only prepared to die for Jesus.

However, not all people got away with it at Stops Camp in Bulawayo. The CIO in detention camps asked the questions while 5 Brigade soldiers, who could not understand or let alone speak Ndebele, assaulted the detainees continuously, indifferent to whether they replied to the questions or not.

Stiff highlights the following account of an unfortunate victim of the CIO at the same Stops Camp in Bulawayo:

"It was the water bag... you can't breathe, for your body won't let you hold your breath forever. After a few minutes you have to drink the water, just to breathe. I drank about a gallon of water. While you're holding your breath, they kick you. They force you to move. You know the feeling when

you get water into your ear? That is the feeling. Of heat building in your head. The pain in your head is the worst. Then you pass out. When I was about to pass out, I could hear: 'Take the bag off, take the bag off, he is about to die.' That is the last I heard... I tried to hold my breath. If they pick me up again, I think I will just start drinking the water from the beginning so I pass out sooner." (Stiff, 2002: 216)

There are more accounts of women being drowned by the CIO. Stiff states:

The perpetrators revived them by jumping on their stomachs until they vomited up the water. They only stopped if the victim threw up blood. Sometimes artificial respiration had to be used to revive their victims. Many did not survive. The torturers brutally beat some victims until they agreed to commit acts of bestiality with donkeys. If they failed or refused to cooperate, the beatings continued. Women, especially the young ones, were raped as a routine and "given as wives" to those members of 5 Brigade who fancied them. Instead of them being released after a few days when they had been cleared of whatever they were supposed to have done, their stays at Bhalagwe were extended by several weeks at a time, while they were passed around until the rapists got tired of them and selected other female detainees. Such repeated rapes often led to uterine disorders and, in at least one case, to a permanent inability to have children. Few of the detainees were interrogated in the real sense. The reasoning behind the torture was difficult to fathom – other than it being mass punishment or sadistic ill treatment the Nazis or Japanese at their worst would have appreciated. (2002: 216)

After deployment the 5 Brigade soldiers made it clear to all and sundry that they regarded themselves above the law. They frequently emphasised to policemen and soldiers from other units who attempted to query their actions that 5 Brigade was answerable to "nobody but Mugabe". Evidence points to the conclusion that 5 Brigade was trained to deliberately target civilians. Wherever they went in the first few months of 1983 they carried out a "grotesquely violent campaign against civilians, civil servants, [ZAPU] party chairmen and only occasionally armed insurgents". Commercial farmers felt that 5 Brigade was more interested in "politicking" than fighting and remarked that when they reported a suspected dissident presence to the Brigade, they showed a marked lack of interest. 5 Brigade was distanced from the rest of the army as a deliberate policy. It was not answerable to the National Army's command structure, nor was it integrated with it. This was not only because it was trained by the North Koreans rather than BMATT, like the rest of the army, but it also wore different camouflage uniforms. It was armed with AK-47s and weaponry of North Korean origin, whilst the National Army had been re-equipped after independence with NATO-style weapons and equipment. 5 Brigade's communications equipment, radios, radio procedures and codes were incompatible with other units, so they could not work together anyway. The recruits were subjected to lengthy sessions of political indoctrination dealing with the niceties of Marxist politics. Other than this, its distinctive red beret would serve to identify it in its infamy. For the Ndebele people, that red beret became the mark of Cain. (2002: 182)

My husband and I visited Zimbabwe late in 1995. We saw my father's youngest brother, uncle Solomon, at my parents' home where a party had been arranged for us. At the party was the late Father Eubank of Cyrene Mission. After that party, my uncle Solomon went to collect his pension in Lupane, where he was killed by Mugabe's henchmen. My father insisted that the police should investigate his youngest brother's death, but the police were not forthcoming. He died for his pension.

We did not understand why there were such food shortages in the country. Little did we know that it was a planned government strategy to deliberately starve and further massacre the people of Matabeleland. People in the towns did not know why there were shortages, although factory workers, who processed all the grain produced in the country, were suspicious that the government was hoarding food. Bags of maize meal were stocked in Bulawayo's producing factories, but this was kept a secret. I personally worked for six months for the Agriculture and Rural Development Authority (ARDA) in Bulawayo in 1989 when forced starvation was still in place. I received telexes of the weekly stock of everything from grain, rice and fruits to livestock from all the farm managers of ARDA throughout the country every Monday and I would submit the weekly stock to the Head Office in Harare. There were evidently enough crops to go round. There was an abundance of everything at the time, but it was not made available to the consumer. We were already an extension of the state of North Korea although we were all ignorant of it, except Mugabe and his friends. The farm managers were doing quite well at the time before all the government's interference.

Apparently forced starvation is still going on. People perished in 2008, even in Mashonaland, for failing to vote for Mugabe while his elite were eating and living lavishly. A friend reported that a private van carrying grain in Matabeleland South was stopped by the police, and the owner forced to get rid of the grain. This was a period when people were dying throughout the country from starvation.

At that time, in a vision, God showed me my high school best friend. I knew that in real life she was married to one of the top people, "the retired Colonels" of ZANLA who are in top ministerial positions. I endeavoured to find her, so I asked a cousin to find her for me and she did. She was very excited to hear that I was looking for her and she sent me a text on my mobile phone to contact her. I did and we had a good laugh. Then out of concern, I asked her how things were for her. She told me that she was very happy in her marriage and had two children who are studying in Australia and that they are doing their second or third degrees. I was happy for her because she is my friend. She related how comfortable she is and how her husband has taken her everywhere around the world, there is no place in the world she has not been to. When I asked her about the fuel shortages, she did not have a problem herself, in fact she has so many cars that she chooses which one to drive every morning. Then I asked how power cuts were affecting them. She said that is not her problem as she has a generator, what we call in Zulu *isthuthuthu*. People in the country were suffering, there was no fuel but endless power cuts and financial hardship and the HIV orphans on the streets; but here is someone living right there amid the suffering. The burden I am carrying for the hurting and suffering of that country is only mine and not hers. Her husband's name is actually mentioned in Stiff's book as one of the elite whose charges for corruption Mugabe authorised to be dropped. My friend may be eating the bread of corruption in ignorance, I do not know. God will judge. What I know is that she is still the same humble girl I knew back in the 1970s at school. In her own words without me leading her, I found out that she loved the Lord. It gets difficult when you get all these revelations, don't you think? I forgive in my heart and continue to love her.

What Mugabe's government has embarked on since it came to power is not normal. Mugabe and his henchmen are controlled by an evil spirit of witchcraft and that of Sodom and Gomorrah – of promiscuity and all kinds of sexual sins. As a result, his state-controlled media and television have in the last year reported half-human and half-goat births by goats in Zimbabwe.

As Saints of God we must wake up because we know the answer and the solution to such problems. We are not wrestling against flesh and blood; we are wrestling against spirits. It is a Satanic government, which is why the Christian Church will be accountable to God for allowing this, especially the Anglican Church that never raises a voice on these issues.

The Catholic priests and bishops tried everything they could but they had no support from the Anglican Church (my own father's employer). There is no record of the Anglican Church opening its mouth about the atrocities in Matabeleland. Western non-governmental organisations like Oxfam also thrive on the suffering of innocent people in Third World countries while they claim to be helping them, in that they are only interested in their own achievements.

Stiff reports that Oxfam was running a programme in Matabeleland at the time of the atrocities:

> *Immediately after the failure of his two journalist colleagues to assist in spreading the word about what was happening in Matabeleland, Nick Worrall contacted several non-governmental organisations who had field*

operations there. With their field staff deployed it was impossible they could have remained ignorant of what was happening. He urged them to go public. Mike Behr, Oxfam's man in Harare, refused to get involved or pass on any information. Oxfam was running a programme in Matabeleland and it did not want to take the chance of it being prejudiced! "If you don't help in stopping the massacres," Nick told him irritably, "there won't be anybody left to benefit from your bloody programme."

Shortly afterwards, apparently finding courage in numbers, a deputation from nine international aid agencies, including Oxfam, sought an interview with Prime Minister Mugabe and his security minister. Those concerned were British Oxfam, American Oxfam, Save the Children Fund, War on Want, the Quakers, the International Catholic Church and three other NGOs from Holland, Belgium and Canada. They pointed out that terrible things were happening in Matabeleland, that 5 Brigade was torturing and murdering people, that hundreds of innocents had been killed and that many more had been injured or forced to flee their homes.

A reliable source said Prime Minister Mugabe dismissively told them to produce concrete evidence. Shortly afterwards at a press conference he similarly demanded concrete evidence when asked what was going on in Matabeleland. The NGO nine jointly compiled a thick report detailing atrocities committed by 5 Brigade and handed in at the Prime Minister's office on 21 March 1983. Sources close to the NGOs said the report contained detailed accounts of deaths, injuries and mutilations obtained from medical personnel and agency staff in Matabeleland. It was supported by photographs. The report's aim, according to Nick Warrall's sources, was to halt the actions of the troops and to prevent repetitions in the future. The aid organisations, despite the volumes of first-hand evidence they had gathered over the previous six weeks, declined to release it to the press or to make press statements. And they never did. There seemed to be a collective naivety that if they passed the report to Prime Minister Mugabe, he would look into the situation and do something about it. By drawing it to his attention, as the country's leader, he was duty-bound to act and put a stop to it. They were living in a dream world.

It is of interest that many years later in 1999, the author [Peter Stiff]
asked Oxfam for a copy of their 1983 report on 5 Brigade atrocities. They
denied one existed. Literally as the NGO-9's report was handed to Prime
Minister Mugabe, troops and police were again moving into Bulawayo's
western high-density suburbs. The Herald, quoting military sources, said
an undisclosed number of people had been detained for questioning and
homes had been searched. Many of those detained failed to return home
and were never seen again. No government comment was available.
Unofficial army sources, shocked by 5 Brigade's tactics, reported that up
to 50 people had been killed during the three-day operation. The bodies
were taken to the city mortuary, but official sources only confirmed three
dead. The army sources suggested the death toll would have been far higher
if 5 Brigade had not been restrained by the presence of the Police Support
Unit and other army units. In one reported incident, 5 Brigade troops
manning a roadblock stopped two regular policemen on police motor-cycles
and beat them up. In another, a group of women were taken to a rubbish
dump and forced to dig through broken bottles and sharp cans with their
bare hands in a supposed search for weapons. In yet another, two men
were forced down a sewer and made to look for weapons. (2002: 186–7)

Stiff's book also records the names of murdered journalists; Joshua
Nkomo's driver; Didiza Ndhlovu, a 25 year old who got interrogated by
the 5 Brigade and shot instantly when he walked passed Joshua Nkomo's
house in Phelandaba; the threat on Joshua Nkomo's life, leading to
his escape from the CIOs and 5 Brigade to Botswana, then to Britain;
the demise of Zipra soldiers after disarmament; Army and Airforce
Commander Lookout Masuku's detention, torture and death at the
hands of the CIOs; tortured teachers and students. I thank God for giving
him the courage to record all he has in his book, because most people
in Matabeleland who lived in the city, like me, experienced less than a
fraction of the suffering of rural folk from the presence of 5 Brigade in
Matabeleland. We were still wondering what happened to the people we
knew. We thought it was HIV finishing people privately, but there was a
worse plague in Matabeleland than HIV.

In October 2008 in a visionary trance while in prayer, I was given the name of the Justice Minister of Zimbabwe. I had never seen him before. I was also shown two solicitors I knew in Zimbabwe. I was then led to ask one of them about the name I was given. He is the one who revealed to me that the name was for the Justice Minister. God then sent me twice to the Justice Minister, and the following is my second letter to him.

3rd March 2009

Further to my letter of 9th February 2009 God is urgently sending me to you again. He has shown me in a vision in the early hours of today, that innocent women have been beaten and humiliated in public by the police or a male security figure. Although there were many fearful women and people there, it was unpredictable who this man would pick to beat up next with his huge leather belt. I was shown these respectful and unsuspecting women being publicly brutalised without any intervention whatsoever. They all ended up somewhere where a door was opened for them to enter in their screaming and terrified state. The atmosphere was very desolate. Such brutality on women should not be ignored because God has been watching. I do not know how many women have been battered or abused by those in authority, but this has to be corrected because God wants justice for these girls and women.

I did not understand why this particular security man was allowed to do this to women, lowering their self-esteem in public like they were animals. He was very brutal and he represents the Security Officials or the Police Officials in Zimbabwe. Justice is required for these women by God; this should not be ignored. It is very urgent to God that something is done about it and that those responsible should be brought to justice. I fear God, and I am only a messenger.

There are women who are hurting right now in Zimbabwe because the laws there are not regarding women as vessels of honour. God always used women in the Old Testament. For example women like Rahab, the harlot in the Book of Joshua, assisted the nation of Israel's transition from the wilderness into the promised land, she saved the nation of Israel and assisted them in their critical time of need and she later became the ancestor of our Lord and saviour Jesus Christ; Deborah the prophetess and wife to Lapidoth in the Book of Judges Chapter 4 and 5 judged Israel at that time, gave a prophetic and strengthening word to Barak to free the children of Israel from the captivity of Sisera and enabled him to defeat the enemy; Hannah in the book of Samuel mothered Samuel and dedicated him for service to the Lord and Samuel became a great prophet and King Soul's spiritual mentor. The list goes on. Our Lord and Saviour Jesus Christ was born of a woman (the Word that was in the beginning of creation became flesh).

As I prayed, I was shown that there was a lot of injustice and prejudice over women in Zimbabwe. God does not like the disrespect women have been given in Zimbabwe over the years, especially by those in authority. Women's bodies or private parts have been exposed in public and God is not pleased with it. God wants justice for these women. God wants the respect of women restored in the land and they should never be treated as lesser beings. They should be given the respect they deserve in every aspect of life, be it at home, at work and even by the Church. To God's eyes, girls and women, especially widows, should be respected and protected. They are equal beings and they deserve equal rights and respect. Men should channel their energy in hard work, not in the abuse of girls and women. Jehovah God is the defender of the weak.

Yes, a woman was created to submit to her husband as unto the Lord, but not to all men. Her husband is supposed to love her as Christ loved the Church and gave himself for it. Eph. 5: 25. Yes, Eph. 5: 21 states that we should submit ourselves one to another in the fear of God. In other words, we should all respect each other. However, we are all (girl or boy, man or woman) commanded to submit to authority. Those in authority should rule with the fear of God. Many laws pertaining to women will need to be changed. For example, a stepmother should not raise a child while the child's mother still lives. The consequences of extra-marital affairs should not put women and children in poverty and at the mercy of a stepparent. Guardianship should be based on merit, not sex. Sexual sins like promiscuity, rape of little girls and women should really be given more consideration and taken very seriously. God hates sexual sins. Because *of the sexual sins of the tribe of Benjamin in Judges Chapter 20, almost the whole tribe of Benjamin was smitten to death. God has watched this sin on women for a long period of time. There are many casualties as a result of this sin of regarding women as lesser beings.*

All I am saying is that I do not need to be in Zimbabwe to know what is happening there. God always reveals things that concern Him to me right here in my own home. I am only in obedience to Him as His servant.

Just to give an example, I was given a vision of a young man who happened to be contemplating suicide because of depression after his military service in Iraq. He had been shocked to arrive there and for the first time to see children begging for food on the streets. He did not anticipate homeless children to be part of the war he had been trained for. God sent me to his mother in good time. His mother believed what I told her because she confirmed her own concerns about her son to me. He had never revealed his feelings concerning his experience in Iraq to his mother.

I am only called to do the work of God. I cannot apologize for being sent by God. Trusting that you too, Honourable Minister of Justice, will understand my position, the burden on me and the reasons God has finally sent me to you, I believe that God has great plans for the restoration of Zimbabwe, if only He could be given the honour that is due to Him. He loves Zimbabweans, 2 Chronicles 7: 14 and 2 Chronicles 20: 20. He has not forgotten Zimbabwe. He has good plans for the nation of Zimbabwe. I believe it.

Trusting that justice will happen for the hurting women of Zimbabwe. Thanking you in anticipation.

Needless to say, none of my letters was answered even though they were sent through DHL. All I know is that God spoke clearly in the early hours of one morning of November 2009 and during the writing of this book that "Justice is coming in the earth". At the end of the day, given the oppressive history of Mugabe's government by way of military power and so forth, it is obvious that the Justice Minister's hands are tied. But God's hands are not tied. Nothing will stop Him from ensuring justice for His oppressed people.

The plight of the abused women and the fatherless children of Mugabe's ZANLA and 5 Brigade

Stiff explains the founding of ZANLA:

During 1997 considerable pressures were exerted on the government by what was described as "50,000 former guerrilla fighters". They called themselves the Zimbabwe National Liberation War Veterans Association. Their leader, frequently mentioned at the time, was Chenjerai "Hitler" Hunzvi, of whom much more would be heard later. The veterans felt that while everyone else in ZANU-PF had prospered, those who had been demobilised in 1980 instead of being absorbed into the National Army had been cheated. They had been satisfied with the earlier two-year demobilisation packages ... It was virtually impossible to say who were truly war veterans and who were imposters, because in the Bush War days no records were kept. Many were undoubtedly former mujibas. When a guerrilla group moved into a tribal area, its political commissar immediately got to work politicising the people there. After witnessing the brutal executions of a few of their neighbours – perhaps the headman, maybe the local school headmaster – everyone soon became pliant and more than willing to cooperate with the guerrillas. They selected mujibas from the young men to be their eyes and ears. Their task was to report on the movement of the Security Forces in the area and everyone else and everything else that was happening.

The mujibas formed the majority of those who reported to the ZANLA assembly points after the cease-fire. Most of the true guerrillas stayed outside to ensure the locals voted for ZANU-PF in the election. Some members of the Zimbabwe National Liberation War Veterans Association were undoubtedly ex-ZANLA with a sprinkling of ex-ZIPRA guerrillas, but it was an open secret that many were mujibas, which hardly entitled them to the title of "war veterans". Others were plainly frauds. Undoubtedly, too, former soldiers of the infamous 5 Brigade were included in their ranks. But whatever their pedigrees, after they stormed ZANU-PF's headquarters in Harare under the leadership of Hunzvi, they *were awarded gratuities of Z$50,000 and tax-free pensions of Z$2,000 a month with effect from December 1997. The average monthly wage of a black worker in Zimbabwe at the time was Z$1,000, which puts the size of the awards in perspective.*

Seeing the ZANLA mujibas so handsomely rewarded prompted the national vice chairman of the Zimbabwe Women in the National Liberation War Collaborators Association, Rose Chizana, to call on the government to make compensatory payments to her members too. When ZANLA guerrillas moved into an area during the war years, they not only conscripted mujibas but also chimbwindos. These were attractive young women or girls who had often not even reached puberty. Like the mujibas they were recruited to keep tabs on the movement of the Security Forces, seek out collaborators and generally provide intelligence on what was happening in the area. They had the additional responsibility of finding and cooking food for the gangs and taking it to their bush camps. At the camps they were duty bound to provide sex for the guerrillas, men mostly much older than they. This was for what was euphemistically called "entertainment only". Rose Chizana, a former chimbwindo herself, said the sexual abuse of defenceless girls by guerrillas left scores of women with children. "Most of the children fathered by freedom fighters are destitute, just like their mothers. They do not know their fathers, so the government should console them."

Their cry for help brought a result similar somewhat to what had happened to them in the bush camps. ZANU-PF's national secretary for administration, Didymus Mutasa, expressed surprise that the group had the audacity to continue appealing for compensation – when they had already been told they would get nothing. "The country cannot stop running just for the sake of compensating all who claimed to have contributed towards the liberation struggle," Mutasa said. He tritely advised them to join "youth groups" and benefit from the projects being run by the ruling party. This response, which understandably was not well appreciated, was the same given to thousands of "comfort women" – women rounded up by the Imperial Japanese Army in Korea and other occupied territories during World War II and forced into prostitution in

army brothels. Those unfortunate women have also unsuccessfully applied
to the Japanese Government for compensation. Disgracefully, like the
chimbwindos, they are still waiting. (Stiff, 2002: 316–17)

Needless to say, the gangs of orphaned street children I saw in Harare
one night a few years ago were really disturbing. They were all following
one boy who had managed to lay his hands on food and like animals
they all began to rush after him and to fight him for his spoil. It was the
survival of the fittest. They live the typical life of an abandoned animal.
My sister cautioned me as we came out of the shop that the children are
very dangerous and we had to move quickly, as they can turn on anyone
with food. I could see that she was scared of them. I wondered where all
those children were going to sleep.

It would not have cost much at all for the government to consider the
plight of the fatherless children and their mothers. If anything, it was an
opportunity they missed. After all, these children belong to unknown
fathers within Mugabe's ZANLA forces and 5 Brigade. There was no HIV-
related disease in Rhodesia before independence; the disease came with
the ZANLA forces. They thrived on raping children, girls and women
of all ages. The orphans on the streets of Zimbabwe are a result of the
campaign of raping women in Matabeleland and all over the country.
Their farms that are designated as "no go" areas, what are they doing
there? They are not growing crops.

In a recent 90-minute documentary, BBC4 showed the plight of
Zimbabwe's forgotten children, picking bones from the dump for a living,
little children that are abandoned like animals in a country where Mugabe
and his elite live in homes that even Ian Smith and his regime never
owned.

When 5 Brigade was first deployed in front of my house, I could
not bear to look at what they were up to. When I saw my neighbour, a
commuter bus driver, being tortured on his way to work, I simply decided
to close my eyes. But did those mothers manage to close their eyes and ears
when their little girls were raped before their eyes? How did the mother of
the twin babies that were buried alive managed to close her eyes and ears?

Stiff further notes:

That the ZANU-PF government collectively approved of the genocide can best be illustrated by tracing the fortunes of 5 Brigade's founding commander, Colonel Perence Shiri – the Butcher of Bhalagwe … he had been promoted to Air Marshall and appointed commander of the Air Force of Zimbabwe. It would have been more appropriate for him to be stripped of his rank and the uniform he had disgraced, arrested and transferred to The Hague for trial before a UN tribunal for genocide and crimes against humanity. This unfortunately they could not do because there were too many other ZANU-PF Chiefs in high office, including President Robert Mugabe himself, who had blood on their hands and were accessories both before and after the fact to mass murder. Shiri's flawed character can be judged by an incident that happened on 21 January 1996. He attempted to flag down a police vehicle on a country road. When it did not stop, he chased after it, and assaulted a police inspector and shot out the tyres of his vehicle. In February 1996 the Attorney General, Patrick Chinamasa, announced that Shiri would stand trial for the offence. Whether this happened or whether the case was quietly filed on order from the top, is unknown, but nothing further appeared in the press about it. (2002: 227)

There is a lot of work for the Church to do in Zimbabwe and those parts of the world where the people are in a cage, completely shut from the outside world, like North Korea. Healing and restoration happen when there is dialogue. Silence will not bring healing and restoration, especially when people in Matabeleland do not know why they were killed. Closure is what we need for the hurting people of Zimbabwe. The justice of being told why things happened the way they did is what they need. The truth will hurt, but it will bring closure and then forgiveness will bring emotional healing and restoration.

My spiritual mentor once said, "There is nothing wrong with you that God cannot fix. In Ezekiel 37: 1-14, the same spirit that carried Ezekiel into his dry bone yard can carry you out of yours. Nothing is so hopeless that God can't fix it. The power is in the Word of God. We need to hear and accept the Word of God because it releases a 'spirit of restoration' in our lives. It turns our stumbling blocks into stepping-stones and our messes into miracles. Glory!"

CHAPTER 8

Will the Free Christian World Continue in Silence?

God is not prejudiced by the colour of skin, because he created all people. Why is the Body of Christ so prejudiced if we all believe and worship the same Jesus?

I have heard well-meaning men and women of God speak passionately on praying for Israel. This is good, but my question is, have they ever prayed for black Jews of Southern Africa, the remnant of King Solomon? The Ndebele/Zulu people of Matabeleland include the Nguni, the Fingo/ Xhosa, the Khalanga, the Venda, the Sutho, the Tonga, the Tswana people and others who were all innocently mutilated in Matabeleland and the Midlands.

One website speaks passionately about a Zimbabwean woman whose books highlight some of the horrible things she has witnessed. Democracy as understood by the "free world" no longer exists in Zimbabwe. Huge swathes of the countryside have been turned into "no go" areas by the ruling party's thugs, who are now known as "war veterans". This means that no news emerges other than government spin doctoring. She writes that when the ugly truth finally comes out, the world will be horrified. The truth is there is absolutely no rule of law. The elections, which were held in 2002, were rigged by the ruling party. Currently, ZANU PF is illegitimately "ruling" the country. Human rights abuses have continued unabated.

She is just one of the people who have the courage and conviction to let the world know what she sees and experiences on a daily basis. The reality is that while you read this, crimes against humanity are in progress and very little, if anything, is being done to stop the madness. State-sponsored terror and anarchy continue unabated.

The starvation currently being experienced in Southern Africa is a direct result of ZANU-PF policies. It is common knowledge that Zimbabwe was the food basket of Southern Africa. It is notable that South African farmers who have not been subjected to the same treatment have produced good grain yields under the same climate conditions. This reinforces the argument that this food shortage is not caused by drought. Most African leaders must shoulder the blame because they have remained silent. As the food supplies dwindled, government ministers continually and categorically stated that there were adequate food supplies. This was a lie.

Meanwhile, Robert Mugabe denies ruining the economy and instead says that his country's problems are a result of the West and Britain imposing sanctions on his government. This is the propaganda he uses to win the support of those he brainwashed.

While Mugabe and his illegal government continue with their campaign of terror on the innocent and suffering Zimbabweans, it is clear that the Anglo-Catholic Church, and Britain in particular, have forgotten all about their contribution in illegally empowering Mugabe over the people of Zimbabwe. The whole country has felt the pain.

The black Jews of Matabeleland continue to be alienated and oppressed in Zimbabwe. There are hardly any Ndebele people left there now. The whole of Matabeleland continues to be under Mugabe's Shona oppression. Is the pain of the Jews of Matabeleland not the same as that of the white Jews that we see highlighted on television? Is Adolf Hitler guiltier than Margaret Thatcher and Lord Carrington's Conservative government that gave Mugabe power over the people of Matabeleland and assisted him in disarming Joshua Nkomo's ZIPRA combatants?

Joshua Nkomo (1984: 245) highlighted the efforts of the brave Zimbabwe Catholic priests and bishops in speaking for the people of Matabeleland, although their statement was criticised by Mugabe's minister of information, Dr Nathan Shamuyarira, as "irresponsible, contrived propaganda". Mugabe said that the bishops were mere megaphone agents of their external manipulative masters, further calling them "a band of Jeremiahs". The bishops responded to Mugabe's attack on their impartiality, but he ignored their protests.

Stiff reports what happened when Nkomo died:

Joshua Nkomo's death at the age of 83 in July 1999 was followed by a state funeral at Heroes Acre outside Harare. In a 90 minute eulogy, President Mugabe lavishly praised Nkomo for helping to forge unity between his Ndebele people and the Mashonas. He appealed for this unity to be continued and made a brief reference to events in Matabeleland in the 1980s, saying the deaths and suffering there had been "regrettable". It was Mugabe's first public acknowledgement that anything untoward had ever occurred in Matabeleland. It appears clear, considering the time lapse since the slaughter, that his move was designed to ward off any troubles that might brew up in Matabeleland with the loss of Joshua Nkomo's restraining hand. Already there were signs of a ZAPU revival with the founding in Matabeleland of a group called ZAPU 2000. They had accused the government of withholding development aid to the province and of corruption. Bekithemba Sibindi, leader of another Ndebele organisation, Imbovane Yamahlabezulu – named after a feared 19th century Matabele regiment – said: "Nkomo has gone with his signature. It is the [end of the unity accord]." Nine days later, Home Affairs Minister Dumiso Dabengwa told the state-controlled Sunday Mail that the government had undertaken to compensate the victims in the affected areas to ensure political stability. "The government will help all those cases requiring assistance."

In December 1999 Zimbabwe's Lawyers for Human Rights and the Legal Resources Foundation filed an application in the High Court for an order to compel Mugabe to make public the report of the Chihambakwe Commission of Enquiry into the activities of 5 Brigade in 1983. They also sought an order to force him to publish the Dumbutshena Report into the fighting at Entumbane in 1982. The Attorney-General, Patrick Chinamasa, in opposing papers, said the two organisations had no right to take Mugabe to court because he enjoyed presidential immunity enshrined in the constitution. The human rights organisation, however, argued that the section on presidential immunities he referred to only covered Mugabe in his personal, not in his official capacity.

On 21 February 2000 Anthony Gubbay ruled that "no presidential immunity is accorded the office of the President". He gave President Mugabe 20 days to challenge the ruling. Justice Minister Emmerson Munangagwa responded by filing affidavits with the High Court on President Mugabe's behalf which, astonishingly, said the reports had been lost.

During an interview with the Deputy Editor of Johannesburg's The Star, Mathatha Tsedu, President Mugabe spoke of the Catholic Commission for Justice and Peace's Breaking the Silence and expressed regret that the war in Matabeleland had been necessary. "We have asked Chiefs to work with government to identify victims and examine the need for assistance and for those institutions to establish who suffered and to determine what compensation may be necessary. But the misguided report by the Catholics is nothing but mischievous. I have asked them why they chose to start their investigations into atrocities in Zimbabwe around the issue and not about atrocities committed by the Smith regime." (2002: 227-8)

Mugabe's legacy of lies and intimidation continues 30 years later

Like Nkomo and others in the past, the new prime minister of Zimbabwe experiences president Mugabe's lies and betrayal.

In a Guardian report on 16th October 2009, Morgan Tvangirai stated that his party was boycotting the unity government over the "dishonest and unreliable" behaviour of Mugabe and his Zanu-PF allies. The report further stated that the prime minister's decision was sparked by the detention that week of Roy Bennet, a Movement for Democratic Change Minister. Apparently there was also frustration over the lack of genuine power sharing since the unity government's formation.

In 1980, Mugabe had used the ways of terror to punish the regions of Zimbabwe that did not vote for him. He forced Nkomo's party into uniting with his in order to benefit from Nkomo's economic strategies that he had fought for all those years. He needed Nkomo's expertise and knowledge and therefore he forced Nkomo to unite under one umbrella with him, as he put it. He then influenced the police force against Nkomo, to frustrate all his efforts to address rallies around Matabeleland by dispersing the crowds with tear gas like Ian Smith used to do, or even worse.

Robert Mugabe had lied at Lancaster House in 1979 when the British asked him what he was fighting for; he told them what they wanted to hear, that he was fighting for democracy. Meanwhile, he had a hidden agenda of a one-party state, like Uganda's Idi Amin. The British government disliked Nkomo because he told the truth, that he was fighting for land, the British's main interest because people in the House of Lords are still holding on to vast areas of unused fertile land in the highest-rainfall parts of Zimbabwe.

Justice on this earth has not been fairly realised concerning African black people. However, God is gracious, compassionate, long-suffering and plenteous in mercy and in truth (Psalms 86: 15). God is a God of justice. He is no respecter of persons. God spoke to me. He said that He is bringing justice on the earth.

Below is an article from an artist in Matabeleland, Zimbabwe (Cont Mhlanga, *Arts and Cultural Activist*, April 14, 2010), which I have permission to reproduce:

30th Anniversary – Where to Zimbabwe?

This weekend of 18 April 2010 is special in Zimbabwe's history as it is the young nation's 30th Anniversary. It is also special to President Mugabe as he celebrates his 30th Anniversary as the President of Zimbabwe. I congratulate him as he has managed to live the dream of the old generation of Africa's nationalist leaders of the '60s, that of being a life President of their party and country despite whatever. When someone achieves the envy of their generation's neighbourhood dream they should be congratulated. This year is also special to me as a cultural activist in that I have been blessed by my Ancestors and God in my thirty years of cultural activism in that I have been able to stamp a solid arts and culture foot print in the nation's cultural landscape. I have one regret though, that all my activism has been under one President, one government by one political party that has found no reason and motivation to financially or technically support my activism for best reasons known to themselves despite the obvious output and national impact of my initiatives to the young nation. Sadly such support and recognition has only come from foreign governments as if my own national leaders see my efforts in the arts and cultural sector of the nation that they lead as criminal. In the 30 years of my arts and cultural activism I can count more incidents of victimization, intimidation and marginalization from the national government that for a full generation has administered arts and culture in independent Zimbabwe in comparison to the material, financial, technical or even partnership linkages that they could have provided within their means. It is sure not inspiring to be marginalized and ignored by one's own government for thirty years! I can only speculate how different it would have been had I the opportunity to do my work under a different government by a different political party or the same political party led by a different President. All I can say is that I now deeply understand why a single President should not lead the same political party, government and or country for as long as thirty years. I am however sure that those that have and continue to benefit from such a political culture in Zimbabwe would vote for it to continue to be the accepted political cultural norm with their hands and feet. I would vote against such a political practice at every opportunity. This is why I teach my children with passion that they should never allow themselves to be led by a single president for over 10 years no matter how bright that president is and that they should never allow a Parliament that initiates new laws on the first Monday of the month and implements them on the last Friday of the same month. This is how the parliament led by Zimbabwe's first and life President functioned for the past 30 years, hence all the new laws they passed only served them and not the majority of the people of Zimbabwe. I will support a new constitution only if it has a clause that will stop this political culture in the future parliament of Zimbabwe. President Mugabe's political legacy; a person who is the only one who has power to skin a lizard with their *fingernail is a danger to society and to all human kind. I love African political satire. I enjoy writing, producing and consuming it. It is to me equal to the African folk story as these focus on character and social development of humans in relation to their environment. In political satire I find freedom to express my opinion and those of the community that is my home. In my political satire plays over the past 30 years I have warned my fans of the very dangerous political legacy that President Mugabe was creating for this beautiful country and its future generations. It is my intention to summarize them here for the nation to remember as we all celebrate the country and President Mugabe's 30th Anniversary as President of Zimbabwe. But before I go on let me pose a question: "Who is President Mugabe to you?"*

I went out to Mthombothemba village where President Mugabe taught in his youthful years to get an answer from an old grandmother who was President Mugabe's student.

"We knew him as teacher Ngwenya. He never used Mugabe. He was always well dressed: white shirts; left hand always in the pocket even when writing on the blackboard. He beat students like hell. Those that did not have guts dropped out of school because of that. He never cooked in his house. There was no stove or fireplace. He went to eat at places we didn't know in town. All the years he stayed at this school he never spoke Ndebele or Shona. Only English."

This is who President Mugabe is to old Mrs Sibanda at Mthombothemba village. This is the man who grew up to be life president and life commander of the national army. His legacy that the majority of people in the country only whisper in the dark is yet to haunt this nation, maybe long after he has taken his number one grave at the National Heroes Palace. The present that belongs to us was the future whose foundations belonged to those that lived before us.

The long walk to freedom
The liberation struggle of this country is the main reason for celebrating this 30th Anniversary. In my opinion the amazing story of the liberation struggle for this country has for the past 30 years been told by untruthful

political servants and agents. I wish one day that as a cultural activist story teller I would be able to tell my version of the story, but here let me give the outline of the story as an introduction to the dangerous legacy of this 30 year presidential term. I can divide the characters in the story of Zimbabwe's liberation into three very distinct waves of movements and phases of collective attitude that can be placed in each decade as follows.

1950 to 1959 – was the movement of pioneer liberators who knew no race, no colour, no tribe, no religion, no gender, no boundaries. For them it was indigenous power and nothing less, Africa for Africans by Africans and then Africa to the world. They focused on growing African allies within their own continent while mobilizing for total citizen participation. This movement was driven by lawyers, writers and labour unions. The standing out motivation in this phase to join the movement was "black power".

1960 to 1969 – was the movement of nationalists who focused on freedom within borders, majority rule with one man one vote. They built guerrilla armies and aggressively mobilized international allies. They used Africa's liberated borders as their operation bases. This movement was driven by educationists now turned full-time politicians. The standing out motivation in this phase to join the movement was "leadership positions".

1970 to 1979 – was the movement of tribalists and looters. Tribal conflicts emerged in the fighting camps and forces. Tribalism grew deep roots in political parties. Looting from villagers and local business in the name of the struggle emerges strongly. This movement was driven by some governments of the now liberated African countries in partnership with political party leaders of their choice. Looting was driven mainly by some armed fighters in commanding positions. The standing out motivation in this phase to join the movement was "personal security and self empowerment".

1980 – is the excitement of independence and one of the biggest deciding factors that had to determine Zimbabwe's future was the turnaround period between the end of the conference on the British soil and the first one man one vote general election in 1980 on the Rhodesian soil. The turnaround period from liberation movements to national government was too short and the 1970–1979 generation moved swiftly and took control of the country. From there on, we are all witness to what happened in the next 30 years after Zimbabwe got its independence. The 30 years we are celebrating this month. As a story teller let me invite you to imagine the story of Zimbabwe this way:

It's a very simple plot. There is a city called Salisbury. It is very wealthy and controls its very rich provinces in natural resources. This is where the corridors of power are controlling. This city is an all settler white club; if you like gang. Two passenger trains travel between Bulawayo and Salisbury every day. Passengers are divided into classes of White, Asian, Coloureds and Blacks. Train drivers and all railway controllers are white. One day a group of blacks, if you like gang, led by Ndabambi and Mabhalane decide that they will jump onto the Bulawayo to Salisbury train and take control of it, destroy the apartheid in the train, remove all white engine drivers and system controllers, replace them with some of their own. Blacks too must drive trains! The resistance they get from the settler club in Salisbury is vicious. They decide to mobilize and take Salisbury down by all means necessary. To do so, they have to take over the total control of the train first and land it in Salisbury. The settler club in Salisbury decides to stop this train from landing in Salisbury. The action and events in the train make a chilling tale. At Shangani train station the now leaders of the small but growing black movement decide to brand and paint the part of the train that they have taken over and call it The Liberation Train. Now the masses can easily identify it and they run to the railway line to cheer it up and give support and service to the occupants in the train. Those that jump into the train are called The Liberators. One has to stay in the train or be thrown out for whatever reason. It takes the train 30 years to get to the great city of money and power. But hold on, it's now not just one train it's now two trains. When the Liberation train got to Kwekwe train station, others decided that they *will jump on a train that was from Salisbury to Bulawayo, take it over and drive it back to Salisbury as they could not stand the heat in this first train any longer. They did not like the Ndebele leader in the train. Citizens now had to choose to jump on which train based on tribal lines. There was now tense competition to arrive first in Salisbury between the passengers of the two trains while the settler white club had now to deal with stopping one more train coming into Salisbury. After all the action adventures and meetings in the two trains they finally both land at the station on 18th April 1980 at the same hour. The 1970 to 1979 movement and generation is in charge. They have the influence and are the opinion leaders. Every one jumps off the train and runs to all directions!! This is Salisbury, the city of money and power. Maye babo!! Questionable History!*

This year we celebrate the 30 years' work of those that arrived in Salisbury on 18th April 1980 and became in charge. It is my wish though that we will one day as a nation find time and reason to celebrate the whole 30 years from when the Liberation train departed for Salisbury from Bulawayo in 1950. You however need to have and respect accurate liberation history to be able to do this responsibly and I am afraid that the current history that is in our schools is a big lie. Zimbabwe's liberation history is a propaganda history pie that will cause serious constipation to the future generations of this country. I wonder what kind of an idiot would write and teach the whole nation wrong history at this age of Facebook? The nation celebrates its 30th Anniversary under very questionable liberation history. Why were non-fiction writers and journalists hired over the past 30 years to write this misleading history?

A foundation for the future

As we celebrate the 30th Anniversary of the country, let's ask the critical question: has Zimbabwe set up a strong foundation for the peaceful development of its citizens to a prosperous future? I have my doubts. In fact all pointers on the ground today show us that over the 30 years the government of Zimbabwe under the leadership of the one and only has laid down a strong foundation for worse future crises. The three most prominent and now advanced foundations are:

Shona xenophobia – It is sad to note that over the 30 years the Zimbabwe government has worked tirelessly and openly to promote fertile ground for Shona xenophobia in the western part of the country. In the next few years the country will be ready to explode and experience this Shona xenophobia. This has been done through a deliberate tribal line based civil service staffing policy for all government departments and government-controlled companies. It has also been promoted aggressively through marginalized education and economic indigenization. The effect of this policy in the western region of the country is so thick that eleven year old kids playing street paper balls will shout to each other tribal venom with such a dangerous and vengeful vigor and words one would only expect to come from drunk adults. The future of Zimbabwe belongs not to us but to these frustrated and angry kids. It is not my intention to list all arguments here but my intention is to say to all Zimbabweans watch out the foundation your government has laid for the future of this country. Don't be silent about this any more especially now that inter-marriages have brought our people so close. Shona xenophobia would be the most painful to both of Zimbabwe's two major tribes. This country has a history of Shona xenophobia, the first in 1929 and the second in 1981. Government is getting it ready for the third. As we celebrate the 30th Anniversary of our country let us all find ways of digging up this very dangerous foundation that the government has laid down for our children. These things can happen if they are left unattended or attended to the wrong way. One more thing is that they suddenly erupt and happen when people list expect them to. I remain convinced that Zimbabwe has prepared very fertile ground for Shona xenophobia and I wait to be proved wrong. Only time will tell.

A foundation for separation – In 2000 when Zapu 2000, a political pressure group I worked with, called for decentralization of administrative power from Harare, most people dismissed it as young crazy youths from

Matebeleland who had nothing worthwhile to do. Today just and only 10 years on, all you need to do is sit in any meeting discussing the new constitution in Zimbabwe's western region of the country and the public cries for separation not even decentralization have become louder and are getting louder each day. The continued suppression and ignoring of the Matebeleland genocide is the major cause of these separatists sentiments that are fast rising. Gukurahundi started off as a way of fixing a "small" political matter between two liberation war parties and it swiftly swung out of control; but then badly handled over the past 30 years and slowly it has grown into a major foundation for the future crises of this country. I am convinced that the nation in the not so distant future will be fighting a separatist movement whose objective is to separate Matebeleland from Mashonaland.

History is very clear that the British colonizers took authority from a King in Matebeleland in 1893 and from Chiefs in Mashonaland early on in 1890 clearly confirming that these were two separate states before colonization. The UN too is very clear on how to proceed with such matters. The Gukurahundi genocide cannot be pushed under the carpet, locked up in cabinets, or be a taboo subject in Zimbabwe that should never be openly discussed any more. It cannot be suppressed for ever. Doing so will only strengthen the cause for calling for separation. And by the way, separationist politics is very fertile ground for civil war. As the nation celebrates 30 years of independence this April it must make it a point that the event cannot be about eating meat and listening to empty self praise speeches. Zimbabweans should call for the Gukurahundi genocide cabinets to be opened. The nation cannot afford to be silent on this. These are sins for this generation and let's not pass them to the next generation of Zimbabweans.

The Zimbabwe government over the past 30 years has carefully set up the agenda of separation politics for this country and has done so on a very dangerous and irresponsible tribal agenda. Zimbabwe has set itself up for serious future internal political conflict in the past 30 years. Only time will have to prove me wrong on this.

A fight for local resources – looting of local district and provincial resources in the name of national development leaving locals in poverty is a trend that has been promoted by the government over the past 30 years. It seems for one reason or the other this government has been very comfortable with rural looting. Rural schools, clinics, roads to name but a few have remained in a sorry state since independence while some employees in government departments, agencies and companies have been used as fronts to loot local resources using some dubious Acts of Parliament and some overzealous ministries and ministers. This is more sensitive in the western region of the country given the tribal employment policy of the government in its ranks. The reality on the ground reads to any local as a "Shona government sending its Shona operatives to come and loot the region and export the resources to Asia while jobless and unskilled locals are left to border jump to neighbouring countries to become economic refugees". This has been made worse by the unbalanced recent land redistribution exercise where local farms have been grabbed from white farmers and given to people from outside the western provinces.

Second is how government has marginalized locals through its financial support programs and tenders to empower non locals ahead of locals to start and operate businesses in almost all of the business centers in the western region of the country.

Thirdly is the protection of corrupt officials and ruling party operatives clearly creating a class structure where the majority Shona tribe over other national tribes have become the super rich class through corruption, favouritism and nepotism.

Fourth is how government has remained silent when tribal elements within its ranks have sought to use public media controlled by government to marginalize all other ethnic cultures and languages to create Shona as the dominant culture and language in the country overriding even the use of local languages at local districts for all public service. Here government has successfully laid a strong foundation for local people to start mobilizing to defend their local resources, languages and culture. One cannot in a modern society collect revenues from locals, take it to the capital to empower a few people in the close circle of those connected to government while local people are left to be victims of poverty, and do it successfully and for ever. One day the locals will sharpen axes and manufacture petrol bombs to defend their local resources and culture. Zimbabwe has set itself well for this conflict in the past 30 years.

Given the three very sensitive issues that I have raised above it is very clear to anyone who cares for peace that the Zimbabwe government under the leadership of the one and only over the past 30 years has handled the Matebeleland question very carelessly and very irresponsibly. They have fooled themselves and everyone close to them that there is no such a thing as "the Matebeleland question". Well all signs on the streets and villages of western Zimbabwe today point otherwise unless one is always flying above everyone or stays in the Diaspora.

As we celebrate the 30th Anniversary of Zimbabwe let's all address the Matebeleland question squarely and stop wishing it away for the good and the benefit of the future generations of this country. Let's not take solace in the fact that we may not be there when it explodes. It is a too dangerous and sensitive question to ignore and the way it is unfolding, it may seriously hurt those innocent kids who are sitting watching satellite television behind those high walls and have no clue of what is going on at the townships or the villages in a country they call home. They could be taken by surprise and that could be your family or your grand children.

A time to reflect

A single fly in a cup of milk throws away the whole value of the milk product until it is removed. I use milk here because I hear it is the president's chosen raw material for his excellent business venture. President Mugabe has sure done a lot of good in his 30 year term as president of this country. No one should take that away from him. He has given Zimbabwe a full cup of milk in his life presidency. However there are three flies in this cup of milk, the flies I have mentioned above, and as long as the flies remain in the cup of milk anyone will see the flies before the milk. It is only natural. In his last years of life President Mugabe should work to remove these flies from this wonderful cup of milk and all of us responsible citizens must assist him to do that. He will never be able to do it when he is dead and no one can do it well on his behalf once he is gone. It is even possible that those that are close to him today or someone else may rewrite history and claim credit for all the good things he has done once he passes on. He will simply then go down in history as a bad person who should be quickly forgotten or remembered only for the bad things that happened during his life at state house. Who of us remember those bad things he did at Mthombothemba village if they are any? I guess not many do. But those bad things he has done while at state house will be remembered by many for ever.

As he celebrates his 30th Anniversary as president of Zimbabwe this month President Mugabe must reflect and consider moving out of the state house now and focus, like a great states man, on removing the three flies in his cup of milk that he has handed over to the future generations of this nation. Trying to do so while he is still in the state house is as good as jumping into the cup and diving to the bottom of the milk to try and remove the flies.

Let me conclude by saying, Zimbabwe is a very beautiful blessed country that does not need nor deserve to be governed and managed on tribal and ethnic lines. It is very unfortunate that a lot of the older generation of Zimbabweans in politics today are still living and advancing their tribal dreams of 1963 and most of our young leaders in politics, business and civil society are learning well this bad culture from them. As we celebrate the nation's 30th Anniversary let's be very mindful where Zimbabwe could be headed to in the next 30 years under the current political culture. Let those that have ears hear. I hope time will prove me wrong.

CHAPTER 9

Time for the People of Zimbabwe to Know the Truth

R obert Mugabe continues to win the support of the SADC leaders who respect him as a revolutionary leader who fought against racial segregation and apartheid, yet he is only in power because he betrayed and murdered true revolutionaries who suffered for the country. He has destroyed the country's economy and continued his campaign of wiping out his enemies, the innocent citizens of Zimbabwe and especially those who are a threat to his rule.

Peter Stiff highlights in his book that after the efforts of the South Africans to destabilise the Zimbabwe Airforce by bombing Thornhill Air Base in 1981, Mugabe's government caught and detained the suspects. I will let him tell the tale (2002: 151-6).

Without a scrap of evidence, the detectives arrested 30 white airmen on suspicion ... Despite protests by Western governments, it took ten months before the officers appeared in the High Court to face charges under the Law and Order (Maintenance) Act. They all pleaded not guilty. The State's case was that the accused had admitted they were part of a "committee" supported by BOSS – South Africa's Bureau for State Security. Its purpose was to bring about the destruction of the Airforce of Zimbabwe and engineer the downfall of Prime Minister Mugabe so he would be replaced by "an extreme radical". They also alleged that three ex-Rhodesian SAS men with the unlikely names of Verwoerd, Jones and Swanepoel had been recruited and sent from Johannesburg to stage the attack on the air base. The State's case included details of "code words", "BOSS agents" etc. – all gained from confessions "freely and voluntarily made". It was obvious from the beginning that it was a trumped up case.

The police investigators, or their political superiors, had decided what had happened at Thornhill, and they set out to build a case around that by means of torture. Judge Enock Dumbutshena, Zimbabwe's first black judge and later Chief Justice, agreed. After a 44-day trial he castigated the State for withholding legal counsel from the accused, found that their "confessions" had been obtained under extreme duress, and acquitted them. ZANU-PF was outraged. As the officers walked from the court as free man, orders for indefinite detention – containing accusations identical to the indictments they had just been acquitted of – were served on them and they were taken back into custody.

The day after their re-detention the government offered Zimbabwean-born Air Vice-Marshall Slatter and British-born Air Commodore Pile, the most senior officers, a deal for their release. They would be deprived of all pension rights and be deported to the United Kingdom. If they agreed to leave the country and said nothing to the press when they arrived in London, the government would consider releasing the others. If they refused, things would get tougher for everyone. Hugh Slatter refused to consider the offer unless everyone was released simultaneously. He was concerned the regime would renege on the deal and leave the others to rot their lives away in Chikurubi. The British Deputy High Commissioner intervened a week later and persuaded him to accept the offer. This was officially announced on 8 September by a government spokesman, who said they would be released from detention the following day. They would be freed, he said, "on condition that they agree to leave Zimbabwe forthwith". He quoted from a statement signed by Minister Ushewokunze, saying: "The decision by the government to release these two men was taken the day following their redetention, but delays in implementing this decision have been occasioned by unnecessary and irrelevant stances and tantrums taken by the officers and their lawyers. Steps are being taken to declare both officers undesirable inhabitants of Zimbabwe in terms of the Emergency Powers (Maintenance of Law and Order) Regulations." They would not be allowed to return even if Zimbabwean-born. There was no mention of the fate of the remaining officers.

On 7 September 1983 Minister Ushewokunze spoke out against Judge Enock Dumbutshena for acquitting the airmen. "During the old regime, in case after case, the High Court justices believed the police and disbelieved the accused. One after another the Smith regime hung [sic] heroic sons of the people on confessions which the accused said the police had extricated by torture. In all those cases the High Court believed police denials. In exactly similar cases since independence, the High Court has invariably believed the accused ... the police brought them before a magistrate to declare in open court whether each accused had made the statement of his own free will, without inducement. The magistrate accepted each accused's statement. The present judgment nullifies the magistrate's court proceeding on the grounds that the police refused the accused access to their lawyers ... A poor man without a lawyer effectively receives different treatment to a rich man without a lawyer ... That a judge could articulate so discriminatory a rule without even apologising for its class character speaks volumes about the ... values of our High Court justices ... In our law, illegally obtained evidence nevertheless remains admissible in court. That stands for the policy judgement and even if the policeman makes a mistake or acts illegally, that does not justify letting the criminal go free ... Mr justice Dumbutshena's judgment reverses that policy ... Finally, Mr Justice Dumbutshena completely underplayed the fact that aeroplanes were destroyed at Thornhill."

On 8 September 1983 Prime Minister Mugabe was bombarded with questions about the detained air force officers at an impromptu press conference held in Dublin, Ireland. It was a question and answer session in which he took a severe drubbing at the hands of experienced journalists who deplored his government's actions. ... Prime Minister Mugabe, who was due to fly directly to New York from Dublin, made an unexpected detour to London where he held talks with British Minister of State, Richard Luce, at Heathrow Airport. The subjects discussed were not revealed, but both governments insisted there had been no attempts to pressurise Mugabe by threatening to suspend economic aid or curtailing the military training mission in Zimbabwe. The talks were described as a normal courtesy. This was unlikely as angry Conservatives had already demanded an end to British aid in retaliation for undiplomatic taunts directed by Mugabe at Prime Minister Margaret Thatcher during his Dublin press conference.

Air Lieutenant Nigel Lewis-Walker was released on 16 November 1983 following a recommendation by a "review tribunal". The Zimbabwe authorities had originally said that the review tribunal's roll was vastly overcrowded, but the priority of the officers' cases was rapidly advanced after a meeting between Margaret Thatcher and Robert Mugabe at the Commonwealth Prime Minister's Conference in New Delhi, India in early December. This was confirmed by Prime Minister Mugabe who announced on his return to Harare that British–Zimbabwean relations, which had gone "sour" since the officers' detention, had been repaired. The cases of Wing Commander John Cox, Air Lieutenants Barrington Lloyd and Neville Weir came before a review tribunal on the 9th and they were released two weeks later. They were given seven days to leave the country, whether they were Zimbabwean citizens or not.

On further issues related to the legacy of intimidation that keeps Robert Mugabe in office, Stiff highlights the following contents of a joint statement issued by the SADC Heads of State after the 2000 poll was over:

We, the SADC heads of state and government, meeting in Windhoek, congratulate the government and people of the Republic of Zimbabwe on the manner in which they conducted their parliamentary elections on 24 and 25 June, 2000. We further express satisfaction that the elections were held in a transparent, peaceful, free and fair environment, in accordance with our shared democratic principles and values. We welcome, with appreciation, the balanced, professional and objective assessments of the election made by the SADC Parliamentary Forum and OAU observer missions. We are disappointed by the partisan and biased manner in which a sector of the international media has misrepresented the land policy of the government of Zimbabwe which seeks to affect a just and equitable redistribution of land in a situation where one percent of the population

owns 70% of the best arable land. We reiterate our acceptance of the urgent
need to affect land redistribution in Zimbabwe to address land hunger and
poverty affecting millions of black Zimbabweans. We welcome assurances
by the President of Zimbabwe that the land reform programme would be
handled peacefully, and within the provisions of the laws of Zimbabwe.
We are convinced that to have a land reform programme which is fair and
just to all stakeholders it is imperative for the UK government to honour
its obligations under the Lancaster House Agreement to provide resources
for that purpose. In this regard, the Summit requested the presidents of
South Africa and Malawi to make representations to the UK government
on behalf of the region. (2002: 467–8)

Did these heads of state actually not know the extent of the intimidation by way of killings, beatings, rapes and threats that were going on in the rural areas throughout the country? God hates false witnesses. How will they answer to God after everything that happened to His people at the time? How much does the SADC know about Mugabe's CIOs and 5 Brigade? They are still raping and maiming and killing and being paid for it from taxpayers' money. Since 1980, the illegal government of Zimbabwe has never respected the taxpayers or even acknowledged their contribution to the state.

The reason political organisations have failed over the years to restore peace in this world is due to selfishness, greed and a lack of unity of purpose. Some member states have their own agenda. The South African Development Community state leaders are rebellious false witnesses, liars, stiff-necked selfish ex-combatants of decades ago, who are doing nothing but great harm in the SADC region of Africa with no consideration for the future generations. They believe that they created this world and therefore that they can override justice and manipulate their way for their own gain. They continue to treat African affairs as their own little family business.

Surely the Lord God will do nothing, but He revealeth His secret unto
His servants the prophets. The lion hath roared, who will not fear? The

Lord God hath spoken, who can but prophesy? Publish in the palaces
at Ashdod, and in the palaces in the land of Egypt, and say, Assemble
yourselves upon the mountains of Samaria, and behold the great tumults
in the midst thereof, and the oppressed in the midst thereof.

Amos 3: 7–9

Who are the revolutionary comrades the SABC regards so highly? What
about the fathers of many in Zimbabwe who also perished in the struggle
for the country and whose graves are not known? They did not suffer so
that the Southern African Development Community (SADC) heads of
state could continue to encourage and condone corruption, selfishness
and cruelty in the region, at the expense of the vulnerable, poor, hungry
and hurting people of God in Zimbabwe.

Does being a president or prime minister make one the creator of
heaven and earth that they should rule in rebelliousness against God?
They all inherited the oppressive principles of their former oppressor in
order to oppress their own black people. They are not even ashamed of
it. It is time for the rebellious SADC leaders to let go and let the Body of
Christ take over the affairs of Africa. Once people have made up their
minds that they do not want unity with you, how can you force them to
agree with you? How can unity succeed if God is not the foundation of it?

The Holy Ghost cannot be involved in any agreement that people
make unless there is humility, prayer and repentance. Unless our unity
efforts are based on the fear of God and on His Word, God cannot be
part of that unity, because only God can bring restoration. "Except the
Lord build the house, they labour in vain that build it" (Ps 127: 1a).

In August 2009, God showed me in a vision that Joshua Nkomo
was the true leader of Zimbabwe and that the younger generations of
Zimbabwe should be told the truth.

The truth has to be written if it can't be openly spoken. "Ye shall
know the truth and the truth shall make you free" (John 8: 32). If the
Bible speaks openly about a terrible betrayer like Judas Iscariot, or Saul
who murdered Christians and was later converted and used by God,
then surely somebody must write about the murderers, haters, liars and

betrayers of this century. What is so special about the people and leaders of today that we cannot write about their obedience and disobedience to God? Was the Apostle Paul not converted after the resurrection of Christ? Are we all not living after the resurrection of Christ?

I would like to clarify here that during the writing of this book I found myself in a predicament with regard to some of the revelations I was given. As I pondered to myself what to do with them on 9th October 2009, I was shown a vision of a very ugly and noisy vehicle. The vehicle was brought to us for our own use. It operated in a strange way. It took time to start, as it was supposed to heat up first and hence its noise when it started. The noise was dreadful to those around. I felt reluctant to use it for fear of upsetting people, but it was the only vehicle we were offered to use. I questioned my husband in the vision and said, "How can we use such a noisy vehicle, it will wake everyone up?" Then the revelation came to me that the vision related to the things I was concerned about putting in the book. On 12th October 2009 at 3.25 a.m., God emphasised in an audible voice about the Gospel Truth. I was woken up to write down the truth, the Gospel Truth, and told that it was not my Book but God's book.

As the Body of Christ, we cannot be silent for fear of being murdered by politicians and their henchmen. God is more fearful to me. His presence visited me in my living room in November 2009 and I will never forget it. Those who wrote the Gospels and the rest of the New Testament were not having a party. Their good and bad were exposed for us all to read in order to learn from them, and not repeat the same failures. Let us do everything possible to fulfil the purpose of God for our lives before He comes. Therefore it is critical for the truth to be highlighted concerning the leaders of our century so that future generations are not deprived of this truth.

Joshua Nkomo's unsuccessful unity strategy

In 1985, while the 5 Brigade was wiping out the Ndebele people of Matabeleland, Robert Mugabe used Enos Nkala, then his Home Affairs

Minister, to coerce the tormented and victimised Joshua Nkomo and his Zimbabwe African People's Union (ZAPU) to unite with Mugabe's government. Mugabe's unity plan was to enforce his current one-party state, like his friend North Korea. Peter Stiff describes what happened:

> *The unity agreement resulting in ZAPU being absorbed by ZANU-PF not only brought an end to dissidence, but also a greater concentration of power in the hands of the President and his ZANU-PF ruling elite. With domination by the executive and without an effective opposition to act as a watchdog, Parliament was relegated to a rubber stamp. Constitutional counterbalances to prevent excesses of political power disappeared. The Senate, which the Lancaster House Agreement had regarded as a sort of House of Lords, was abolished. The 20 seats reserved by the Lancaster House Constitution to give the white minority a forum for a period of 10 years had also mostly gone. Parliamentary seats were increased from 100 to 150, but of these only 120 would be up for election through the unitary voting system. The remaining 30, increased from 20, were the seats previously preserved for whites which should have been abolished. Instead, they were reserved for chiefs, provincial governors and political cronies nominated at the discretion of the President, which 30 members of ZANU-PF got seats without winning a single vote. The effect is that if the ruling party wins 46 seats and the opposition wins the balance of 74 seats in an election, the ruling party wins the election. With the 46 seats properly won plus the Presidential nominations of another 30, it winds up with a simple majority of two. These electoral "reforms" did not raise a storm of protest and neither did they become an issue in the 1990 elections. The truth was that ZANU-PF had slipped them virtually unnoticed, like an assassin's knife, into Zimbabwe's chances for true democracy. (2002: 245)*

Mugabe did not stick to the Unity Agreement with Nkomo because of his own one-party state agenda. He was not spiritually united with Nkomo in the first place. This is a man whose strategy for the extinction of the Ndebele people had been finalised and documented by his party a year before the Lancaster Agreement was even signed. According to his ZANU party's red policy handbook, his strategy was born and documented in January 1979, whereas the Lancaster Agreement was signed in December 1979.

After independence, Mugabe and his government simply prepared to implement and enforce their strategy to exterminate the Ndebele people of Matabeleland. His government of mass murderers and criminals was driven by revenge, anger, unforgiveness, greed, selfishness and a hunger for power. Political difficulties imposed on black people by the Rhodesian government only contributed to a greater extent to the anger and bitterness that were already there in Mugabe's life, the pain of being rejected. Prior to him marrying Sally Hayfron in Ghana and becoming a politician in the 1950s, Mugabe had already had experienced rejection by the family of his Ndebele girlfriend. They loved each other, but the tribal hatred and division in their families forbade the relationship. The vendetta remained in Mugabe's heart. Therefore, his revengeful actions were premeditated long before he even knew he would be the first president of Zimbabwe.

Unity was Nkomo's wish, but what he forgot was that he needed to go back to God to correct the mistake he and his friends had committed, before he could go forward with his Unity Agreement. According to his book (Nkomo, 1984), God gave instructions to him and his friends that they failed to obey. By his own confession Nkomo admits that he disobeyed the voice of God when he resolved to fight Ian Smith and his government of the visitors, the white settlers. The oppression of his African people was too painful for him to wait on God for the restoration of their land. He did not take account of the fact that God is a God of recompense. When God told Abraham to sacrifice Isaac, Abraham did not argue or disobey God. God saw his obedience and therefore blessed him. Obedience is better than sacrifice.

When Moses disobeyed God's instructions and hit the rock twice in his anger, instead of speaking to the rock as instructed by God, it cost him the opportunity of setting foot in the promised land after 40 years in the wilderness.

And the Lord said unto Moses, get thee up into this mount Abarim, and see the land which I have given unto the children of Israel. And when thou hast seen it, thou also shall be gathered unto thy people, as Aaron thy brother was gathered. For ye rebelled against my commandment in the desert of Zin, in the strife of the congregation, to sanctify me at the water before their eyes: that is the water of Meribah in Kadesh in the wilderness of Zin.

Numbers 27: 12–14

Like Moses, King Lobengula, the last king of the Ndebele people, did not live long after he rebelled and fought the settlers. Joshua Nkomo, after being warned by God not to repeat the mistake that King Lobengula had made, went ahead and fought the Rhodesians for the land and to free his people from racial oppression and segregation. He also died without seeing peace in the country he had long suffered for.

CHAPTER 10

Why Should We Forgive?

We cannot continue the legacy of unforgiveness and disobedience to God, especially as a people and as the Body of Christ. Jesus is coming soon. I am saying this because as believers in Christ we need to be quick to confront our own bitterness and unforgiveness and ask God to remove it from our hearts. The dead are dead; we cannot bring them back. However, there is nothing too big for God to fix. God is a big God. In the book of Ezekiel He told Ezekiel to prophesy to the dry bones and the dry bones came together. The dead will be raised and they will testify about what happened to them. The truth will be known. The Word of God tells us:

> Let us hear the conclusion of the whole matter. Fear God, and keep His commandments: for this is the whole duty of man. For God shall bring every work into judgment, with every secret thing, whether it be good, or whether it be evil.
>
> Ecclesiastes 12: 13–14

I would personally encourage the people of Zimbabwe and other affected African countries to forgive, because unforgiveness only creates a terrible cycle, as we have all seen from the examples of the Matabeleland holocaust and massacres as well as other examples around the world. Jesus is coming soon, why miss eternity with Jesus just because of unforgiveness? Vengeance belongs to God.

We forgive because the Word of God commands us to forgive. The Word of God does not define what type or size of offence or trespasses we should forgive, but simply commands us to forgive men their trespasses. Jesus said, "For if ye forgive men their trespasses, your heavenly Father will also forgive you: But if ye forgive not men their trespasses, neither will your Father forgive your trespasses" (Matthew 6: 14–15). So not to be forgiven by God is such a terrifying thought.

Unforgiveness creates grudges and therefore opens our minds to Satan's manipulation. Because of unforgiveness and grudges, Robert Mugabe's mind became open to manipulation by Satan. Unforgiveness leads to madness. He began to follow his mind and therefore ended up with the Gukurahundi strategy against his enemies. Once the strategy was put on paper, it was consequently enforced.

Satan should never be given room in our minds. His ideas stink like hell. He knows that his time is short and therefore he wants to manipulate, condemn and destroy God's people. He does not want to perish alone. He is trying hard to defy the purpose of the Cross of Calvary. The sacrifice Jesus made for us cannot be defied. Jesus demonstrated the power of forgiveness on the Cross of Calvary. Unfortunately God cannot force us to make the right choices, like forgiving one another. He made His will known to us and even sacrificed His son for us. So, what more can He do for us? It is entirely our choice to obey Him or not.

As I have been writing this book, God has dealt with me in the area of forgiveness as far as the suffering of the people of Matabeleland is concerned. If I do not forgive the perpetrators of all the suffering of my people, I would be empowering them to make me angry over what I cannot undo and anger would lead to mental illness, as I discovered in my years of psychiatric nurse training. I cannot undo the beatings, the sexual abuses of babies, young and old; I cannot undo the sexual humiliation of our girls and women; I cannot undo the killings; I simply cannot undo the experience of the people of Matabeleland.

Therefore I choose to surrender my pain back to God, who knows how to heal the human mind, as He is the Creator of it. Forgiveness is a choice and I definitely choose to forgive all involved in the extermination of my people in Matabeleland, Zimbabwe. Therefore, I can boldly say that I forgive the Government of Margaret Thatcher, Lord Carrington, Julius Nyerere and all those who supported the secret meeting in Tanzania that illegally gave Robert Mugabe power over the people of Zimbabwe.

I choose to forgive the white Rhodesian forces together with the British who ensured that ZIPRA forces were disarmed and all their ammunition seized from them so that Mugabe's 5 Brigade/Gukurahundi would easily round them all up and wipe them off the earth. I choose to forgive Robert Mugabe, his defence ministers and all his cabinet ministers, dead or alive. I also choose to forgive all Robert Mugabe's henchmen, every CIO involved in the betrayals, illegal evil-driven arrests, tortures and killings, Mugabe's 5 Brigade, also known as Gukurahundi, and Mugabe's youth militias for all they did to our fathers and to all our elders, mothers, sisters and brothers and children in Matabeleland North, Matabeleland South and the Midlands. I also choose to forgive them for what they continue to do. It is the choice they embarked on, to pursue their satanic campaign of hate and revenge.

I choose to continue forgiving because unforgiveness only gives the enemy power to keep us in bondage by tormenting our mind with bad memories and feelings of depression. I refuse to give Satan that power. I choose to bury the past and focus on bringing healing and restoration to the lives of those who are still affected, the people of Matabeleland. However, I also realise that there are innocent people in Mashonaland who have not been part of the clean-up strategy and who never accepted it. I also forgive the people of Mashonaland who still believe that the people of Matabeleland deserved to be punished. I forgive those who encouraged and enjoyed the holocaust of the people of Matabeleland.

It is my prayer as I write this book that the people of Matabeleland will find it in their hearts to surrender their enemies to God and ask God for his forgiving grace. From my experience, I find it easy to ask for God's help when it comes to forgiveness because on my own effort I fail; I still meditate on the pain done to me. It is dangerous to meditate on the pain done to you. You must surrender your abusers, your persecutors and all who have hurt you to God, because He is God. He created them, therefore He knows them better than I do. He knows why they do what they do. I have learned not to bother myself trying to figure out why people find it so easy to hurt me and never apologise to me. Surrendering to God is the way forward because He helps me to forgive and carry on with my life.

Unforgiveness binds you; it gets you so stuck that everything around you breaks into pieces, even the cups and glasses in your kitchen; the washing machine stops working at the same time as the cooker and the microwave oven; the toilets refuse to flush, and all your money begins to go to the handymen you hire to fix the broken things. Unforgiveness stinks! It deprives you of your peace; it leads to disease (high blood pressure) and a dependency on prescribed drugs. Unforgiveness leads to hatefulness, which leads to grudges and for some vendettas; that is witchcraft, the ultimate consequence of which could be murder or mass murder, and genocides such as we have seen or heard of in the last years, as seen on 11th September 2001, in other parts of the world and clearly in Matabeleland since 1980.

Some would say, but where was God when all was happening? Some would say God was where He was when His only begotten Son Jesus was whipped 40 times by the Roman soldiers, spat at, insulted and kicked by the crowd of haters and crowned with huge thorns that dug into his skin while he was being nailed on the cross. Not only God saw it, His natural mother Mary watched in travail, but all who loved Him and those He had healed and helped also watched. It was not easy for them, but they watched because they loved Him. Jesus did not resist; He did not insult his persecutors back; but in silence like a lamb to slaughter He endured it all to His death as He went to Calvary. The prophet Isaiah was given this event in the spiritual realm, but did not live to see the fulfilment of it. I wonder what names Isaiah got called by those who heard him when his prophecy was not fulfilled during their lifetime; a liar and a false prophet I suppose. But Isaiah had seen it in his spirit. Boldly he spoke it, and we read it in the book of Isaiah 53: 5: "But He was wounded for our transgressions, He was bruised for our iniquities: the chastisement of our peace was upon Him and with his stripes we are healed."

What a shameful way to die, paraded on the cross for everyone to look at you when you did nothing wrong! Yes, He took all our curses upon Himself. He took our shame upon Himself. Our sickness and disease, our sins and rebelliousness, the insults that were meant for us, failures, poverty, all the evil in our hearts became His at that time as the crowd yelled at Him and called Him all sorts of things He was not. Jesus did it all for you and I. When we receive Him into our hearts as our Lord and our Saviour, we receive life and freedom from condemnation. We are made righteous in Him. We are made whole, nothing broken, nothing missing. Yet we still deny Him today, but He has not given up on us because he paid a painful price for us. He never stops loving us.

We don't hate our children because they have done wrong, we still love them. So how much more is the love of Christ for us? When we surrender our burdens to Him, He gives us peace of mind. Jesus forgives those He died and suffered for. When we hit rock bottom because of circumstances in our lives and we turn to Jesus, He is ready to receive us into His arms, forgive us for rebelling from God, and restore us as we continue to trust Him and to believe in the principles of His Word.

Thank God that death has no sting in the life of a believer because of the hope that we have in Christ because Jesus died and rose again. He sits at the right hand of God in heaven. interceding for us. He is coming soon for us, his bride and his church.

CHAPTER 11

The Vision

I was shown this vision in February 2008. As I said at the beginning
of this book, I have come to realise that some of these visions,
dreams and revelations are for the benefit of the Body of Christ and
therefore I cannot keep them to myself. I have heard God's great people
say, "Delayed obedience is still disobedience to God."

In the vision, I saw a large group of men on their knees. It was a place
in Africa called Zimbabwe and these were black men. The men were being
trained in how to worship God, hours of worship on their knees. As a
worshipper myself, I was attracted to make my way towards this place
and as I got closer, I heard a loud voice saying, "Worship! Your tool to
departure as the world economy system changes!" Then it was suddenly
at the end of the session and they all quickly stood up to leave. No one
was talking. They all left in silence and in great speed.

When these men left this place of worship, I realised that some were
still silently consumed in worship as they walked away. I was greatly
impressed by this. As I walked out of the area, I tried to ask one young
man where I could find toilets in this place, but I realised that his eyes
had a "faraway look" in them. He was physically on earth, but I could tell
from his eyes that he was spiritually in heaven. Then I realised that it was
important that I ignore the pressure I had and also continue worshipping.
I was quite impressed with this young man.

As I continued walking, I found myself at a house where I eventually
found the book I had long been looking for. It was green in colour and was
about the economy. A man was keeping it in his house. I was not shown
clearly who the man was, but I'm sure it was Satan. I left and continued
my journey.

I still needed the toilet desperately. I entered a dormitory where I saw beds, all of which were made and all covered with white linen or white bedcovers, but nobody was in the room. It was quiet. At last I spotted the way to the toilets and I felt hopeful as I made my way there. Then suddenly, further ahead to my right, the double doors opened. This was not the entrance I had used to enter. As the double doors opened, I saw a sister I knew from my teenage years.

She had been my neighbour in Bulawayo, Rhodesia (now Zimbabwe) in 1978. She encouraged us all in the Lord in our neighbourhood. Her and her husband lived in a house just behind my parents' house. She was a state registered nurse and her husband was a bank manager. They were both successful and they loved the Lord. They would, with other young Saints of God, hold prayer meetings around the community. Whenever the prayer meeting would be in their home, they would invite all their neighbours to attend. I was not born again myself, so I would attend mainly because I enjoyed their songs and I was also curious to know the reason behind all their motivation and passion for the Lord. This was also a time of the revolutionary war against racial segregation, oppression and inequality in Rhodesia. After I got born again in 1979, I was thrilled when she invited me to join her in teaching Sunday school. In 1979–80, we used to teach children in the community whose parents never went to church. I learnt much from this sister which I never forgot. She had great love and great respect for children. She used to make children feel good about themselves and I greatly admired her skills. She was very special to these children and to me.

I thank God that I have, since this vision, been rejoined with her again. She is still the same, a humble woman of God. We cry and laugh together on the phone. She is in the USA. I love her so much and I thank God for her. She told me that God removed her from nursing in the year 2000 for His purpose. I am not surprised to see her with the children in this vision. I have since established that her husband is now gone to be with the Lord in heaven, so she is a widow and still a great woman of God. The political and economical difficulties she faced in Zimbabwe pushed her out to seek refuge in the USA and she left her family in Zimbabwe, as she could not financially afford to take them with her.

In the vision, at the entrance of these double doors I saw this sister. She was arriving with about four or five nicely dressed little children between the ages of approximately 2 and 5. I assumed that these were orphans who lived in this dormitory. The children looked well groomed with pretty clothes on. I remember one had a pink dress with white lace trimmings and a pair of white socks. These children were quite well looked after. I was excited to see this sister after such a long time, but I could not talk to her at that moment because of the pressure I had and she did not see me. She had just put down one of the children she had been carrying and was busy focusing on the children, while I went into one of the cubicles of the dormitory to find the toilet. I saw it at last.

As I went in to use the toilet, someone raised their head from one of the beds. I was surprised that someone was actually sleeping on one of the beds in the dormitory. There had been no sign of anyone in these beds, all of them looked flat as if there was nobody in the dormitory. I then realised that the Holy Angels of God were keeping the place.

One remarkable thing I remember is the atmosphere of loneliness and desolation that seemed to be all around. Even the worshippers I had seen at the beginning were all focused. Once they were dismissed they rapidly left in speed and in quietness. I thought this must have been a time of tribulation.

Then I was suddenly somewhere else listening to a testimony by one man of God who was overwhelmed by the love and support the brethren he served were showing him. He was testifying about how the people had bought him a nice car and how they ensured that he had the best. It was clear that the people here appreciated their man of God and therefore enjoyed giving to him and demonstrating their love and support for him. Their love was too overwhelming for this servant of God. There was unity of purpose among the members of his congregation.

At the time of this vision, the credit crunch was not being discussed. People were still borrowing from the banks and overspending. People were selling houses successfully and the property market was doing very well. There was no media warning of a forthcoming economic slowdown – but suddenly, things changed.

The worldwide economy rapidly collapsed towards the end of 2008. The UK and the US began the struggle to stabilise the rate of inflation. Most banks were struggling too and some were closing as investors withdrew their money. The property market suffered as mortgage lenders stopped lending to first-time buyers. Businesses in general began to feel the pinch as the public started to spend less, leading to more job cuts and suffering for more families. Homes were auctioned as mortgage repayments became unaffordable, especially for most young people. Those who were made redundant lost their homes to building societies. Only the auctioneers gained business. As fellow Southern Africans say, "One man's fall is the rise of another."

This sudden crash of the economy worldwide could have been worse had it not been for the Saints who interceded in prayer. It is very easy for the logical minded to overlook the power of prayer in such situations.

There are many religions on earth and many religious people. Saints are not religious people; they are born-again, God-loving, sanctified and dedicated Believers and followers of Jesus Christ, His Church. They are the redeemed of the Lord through Jesus Christ. The "Church" does not refer to the building or any religious place of worship, but the collective Body of Believers in Jesus Christ, regardless of which denomination they belong to. Every Saint, whether male or female, is then referred to as the Body of Christ, which is also the Bride of Christ, the soon and coming Groom.

The green economy book

God is empowering His Saints to take back control of the economy of the world from the enemy. He is preparing His people to take the "green economy book" from the corrupt hands of greedy, evil and uncaring politicians and world leadership. The colour green is symbolic of prosperity. This means that God will prosper His people in difficult times of economic hardship. This is the shaking that was prophesied by the prophets of God in the Old Testament. It is important to believe what the prophets of God say. God spoke to His prophets decades ago.

For thus saith the Lord of hosts, Yet once, it is a little while, and I will shake the heavens, and the earth, and the sea, and the dry land; And I will shake all nations, and the desire of all nations shall come: and I will fill this house with glory, saith the Lord of hosts. Silver is mine, and the gold is mine, saith the Lord of hosts.

Haggai 2: 6–8

A prophet of God is His mouthpiece. Listening and believing what a prophet of God says would not only protect one from the enemy's traps but would cause you to prosper, in that you would be able to progress and achieve whatever God has ordained for you to achieve. Knowing the Word of God is very important. Everyone has a choice to read the Bible or to ignore it. However, there are consequences associated with every choice we make, more so when we depart from God's commandments and statutes. "Believe in the Lord your God, so shall you be established, believe His prophets, so shall ye prosper" (2 Chronicles 20: 20). I believe that being established would mean that one is well secured and rooted; whatever work you do will succeed because God Himself is the foundation of all you set out to do. Prospering, I believe, would mean continuing without any hindrances or blockages.

Satan and those who allow themselves to be used by him have for decades abused the economy of the world. They have for a long period been monopolising the economy of the world as if it belonged to them when it did not. The evidence of their greed, their selfish stewardship and evil ways, is seen all around the world: the broken hearts, the homeless, neglected and abused orphans, young and old, the destitute, vulnerable widows and the hopeless and hungry poor people on the streets and in the dirty corners of this world. Selfish leaders have invested in weapons of mass destruction when their cities are full of suffering poor people. It is not God's will for His church buildings and places of worship to be turned into public houses and homes while much investment is put into leisure centres, football or sports grounds in general. Jesus got very furious when He found people doing their own business in the house of God. "Is it not written, 'My house shall be called of all nations a house of prayer?' But ye have made it a den of thieves" (Mark 11: 17).

It is not the will of God for anyone in the world to suffer poverty and isolation. God understands the pain of the poor; that is why He chose to be born in a poor family by a poor virgin, Mary. He did not come to earth in any other way but the way of poverty. He was born in a stable that belonged to animals. He was not born in a posh hospital. This is why He bears the burden of the poor. The prophet Isaiah prophesied about Jesus' birth and crucifixion in the Old Testament:

> He is despised and rejected of men; a man of sorrows, and acquainted with grief: and we hid as it were our faces from Him; He was despised, and we esteemed Him not. Surely He hath borne our griefs, and carried our sorrows: yet we esteem Him stricken, smitten of God and afflicted. But He was wounded for our transgressions, He was bruised for our iniquities: the chastisement of our peace was upon Him; and with His stripes we are healed. All we like sheep have gone astray; we have turned every one to his own way; and the Lord hath laid on Him the iniquity of us all.
>
> Isaiah 53: 3–6

For decades, hard-working believers and followers of Christ in the world have been expected to meet the needs of the poor and oppressed around the earth, yet they have also been subject to all kinds of financial constrictions like high costs of taxation and levies of all kinds, while the politicians earn very high, unrealistic salaries but hardly consider helping the poor.

This is why Jesus spoke to the multitude, and to His disciples, saying:

> The scribes and the Pharisees sit in Moses' seat: All therefore whatsoever they bid you observe, that observe and do; but do not ye after their works: for they say, and do not. For they bind heavy burdens and grievous to be borne, and lay them on men's shoulders; but they themselves will not move them with one of their fingers.
>
> Matthew 23: 1–4

God created us all to worship Him, but we see a lot of rebelliousness and injustice in high places, by those in authority. This will not be the case any longer in the end time because it is not in the will of God. This is why in my vision men were being taught how to worship God. As we worship God, instigators of pain and injustice on the poor will be removed from power.

God is now in the business of preparing His people for the coming of the Lord Jesus Christ. Worship is what keeps us connected with the Holy Spirit, our tool to departure as the world's economy system changes. The current economic situation around the world is significant of the coming of the Lord Jesus Christ. So we are warned here that He ought to find the spirit of worship in every believer's heart. It is when we praise and worship God that He fills us with the Holy Spirit. The Holy Spirit is the enabler; He enables us to experience the love of God and to appreciate His Grace through His Son Jesus Christ, our Saviour and our Redeemer. The Holy Spirit empowers us to worship God.

What is the will of God for us here on earth?

Justice on earth is the will of God for the fulfilment of His plan and purpose for mankind. He is a God of justice. God wants to see justice for the vulnerable, the weak and helpless and the poor. What the enemy meant for harm, God is turning it around for the good of His people. However, the Body of Christ has the ultimate decision for this to be realised. Obedience to God, love, humility and holiness are the essential keys to unlocking the God-ordained potential within each of us.

People do not realise when they are given the opportunity to be in positions of authority that God's eyes are upon them. God knows the name of everyone under the sun. He knows the name of every politician. He is watching how everyone operates from those positions. Others were long deceived by Satan and blinded to the fact that the economy of the world belongs to God. Those who read the Word of God know that it is written that "The earth is the Lord's and the fullness thereof, the world and they that dwell therein" (Psalms 24: 1). For decades, most of the world's leaders and most of those in positions of authority have been in a slumber, thinking that they were the ones in control, thereby ignoring the authority of the Church in the affairs of the world. The voice of God can only be heard through those vessels that are separated for His purpose, His Servants, the Ministers of His Word. Persecuting and ignoring God's prophets is literally shutting the mouth of God, the consequences of which are seen everywhere in the world today.

God has allowed politicians to be in those positions for a reason, and for a season. He knows them all by name! Therefore justice on the earth in these last days is a priority on God's agenda. Some of the issues related to the injustice suffered by the needy, the helpless and the poor will be highlighted throughout this book as the Spirit of God leads me.

We do not know who we are until God reveals it to us. He knows us by our very names and He knows us best. He also sees how we operate in the positions He has placed us in here on earth. He is no respecter of persons. The street and public place cleaner, the refuse collector, the homeless, the abandoned baby, the orphan, the rich and the poor are equally important to God. He created us all in His own image. That is why He sacrificed His only Son, Jesus Christ, to be crucified on the cross in our place. Being holy and blameless, Jesus was condemned, accused and crucified for sins you and I commit. He did it so we do not have to carry the condemnation of our sins any more. This benefit is available to all who acknowledge and accept Him as Lord in their lives.

Christ hath redeemed us from the curse of the law, being made a curse for us: for it is written, Cursed is every one that hangeth on a tree: That the blessing of Abraham might come on the Gentiles through Jesus Christ; that we might receive the promise of the Spirit through faith.

Galatians 3: 13–14

How else would God have demonstrated His love for His own creation?

In the vision, I eventually found the green economy book I had been looking for. Who was the man with the economy green book? The man was Satan and his beneficiaries, the wicked.

After God delivered the children of Israel out of the bondage in Egypt, He promised to protect them and to provide for them. Through Moses, He warned them concerning obedience to Him and gave them His Law of Order, the Ten Commandments, teaching them how to live. God further warned the children of Israel not to forget His commandments. He reminded them about the Covenant He made with their ancestors Abraham, Isaac and Jacob. He further warned them concerning the consequences of sinning against Him.

> *And thou shall say in thine heart, My power and the might of mine hand hath gotten me this wealth. But thou shalt remember the Lord thy God: for it is He that gives thee power to get wealth, that He may establish His covenant which He swares unto thy fathers, as it is this day. And it shall be, if thou do at all forget the Lord thy God, and walk after other gods, and serve them, and worship them, I testify against you this day that ye shall surely perish. As the nations which the Lord destroyed before your face, so shall ye perish; because ye would not be obedient unto the voice of the Lord your God.*
>
> *Deuteronomy 8: 17–18*

Remember when Jesus walked this earth that the Jews and the Israelites were under the oppression of the Roman Empire. Therefore they hoped that Jesus was the new king they had been waiting for to deliver them from their oppression. What they did not realise was that the bondage that Jesus came to deliver them from was not just a physical one but a spiritual bondage. They were bound by sin, due to lack of knowledge, wisdom and understanding. Jesus came to teach them how to live in a holy way. Their spiritual bondage was the result of the rebellious, sinful ways of idolatry they had practised since the time they were captured by the Babylonians.

> *And they watched Him, and sent forth spies which should feign themselves just men, that they might take hold of his words, that so they might deliver Him unto the power and authority of the governor. And they asked Him saying, Master, we know that thou sayest and teachest rightly, neither*

acceptest thou the person of any, but teachest the way of God truly: Is it lawful for us to give tribute unto Caesar, or no?

Luke 20: 20–22

He said, Shew me a penny. Whose image and superscription hath it? They answered and said, Caesar's. And He said unto them, Render therefore unto Caesar the things which be unto Caesar's, and unto God the things which be God's.

And they could not take hold of His words before the people: and they marvelled at his answer, and held their peace.

Luke 20: 25–6

God wants His gospel to be heard by all the people on the earth before Christ comes for His Bride, the Church. He wants His gospel to reach all the ends of the earth, the rich and the poor, for His glory, but this costs money. He wants justice for all. He wants the weak and vulnerable people to be properly cared for, the hungry and poor to be reached, fed and clothed. He wants the homeless to have proper shelter. He wants the hurting orphans removed from the streets, given hope, loved and protected. God wants the captives set free.

Therefore in these last days before Christ comes for His Bride the Church, it is the will of God and His plan for the control of the economy of the world to be removed from Satan and his cohorts, the corrupt, selfish and cruel world leaders and their beneficiaries, and to be placed in the hands of the heirs of Salvation, the Saints, God's loyal stewards who have sowed seeds in tears, for the benefit of all concerned. God's Word tells us: "The wealth of the sinner is laid up for the just" (Proverbs 13: 22b). In the Book of James 5: 1–3 it is written:

Go to now ye rich men, weep and howl for your miseries that shall come upon you. Your riches are corrupted, and your garments are motheaten. Your gold and silver is cankered; and the rust of them shall be a witness against you, and shall eat your flesh as it were fire. Ye have heaped treasure together for the last days.

The Book of Job also tells us:

> *This is the portion of a wicked man with God, and the heritage of oppressors, which they shall receive of the Almighty. If his children be multiplied, it is for the sword: and his offspring shall not be satisfied with bread. Those that remain of him shall be buried in death: and his widows shall not weep. Though he heap up silver as the dust, and prepare raiment as the clay; He may prepare it, but the just shall put it on, and the innocent shall divide the silver.*
>
> Job 27:13-17

Concerning the orphans I saw in the vision, I saw beds covered in white linen and an Angel of God guarding the children's dormitory was in one of the beds. Jehovah God is the keeper. He is the father to the fatherless.

Prior to this vision, from 2007 to early 2009, I was also shown several other visions of children and young people. I saw African children in a familiar setting like Zimbabwe, whose parents neglect them and were being raised in unsafe homes. These parents, due to economic pressure, were opening their homes to sin without any regard for the children.

In one particular dream I was running from bad people with these little children. I had to help one who was struggling to run. But when I reached their home I realised that their mother was too consumed in sin to care. Strangers occupied all the children's bedrooms. It was not a safe environment for these little ones at all and I felt great pain to leave them there, as I could see that they were the ones turned to strangers in their own home. These children were very vulnerable. The environment their mother subjected these children to was very immoral and demonic.

I was also shown beautiful flowers that are ready to bloom in dry places where they only got their water from the rain, if by any chance it rained. They were not in proper flowerbeds where they could be watered and groomed. These flowers were growing at random along the walls of buildings where people passed by. They were in danger of being picked by anyone in their blooming stage, as they were easily noticeable for their beauty. As I looked around, there were many empty spaces in the flowerbeds. These flowers could easily have been transplanted into the flowerbeds where they could have been watered with the rest.

It was then revealed to me that these beautiful flowers that were about to bloom were actually children in foster homes in the West and those growing on the streets in poor Third World countries and particularly in Africa.

Most of these children were being raised without any spiritual grooming whatsoever. They grow up not belonging to anyone. They are like the property of the state. The Social Services Department manages their lives. These children are the future generations of our world. Most of them move from one prayerless home to the other, they have never been taught how to pray. Those who care for them are legally not allowed to show affection by touching them for fear of abuse.

This is another deception of Satan, his strategy for the Western world to raise future generations that have never been shown affection. He has used a few of his immoral agents to set a bad example for the system of this world to remove love and affection from children. Those growing up in prayerless homes are vulnerable to Satan because they do not know the truth in God. But there is state funding involved in the fostering of these children; another example of the economy in the wrong hands.

What does the future hold for those children who grow up in love and are taught the Word of God, loving and giving? Are they not vulnerable?

Is the social care system in the Western world successful in dealing with the problems of society, or is it desperate for the intervention of God? But how can God help if He is not given the upper hand in the state's decision making? The schools are stripped of any power to discourage children and young people from practising sex outside marriage. The school nurse is statutorily authorised to facilitate teenagers below the age of 16 who approach her for birth control tablets, without having to seek the approval of their parents first. The student has her right to privacy and therefore the school nurse must maintain confidentiality on their behalf. It appears to me that such policies completely rule God out.

The devil is fully aware of his strategy to destroy the future generations and create ruthless evil beings out of them. Can politicians give advice on how those who are raised in Bible-based, loving homes can defend themselves from the children who grow up on the street? Kicking God's voice out of the justice system of this world has its consequences for future generations. Disobedience to God always has its consequences.

Except the Lord build the house, they labour in vain that build it: except the Lord keep the city, the watchman waketh but in vain.

Psalm 127

Concerning needy young people, I saw a vision of hungry and desperate young boys somewhere in Africa, planning to go and burgle some houses a mile away, just for food. These were good boys, but I could see the desperation in them. They were genuinely hungry. I feared for them and for the ones they were to burgle too. I also saw the homeless and lonely young boys in the early hours of the morning. They had just woken up from the streets and they were hungry. Yes, it is the will of God for the orphans of all ages to be fed, assisted, comforted, educated and taught the ways of God and the love of God. They also need healing and salvation.

Concerning the poor widows or single mothers, yes, it is the will of God for the widows and single parents to be assisted. He wants the widows and poor single mothers to be comforted and assisted with the upbringing and education of their children. I will discuss the visions I saw concerning this group of people as I continue in the book.

Concerning the old and frail, yes, it is the will of God for the old and frail to be visited and loved, that they get proper respect in their old age and that their lives are valued and not seen as a burden by those controlling and monopolising the economy. Longevity is a blessing from God and the right of every human being. There is a lot that younger generations can learn from the older generations. Older people like to reminisce about their experiences and this is a gift to young people. The first-hand knowledge they have is not written in history books and you will not find it in the National Archives.

For example, during the time of my mental health nurse training, I met an old Polish woman who told me things I had no clue about. She told me that people think Hitler was the bad one but from her knowledge, it was Mussolini who was terrible and people have got it all wrong. She then told of her suffering under the brutality of Mussolini. She was not mentally ill at all and she was fully aware of the attitudes around her. She was very lonely where she lived and she was in a lot of physical pain. She only needed love, reassurance and respect from those around her.

It is the will of God for families to be reunited in love and harmony and that old people are not left lonely in a world full of people, but are visited and loved. It is the will of God for the oppressed to be delivered and set free. These groups of vulnerable people are the reason certain jobs and professions are in place. But is God pleased with these positions as far as meeting the needs of these vulnerable groups of people is concerned?

The voice of God has to be restored in the affairs of the world for the will of God to be fulfilled

Unless the Body of Christ takes an upper hand in ensuring justice for the poor on the earth, God's poor people around the world will not get much help from politicians.

> *He that oppresseth the poor reproacheth his Maker: but he that honoureth Him hath mercy on the poor.*
>
> *Proverbs 14: 31*

> *The righteous considereth the cause of the poor: but the wicked regardeth not to know it.*
>
> *Proverbs 29: 7*

In a sermon preached by Bishop Eddie Long on Kingdom wealth, he stated that the Body of Christ does not have a voice because of its poverty state. He further clarified that Jesus loved the poor, He ministered to the poor, He took good news to the poor, but that did not mean they had to remain poor. He further stated that riches are something that we have, but wealth is something that we own. The reason the Body of Christ has no dominion here on earth is because the Body of Christ is financially poor; ungodly people, who have very little understanding of what God ordained for this world, are the ones in control of the economy because they are rich and they get heard; poverty is a curse. Being poor is not a mark of spirituality. Quoting the multiplication principle in Matthew 25: 14-30, he stated that God expects us to be fruitful with the little that He has entrusted us with. Poverty is a result of not sowing or not sowing enough, and not tithing. Without sowing there is no reaping (Product No. IGC99/230 from kicc.org.uk).

For decades, the will of God has not been effectively implemented here on earth due to financial constrictions that God's servants face every day. The plight of the Church concerning poverty has never been taken seriously. This is not because it cannot be done. There is enough money in the hands of a few rich people that can actually cancel Third World debt. It has been very difficult for the gospel to reach the poor and especially the hungry, due to political problems experienced in most parts of the Third World. Most politicians have for decades been driven by greed and selfishness. As a result, they have ruled their respective countries with an iron fist. They have controlled and monopolised the good of the land, turning a blind eye to the needs of their own people. Corruption and neglect of the needs of people by those in power has resulted in groups of armed rebels and the violence caused has been very extensive and atrocious to the vulnerable poor of the world.

Therefore the burden of caring and helping the poor in such situations is usually left to the Saints of God, as it is the Saints who feel their pain. Politicians have for decades enjoyed listening to the Church's pleas without moving a finger to assist the Church. The efforts of God's Servants in reaching the poor and meeting their needs have been met with great difficulty, making the spread of the gospel practically impossible. How can God's servants preach to the hungry and homeless without first feeding them? Food, clothing, water supplies and shelter are much needed in most parts of the Third World, hence the need for the Gospel to reach such parts where the hungry, orphaned and homeless are. Nobody requires a PhD to work out the needs faced by those in missionary work.

Why should the servants of God be appealing for public donations in order to feed and clothe the hungry, when politicians who are entrusted with public funds are totally ignoring their responsibility? They are busy accumulating wealth at the expense of those whose welfare is assigned to them. They simply do not care. Not very long ago, we had on the news many politicians exposed for misuse of funding, due to their selfish and greedy desire to hoard wealth. God lifts up, and He brings down.

And he said unto them, Take heed and beware of covetousness: for a man's life consisteth not in the abundance of the things which he possesseth.

Luke 12: 15

In the UK we recently heard the shocking news of a young mother of a disabled daughter, who for a long period had been reporting abuse from her neighbours to the police and the authorities concerned. All her efforts to stop her neighbours from making her life more difficult were ignored. She was suffering abuse and isolation because she had a disabled daughter. Nor was she getting any help with her daughter. As a result of her long-suffering and hopeless life, she drove her car to a nearby lay-by and burnt herself and her daughter to death. She took her daughter with her because she was concerned that no one would be there to look after her. The police and those in authority in the area neglected this young woman. She was lonely and isolated in a world full of people. Even the state-employed authorities turned a deaf ear. This story would not go down well for anyone who is a carer of a disabled child. How could the police not protect her from her own neighbourhood? What was she expected to do? God is a God of justice.

Politicians around the world and those entrusted with authority will have to reconsider their ways because all wealth is being supernaturally removed from the hands of the undeserving selfish stewards and being transferred into the stewardship of God's holy people, the righteous ones.

I returned, and I saw under the sun, that the race is not to the swift, nor the battle to the strong, neither yet bread to the wise, nor yet riches to men of understanding, nor yet favour to men of skill; but time and chance happeneth to them all.

Ecclesiastes 9: 1

Saints of God require money to do the work of God around the earth before Christ comes. The gospel has to reach the uttermost parts of the earth and the poor need proper shelter, proper food, clean water, education and all the good things that God has ordained for His people to enjoy. Nothing can stop this from happening, not even the devil or his demons combined. God Himself is in charge of the wealth transfer for His will to be done on earth as it is in heaven.

And I will shake all nations, and the desire of all nations shall come: and I will fill this house with glory, saith the Lord of hosts. The silver is mine, and gold is mine, saith the Lord of hosts.

Haggai 2: 7–8

The Saints around the world are being supernaturally empowered for the stewardship of God's wealth. All wealth belongs to God.

I will take no bullock out of thy house, nor the goats out of thy folds. For every beast of the forest is mine, and the cattle upon a thousand hills. I know all the fowls of the mountains: and wild beasts of the field are mine. If I were hungry, I would not tell thee: for the world is mine, and the fullness thereof.

Psalms 50: 9–12

Therefore the Saints of God realise the urgency of preaching the gospel in all the earth, as it is when this is accomplished, that the end shall come, the rapture of the Saints. Before Christ comes for His Bride, the whole world will have at least been given the opportunity to know the Lord Jesus Christ and to receive Him as their Lord and Saviour.

And this gospel of the kingdom shall be preached in all the world for a witness unto all the nations; and then the end shall come. When ye therefore shall see the abomination of desolation, spoken of by Daniel the prophet, stand in the holy place, (whoso readeth, let him understand).

Matthew 24: 14–15

Before His crucifixion, Jesus prayed in John 17: 18-20:

As thou hast sent me into the world, even so have I also sent them into the world. And for their sakes I sanctify myself, that they also might be sanctified through the truth. Neither pray I for these alone, but for them also which shall believe on me through their word.

After His resurrection, Jesus commanded His disciples in Mark 16: 15–18:

And he said unto them, Go ye into all the world, and preach the gospel to every creature. He that believeth and is baptised shall be saved; but he that believeth not shall be damned. And these signs shall follow them that believe; In My Name shall they cast out devils; they shall speak with new tongues; They shall take up serpents; and if they drink any deadly thing, it shall not hurt them; they shall lay hands on the sick, and they shall recover.

Jesus is coming soon for his bride. What will happen especially to religious people or others who have rejected Him? What will happen to those who refused to accept Jesus Christ as their Lord and Saviour or those who have not believed in the Holy Spirit?

The Saints will be suddenly taken. There will be no warning of the day or the time, because Jesus Himself said it in Mark 13: 30-37:

Verily I say unto you, that this generation shall not pass, till all these things be done. Heaven and Earth shall pass away: but My Word shall not pass away. But of that day and that hour knoweth no man, no, not the angels which are in heaven, neither the Son, but the Father. Take ye heed, watch and pray: for ye know not when the time is. For the Son of man is as a man taking a far journey, who left his house and gave authority to his servants, and to every man his work, and commanded the porter to watch. Watch ye therefore: for ye know not when the master of the house cometh, at even, or at mid-night, or at the cock crowing, or in the morning. Lest coming suddenly he finds you sleeping. And what I say unto you I say unto all, Watch.

Reading and meditating on the Word of God is important. "Thy Word is a lamp unto my feet, and a light unto my path" (Psalms 119: 105). It is the fundamental act of obedience to God. "Thy Word have I hid in mine heart, that I might not sin against thee" (Psalms 119: 11).

There are many reasons that have caused many of God's people to depart from His ways. In the Third World countries and mainly in Africa, ignorance was the main cause, in that God was not so much worshipped. African people's traditions and cultural ways encouraged the belief that their ancestors determined their livelihood and success. They put ancestors up front and believed that Christianity was brought to Africa by the oppressor. They believed that the European missionaries came to oppress them through religion. This was because they could not reconcile or link racial discrimination and the oppression the missionary imposed on the black man with the sacrificial love of the Cross and that the Grace of God through Jesus Christ included them. I have no doubt in my heart that God sent the white missionaries to Africa; but did they do exactly what God sent them to do or did they disobey Him?

In Europe, most people are born in families that had for decades stopped worshipping God. The main reason for this is civilisation, because civilisation changed people's occupation as they became more educated, diverting their focus from God as their source of provision to self-sufficiency and career development and advancement. So as more people became educated, more knowledgeable and prosperous, Satan began to lie to them as he did to Eve in the Garden of Eden. He began to convince God's people, the scientists, that their research and discoveries showed that man was clever. He began to lie to them in making them believe that they could come up with all sorts of inventions themselves, independently of God. Scientist began to challenge God in that they were in control of their own lives. Therefore Satan led people to believe that they did not need God for anything and eventually people forgot that their intelligence, success and comfort were from God, yet God had actually forewarned that they should never think that way in the first place. We read in Deuteronomy 8: 10, 17 & 18:

> *When thou hast eaten and art full, then thou shall bless the Lord thy God for the good land which he hath given thee. And thou say in thine heart, My power and the might of mine hand hath gotten me this wealth. But thou shalt remember the Lord thy God: for it is He that giveth thee power to get wealth, that he may establish His covenant which He sware unto thy fathers, as it is this day.*

As God's own creation, we began to enjoy our riches and forgot about praying to God or trusting Him as our source of provision. Eventually generations of people stopped going to church as they now enjoyed luxuries and comfort in their homes. As we continued to acquire more of our own knowledge, we began to deny our God because we saw ourselves as the masters of our destiny. But there is a difference between the knowledge that comes from men and that which comes from God. God warned in Hosea 5: 6:

> *My people are destroyed for lack of knowledge: because thou hast rejected knowledge, I will also reject thee, that thou shalt be no priest to me: seeing thou hast forgotten the law of thy God, I will also forget thy children.*

The truth is, if God created heaven and earth and all that is in the earth, which includes us, how could we be fooled into believing that we could claim as our own the new discoveries and inventions we make in a world that we did not even create?

To this effect, I would like to quote the late Joshua Nkomo's words (1984: 15):

In 1974, when I was released after more than ten years in prison, I was
told that the voice of the shrine had issued a message. It had said farewell,
and ceased speaking to the people, but their complaints and pleas would
still be heard. Perhaps as people become more "civilised", God takes a
step back.

It appears to me that even Nkomo, also known as Father Zimbabwe,
recognised the disadvantage of civilisation as far as obedience to God
and honouring God are concerned. I believe that as God's people we have
rejected Him by failing to acknowledge Him as the source of our witty
inventions and by letting the devil take over and twist things.

The Bible confirms that before we were even conceived, God had
already deposited his creativity in each person:

Before I formed thee in the belly I knew thee; and before thou camest
forth out of the womb I sanctified thee, and I ordained thee a prophet
unto the nations.

Jeremiah 1: 5

The important question is, who should be getting the glory from our
creativity, Satan or God? God gave us all the free will to choose our
destiny. He simply gave us the guidance we need through His Word. He
clearly warned and stated some of the consequences of being disobeyed
in Exodus 15: 26:

And said, If thou wilt diligently hearken to the voice of the Lord thy
God, and wilt do that which is right in his sight, and wilt give ear to his
commandments, and keep all his statutes, I will put none of these diseases
upon thee, which I have brought upon the Egyptians: for I am the Lord
that healeth thee.

We still chose to disobey God because we stopped worshipping Him as
our Creator and we did not keep His statutes, as He had warned in the
beginning.

The devil likes to lead people astray by stealing what God has already created and then twisting it, so that it looks like the secular world owns it and not the Body of Christ, His Church. For example, clapping and dancing in the church is seen by other religions as out of order. This is one of Satan's deceptions. Satan is not the one sitting on the throne; Jesus is because He paid a price for the forgiveness of our sins. Who created the dance and for whose joy was it created? In John 10: 10 Jesus said:

The thief cometh not, but for to steal, and to kill, and to destroy: I am come that they might have life, and that they might have it more abundantly.

Praise, worship and dance belong to God's people and we do it for His Glory, not men's glory. God created music, song and dance to give Him pleasure. The lyrics in a song speak for themselves; they will tell you if the source of the song is God or a counterfeit. The Holy Spirit gives us discernment, because not all songs are holy. Some songs are filthy and so are the dances associated with them. As a Church, we should be careful what we listen and dance to. Our bodies are temples of the Holy Ghost. We cannot afford to grieve the Holy Ghost by singing and dancing to the lyrics that come with secular songs.

In the New Testament, Jesus was very creative in His preaching: He told a lot of stories because He wanted us to have a real scenario or picture in our minds to enable us to understand the things He was saying. For example, in His warning to us to be vigilant, watchful and ready in our daily living, He told the story of the ten virgins (Matthew 25) who waited for their Bridegroom; some were fully prepared in their waiting but some of them were not prepared because they ran out of lamp oil in the middle of the night, as a result of which they missed the ceremony.

Jesus was not boring, which is why crowds of people always followed Him. The large numbers of the people drawn to Him did not all need healing or any particular help, they simply enjoyed listening to Him because He brightened their day. He gave them hope and a reason to live.

The fact that some of us, in our childhood, enjoyed hearing bedtime stories from our parents or grandparents is evidence enough of the joy of listening. We never liked it when the story ended, we asked for more stories until the storyteller got tired. It is not true that going to church is boring; it is the way that this very important practice has been portrayed over decades by ignorant people, leaving it as nothing but a boring place to be, thus putting people off believing in and worshipping the Creator of Heaven and Earth, their God. If Jesus used stories and parables to preach to the people, what is stopping us from learning from Him? Only a few people now are drawn to Jesus in proportion to the large numbers of people who are in this world. This is all due to the lies and the deception of the enemy through false and judgmental church doctrines that have put people off believing and worshipping their Creator.

What will happen to those who have not been told about the hope that is in Christ?

In certain parts of world, the efforts of the servants of God to reach people with the Gospel of the Lord Jesus Christ are being crushed. They are being persecuted by killings and massacres, as seen in the Middle East and Asia. What people believe in is a matter of choice. Nevertheless, the gospel of the Lord Jesus Christ has to be preached and oppressed people have to be reached. The following is a special quote of the words of Jesus to His disciples after He rose from the dead:

> And Jesus came and spake unto them saying, All power is given unto Me in heaven and in earth. Go ye therefore, and teach all nations, baptising them in the name of the Father, and of the Son, and of the Holy Ghost: Teaching them to observe all things whatsoever I have commanded you: and, lo, I am with you always, even unto the end of the world. Amen.
>
> *Matthew 28: 18–20*

There are many of us who are talented or gifted in creative art like singing, dance, speaking, drawing, poetry or comedy. These are the gifts God has given to us to use in preaching the Gospel to the lost, but we have given up telling God's lost people about the Lord Jesus Christ. We have lost our oil out of fear of being ridiculed, shunned or labelled as weird. We have become too accustomed to the system of this world and our daily routine is not different from those who are living in darkness. We are too embarrassed to be known in our neighbourhood as Saints of God, the Bride in waiting. The Groom is watching us with great sadness. A lot of God's ignorant people perish in their depression and desperation because nobody has reached out to them with a true message of the Lord Jesus Christ, a message of hope. This is why there will be Judgment Day for all. Jesus Christ is the only hope of the dying world. Nothing will stop Him coming for His Bride.

The invitation to receive Jesus is still available to all on the earth today. Others are receiving Him and others still do not believe that He was the Son of God. Others believe that He was in the beginning of the world and that the earth was created by Him; others do not.

> *He was in the world, and the world was made by Him, and the world did not know Him: He came to His own, and His own did not receive Him: But as many as received Him, to them He gave Power to become the sons of God, even to them that believed on his name: Who were born not of blood, nor of the will of the flesh, nor of the will of man, but of God.*
>
> *John 1: 10–13*

Knowing the Word of God is important, because in I John 1: 1 we are told that in the beginning was the Word, and the Word was with God, and the Word was God. Some people prefer to stay out of it all. They do not think the Word of God is logical. 1 Corinthians 3: 18–20 says:

> *Let no man deceive himself. If any man among you seemeth to be wise in this world, let him become a fool, that he may be wise. For the wisdom of this world is foolishness with God. For it is written, He taketh the wise*

*in their own craftiness. And again the Lord knoweth all thoughts of the
wise, that they are vain.*

Those who choose to believe in Him get saved from the wrath to come.
He is still the same yesterday, today and forever. He still forgives the sins
of those who ask Him to. 1 John 1: 8 & 10 state "If we say that we have no
sin, we deceive ourselves, and the truth is not in us: If we say that we have
not sinned, we make Him a liar, and His Word is not in us." According
to 1 John 1: 9, "If we confess our sins, He is faithful and just to forgive us
and to cleanse us from all unrighteousness." This is further clarified in
Romans 10: 9: "If you shall confess with your mouth that Jesus is Lord,
and believe in your heart that God raised Him from the dead, you shall
be saved."

However, after the Lord Jesus forgives us our sins the Word of God
says that we become new creatures, old things pass away and all things
become new. This is what Jesus meant by being born again to Nicodemus
the Rabbi, in John 3: 3.

*Verily, verily, I say unto thee, Except a man be born again, he cannot
see the kingdom of God. If we say that we have fellowship with Him and
walk in darkness, we lie and do not tell the truth: But if we walk in the
light as He is in the light, we have fellowship one with another, and the
blood of Jesus Christ His Son cleanseth us from all sin.*

1 John 1: 5–7

Our ever present help and our comforter, the Holy Spirit

Jesus promised His disciples that His Father would send the Comforter to
abide with them for ever. The Holy Spirit is our Helper and our Comforter.
He dwells in us as the Word of God says, that the physical body is the
Temple of the Holy Spirit. Jesus made this promise to His disciples in
John 14: 16: "And I will pray the Father, and He shall give you another

Comforter, that He may abide with you forever." He then proceeded to say, "Even the Spirit of truth; whom the world cannot receive, because it sees Him not, neither knoweth Him, but ye know Him; for He dwelleth with you, and shall be in you" (John 14: 17). So the Holy Spirit dwells with the Believer and within the Believer. Which means that the Holy Spirit is supposed to have complete ownership of the Believer.

The Holy Spirit helps the Believer to rely completely on Him and to trust in God for guidance in their everyday life. The Believer recognises that every decision they make should be brought before God in prayer. The steps of a good person are ordered by the Lord (Psalms 37: 23). Therefore, it is the responsibility of the Believer to consult the Holy Spirit for help with guidance and direction in their everyday life and to be sensitive to His presence. He is always waiting to be consulted. He is the One we were given to help us here on earth. The Holy Spirit helps us whenever we pray for direction with our lives and He comforts us in difficult times, in times of grief and sadness.

The Holy Ghost's power enables us to mature in Christ and become the sons of God, but if we receive Christ and fail to recognise the need to be filled with the Holy Ghost's power, how can we function as Believers? John I: 12 states, "To all who received Him, He gave them power to become the sons of God."

In the Book of Proverbs we are told, "The fear of the Lord is the beginning of wisdom: and the knowledge of the holy is understanding" (Proverbs 9: 10). This is demonstrated by a life of integrity, a life of honesty. Quite often, when a Believer fails to be watchful or vigilant, circumstances may control our thoughts and speech. David came before God in humility because he recognised that he could not rely on his own wisdom. In Psalms 19: 14 David prayed: "Let the words of my mouth, and the meditation of my heart, be acceptable in thy sight, Oh Lord, my strength and my redeemer."

Our thoughts are hidden to the other person, but not to God. A life that fears God, a life of holiness, is also demonstrated by careful talk as opposed to careless talk. In Psalms 141: 3 David also prayed: "Set a watch before my mouth; keep the door of my lips." Those who recognise the need to walk in uprightness before God and for holiness in their lives usually recognise the need for humility before God in acknowledging to Him that we need His help in doing this because on our own, we could not possibly do it.

> *Jesus said to His disciples, It is easier for a camel to go through the eye of a needle, than for a rich man to enter into the kingdom of God. And they were astonished out of measure saying among themselves, who then can be saved? And Jesus looking upon them saith, With men it is impossible, but not with God: for with God all things are possible.*
>
> Mark 10: 26–27

What Jesus meant here was that we cannot change ourselves, but God can, if we ask Him to. So instead of struggling trying to do good in order to appease God when inside our hearts we are not pure, all we need is to humble ourselves to God and cry "Help!" The transformation has to begin inside out, not outside in, and only Jesus can transform us.

God is moved when we pray His Word. He is not interested in emotional empty prayers, like those the Pharisees were in the habit of making. He wants to see our humility in acknowledging His Word and trusting in His promises to us, which are found in His Word. He wants to see His Word written in the hearts of His people. This is what moves Him, only when we cry out His Word, the scripture. When hardship strikes, we should only cry out His promises to us, based on the scriptures.

The power of the Holy Spirit will not be available on the earth for those who have rejected Christ or those who believed in Christ but lived lives that deny Him, unholy lives. God will not force Himself on anyone unless we choose to live according to His Word. The presence of the Holy Spirit in us (the Bride) is our connection with Christ (the Groom). So this connection will be made complete when Christ comes for His Bride.

It will be like when two magnetic fields attract each other. The Bible says that when Christ comes, those who died in Christ will be raised from the dead and they will be the first ones to be caught up in the sky with Him; then those who are living in Christ will follow and be caught up with Him too. It will be an intimate moment between the Groom (Jesus Christ) and His Bride (the Holy Spirit-filled Saints of God, the Saints). So there will be no more divine protection for those who remain when the Saints are suddenly raptured from the earth. The most painful reality is that, because of compromising and unholy lifestyles, not all Believers in Christ will be taken up. Holiness is a choice that every Believer is free to make.

An urgent call to every Believer for intimacy with Christ in this end time

On the afternoon of 11th October 2008, I fell into a deep sleep amid great noise from my family, who were all watching television. I was in a vision again. In the vision, I saw a young woman interviewing people for the position of an accountant. I then saw a young couple arriving. The young man was black and his wife was Caucasian. The young man told a lot of lies. At first he said that he really needed the job, then it turned out when the woman interviewing looked for him that he had disappeared with his wife. When I looked outside for him, they had gone. Then the man who was working outside told us that the young man said he could not take the job because he had two groups of churches that he was contracted to as an accountant, but he never mentioned this to the interviewer in the first place, he secretly vanished. So I thought, why did he come to this interview to start with if he was committed elsewhere? I kept repeating to the man outside that the man was a liar and a deceiver, because the interviewer was ready to give him the job and he let her down and caused her great embarrassment and pain.

In the same room where that young man was supposed to be waiting was a young white woman. She was not here for an interview but she was waiting. Outside, I could hear the voices of black men advising a man who was about to propose to his girlfriend to go on his knees. They were very concerned for him because he had been through a series of disappointments. They were all feeling sympathy for him and they did

not wish to see him rejected again this time. I noticed that the young
white woman in the same room as me was acting strangely. She seemed
to be embarrassed as if she was trying to hide herself from me. It took
a while for me to work out that she was the one the men outside were
waiting for. She was not dressed well enough for the occasion. She was
in jeans and she looked unprepared for the occasion. I then realised that
she was dreading being engaged, which is why she was embarrassed and
trying to hide.

She suddenly stood up and was now dressed well, in a pinkish outfit.
She looked very attractive now. She went outside and then through the
gate to the area where the men were. There was a chair there where she
sat. As her man started walking towards her, she suddenly stood up again
and walked towards the gate, as if she had changed her mind. The man
who had been at the forefront of couching the man on how to propose to
a woman suddenly cried loudly "Oh! Not again!" and buried his face in
his hands, shaking his head as he looked down in great disappointment.
But the young woman was not leaving. She had dropped something of
value to her nearer the gate and she was going to pick it up. When the
other men noticed that she was coming back again, they rebuked the one
who was crying for giving up so easily. Everybody was happy again as the
engagement proceeded. I wondered what it was that was so valuable to
this young woman that she had dropped and had to go back for, creating
confusion to everyone in the process.

Then I heard the noise of a second drama, a commotion, at a different
place. As I looked, it was a different couple whose engagement had just
been broken. The man was running after the woman, who did not want
anything to do with him. She was completely rejecting him and running
away from him. She threw his ring back at him, shouting abuse. It was
such a sorrowful site as the man ran after her, begging her to come back
to him.

Another commotion, a third one, was taking place a few yards away. It
was now like watching drama all around me. This time there were three
brides running away from a wedding ceremony. Whether they were all
sisters or friends I'm not sure. Their mother and others were running

after them, trying to get them back to the wedding ceremony. What a sight! After they disappeared down the road, I looked back at the couple who had just broken their engagement and the man was still trying to persuade her to come back. While I looked at the scenario of the begging man, feeling sorry for him, I saw the mother of the three brides and others all passing again, having managed to catch the three brides. They were holding on to them and unceremoniously walking them back to the wedding ceremony like captives. The mother looked in the direction of the begging man who was still struggling to persuade his fiancé and she gave them a dirty look of pride and victory, obviously showing off that she had managed to persuade her daughters back to their wedding ceremony.

She behaved as if she was in competition with the other woman who had broken her engagement. There was no compassion in her for the couple, bearing in mind that other people were still in pain and going through the disappointment of being rejected. But I noticed that the mother was actually forcing her daughters back to the ceremony against their wishes. She was holding one tightly with both hands and the rest of the bridal party was such a sorrowful sight as they went back against their wishes. I also found it very awkward that the brides were all dressed in red. I did not understand why this mother had to force her daughters to commit to marriages they did not want. They were going back for their mother's sake. Watching them all heading back to the wedding ceremony was like watching a funeral, or like captured slaves being taken back to their master.

I suddenly woke up, feeling exhausted from what I had just witnessed. I stood up and left the room, feeling very confused at all this drama around me. As I asked the Lord in my tired state what the meaning of it all was, He revealed to me that His Bride is refusing to commit to Him. This broke my heart and I began to cry. During the drama I had felt the pain of those men who were being rejected. The women were all rejecting commitment and intimacy with their men. Then as I wondered why the three brides were dressed in red, I realised that the red stood for blood. This is when I was given the revelation that these women represented the Church, the Bride of Christ, and His lover, for whom He bled.

Other Believers are still compromising their lives, in that they are going back and picking up what they threw away when they got born again, when they first entered the gate. Their focus is divided to a double-standard way of life, and they prefer to hold on to things that are hindering them from totally surrendering to Jesus. Even though most Believers in Christ benefit from the blood covering, they prefer not to be too committed to Jesus because they enjoy their independence. They want to remain free to do their own will.

After these visions in 2008, I was taken on a journey of discovery, where I was led to some pastors and others in Zimbabwe. This journey confirmed that others enjoy a life of compromise so that they really do not have to fast and pray for breakthroughs in their lives, they simply trust or expect other people to meet their needs, not God. Other pastors actually cause the people of God to sin in order to impress them by supplying their needs through sinful ways. Their ministries look good on the outside, but things obtained through ways of compromise are hidden inside their ministries. Selfishness and pride are hindering them from seeing the truth. They prefer being neither hot nor cold; they do not want total surrender to Jesus, the Groom. Therefore there is not much intimacy with Christ among most Believers in the Body of Christ.

Most of the Believers in Christ are either rejecting His love or refusing intimacy with Him outside the church. The reason for this is because of laziness to pray and to read and meditate on the Word of God. I am living proof of it, because I received Jesus as my Lord and Saviour in 1979, yet I did not know the Lord the way I know Him now. It took one message of rebuke from a young woman who probably was not even born again by that time in 1979.

The Bible recommends that we rebuke each other unto righteousness. Open rebuke is better than secret love (Proverbs 27: 5, 6). Quite often we give more time to our jobs and to our own personal interests than we give to God. Most Believers even hate the preachers who preach about tithing and sowing seeds, yet we all still expect God to meet our needs and to hear our prayers. This is selfishness and lack of appreciation of the

Grace of God. The Word of God is clear in Malachi 3. There are always consequences associated with rebelliousness and disobedience to God.

Most people think obeying the statutes and commandments of God is only for Christians. Christianity is only a name of the movement given to the group of people who believe in Christ. The bottom line is that religion is not what Jesus suffered and died for on the cross, He died for our redemption from sin in order to be reconciled back to God. He died for all nations to be reconciled back to God. His blood is pure and holy and powerful because Mary was a virgin when she conceived Him and remained untouched until His birth. This is why Jesus taught that He came from the Father to earth, that He is the bread of life.

> *Now the birth of Jesus Christ was on this wise: When as his mother Mary was espoused to Joseph, before they came together, she was found with child of the Holy Ghost.*
>
> *Matthew 1: 18*

The fundamental issue is that God is not interested in any religious doctrine unless it is based on His Word. No religion on earth is important if is not founded on God the Father, God the Son and God the Holy Ghost. Jesus preached about Himself and His purpose here on earth to the Jews, but they would not listen.

> *The Jews then murmured at him, because he said, I am the bread which came down from heaven. And they said, Is not this Jesus the son of Joseph, whose father and mother we know? How is it then that he saith, I came down from heaven? Jesus therefore answered and said unto them, Murmur not among yourselves. No man can come to me, except the Father which hath sent me draw him: and I will raise him up at the last day.*
>
> *John 6: 41–44*

The gospel is easily available to all nations on the earth today. We have no excuse nowadays because apart from the radio, we now have a series of television channels and the internet, all powerfully projecting the gospel of the Lord Jesus Christ. This confirms Jesus' own words to the Jews when He said to them:

> *It is written in the prophets, "And they shall be all taught of God. Every man therefore that hath heard, and hath learned of the Father, cometh unto me." Not that any man hath seen the Father, save he which is of God, he hath seen the Father. Verily, verily, I say unto you, he that believeth on me hath everlasting life. I am the bread of life.*
>
> John 6: 45–48

Therefore God expects us as His people to humble ourselves before Him and cry out to Him in prayer.

> *Therefore said I unto you, that no man can come unto me except it were given unto him of my father.*
>
> John 6: 65

God only wants the Truth to be told to His people. He wants us all to live according to His Word, simply trusting Him. Jesus paid the ultimate price when He was crucified on the cross. There is power in the blood of Jesus. His Blood was shed to cleanse us from sin and to protect us from all evil. It is about Jesus, not religion. All He wants is for His Bride, those who receive Him, to have an intimate relationship with Him, and this can only happen through fasting and prayer and worship.

It is a wonderful thing to desire to know God and to live for God. Laziness in getting intimate with Him is a serious and selfish stumbling block, because each one of us has a different part to play or an assignment that has to be accomplished for the kingdom's purpose before Christ comes for His Bride, the Body of Christ. It is like a jigsaw puzzle where eventually the pieces all join up together and the picture becomes clear. Without you the puzzle would not develop the full picture it is designed for. It does not matter how tiny a branch you may appear to be in the eyes of people, you still have a very vital purpose to the vine, Jesus Christ.

I am the vine, ye are the branches: He that abideth in me, and I in him, the same bringeth forth much fruit: for without me ye can do nothing. If a man abide not in me, he is cast forth as a branch, and is withered; and men gather them, and cast them into the fire, and they are burned. If ye abide in me, and my words abide in you, ye shall ask what ye will, and it shall be done unto you.

John 15: 5–7

I heard one great man of God state that every person is born to solve a problem. How could we know such wise words if we do not take time to listen to God's great preachers? The Apostle Paul endured shipwrecks just to reach some parts of the world with the good news of the gospel of the Jesus Christ. God has given each of us a free will to choose what we want to hear and watch.

For God so loved the world, that He gave His only begotten Son, that whosoever believeth in Him should not perish, but have everlasting life.

John 3: 16

Most of us Believers in Christ are not keen to know the purpose of God for our lives here on earth just in case it interferes with our own desires. This is how the devil deceives and lies to God's people. He knows that if we listen to the gospel of Jesus Christ our lives will be transformed for the best. But the Word of God tells us:

Trust in the Lord and do good; so shalt thou dwell in the land, and verily thou shalt be fed. Delight thyself also in the Lord; and He shall give thee the desires of thine heart. Commit thy way unto the Lord; trust also in Him; and He shall bring it to pass.

Psalm 37: 3–5

God cares about us and He knows our desires because He created us. Nothing is hidden from Him. The devil is a liar.

The Word of God states that a thief comes not but to steal, to kill and to destroy (John 10: 10a). In Haiti, Satan caused God's people to reject Him by deceiving them. Now he has stolen those lives, because Satan knows that his time is short, he wants many to perish with him. Hell is not for people but for Satan and his angels who rebelled with him against God their creator.

Satan caused God's angels to rebel against God and God struck them all down. Hell is for them not for people, which is why God gave us His only Son Jesus to come and redeem us from the curse that came with the fall of Adam and Eve (see Genesis 3). If Jesus had refused to die on the cross, He would have disobeyed the will of God and we would not all qualify for eternity, because the Holy Bible states: "For as by one man's disobedience many were made sinners, so by the obedience of one shall many be made righteous" (Romans 5: 19). It is the obedience of Jesus to God that qualified us to eternity, His Grace. Our good works alone would not qualify us because the nature of sin can only be uprooted when we receive Christ as our Lord and Saviour. Jesus Christ conquered death on our behalf and took the keys of hell. Satan does not have the power to take anyone to hell except if we give him the power to take us. Jesus has the power to save us from damnation and he also has the power over our destiny, heaven or hell. The question is, how wise are the choices we make?

CHAPTER 12

How Do We Get Intimate with Christ?

It is the same as asking the question, how do we get intimate in a marriage? Most people think that intimacy in a marriage is only about sexual intercourse between the husband and wife, which is the reason relationships do not last long at all. If your spouse only comes closer to you because they are after sex, then they are selfish and unloving. They are nothing but a blood-sucker. Intimacy is more than just sexual intercourse. It is mutual. It is not only one sided. It is a give-and-take kind of relationship. Intimacy should happen in good times and bad times.

Most of us believers in Christ think we can bribe our way to heaven. God cannot be manipulated. He looks at the heart: how much do we love Him? Do we only love Him when all is going well for us, or do we love Him even if all hell is breaking loose around us? Is He God in good times but we denounce Him in bad times, when an earthquake hits? Is He God when we are surrounded with friends, receiving gifts and good things and money from everywhere; is He still God when we are only one meal away from starvation and all our friends have deserted us? God is always God, in good times or in bad times; our circumstances do not alter His Sovereignty. He is God and He is Holy.

Therefore intimacy with God is enhanced through communication. We communicate with God when we humble ourselves before Him in reading His word, in fasting and talking to Him in prayer, in praise or dance, and in worship. He deserves our praise and worship because He did not only create us, He also provided a way to reconcile us back to Him after the disobedience and fall of Adam and Eve. We did not stop disobeying and sinning against God even after Adam and Eve were spared.

The Holy Bible shows us in the Old Testament, that forgiveness of sin was through the sacrifice of an animal, the scapegoat. This took all the sins of the people and the High Priest brought its blood before the Holy of Holies. If the High Priest came out alive it meant the sins of the nation were forgiven. However, this did not deter His people from sinning. Bringing before God the blood of the sin animal became a routine. As we read from the scriptures we see that the Israelites, God's chosen people, constantly continued in ways of rebelliousness against Him. This annoyed God. He could have wiped all humanity off the face of the earth, yet He chose to go silent. God honoured His covenant with Abraham. After all those years of silence, He still felt compassionate enough to fulfil His promise as prophesied by His prophet Isaiah, in Isaiah 53, to provide himself as a sacrifice for our sins in order to reconcile us back to him through Jesus, thus fulfilling the prophecy that the Word became flesh and dwelt among us, and the government was upon his shoulders.

He walked this earth, teaching us the principles of life. His perfect life was an example that we should all follow, but His own people still denied Jesus because they were too engrossed in their religious beliefs and traditions. They were too accustomed to their oppressed lifestyle under the Roman Empire to recognise the liberating opportunity from God: Jesus, the ultimate living sacrifice for all humanity. His blood is still very powerful today and it still protects us from all evil and cleanses us from all unrighteousness. It is not the blood of a human being, it is God's own DNA. When we receive Jesus as our Lord and Saviour, His blood washes all our sins away and protects us from all evil.

This is why God is worthy of our praise and worship. He loved us first before we even knew Him. He paid a price for every human being in the earth, born and yet to be born. This is why we worship Him. He cancelled our death penalty in advance, through Jesus His Son.

Even if Satan can try to touch my body, he cannot touch my spirit. Jesus Christ determines the destiny of my spirit, not Satan. He is my Redeemer.

He was wounded for our transgressions, He was bruised for our iniquities, the chastisement of our peace was upon Him, and with His stripes we were healed.

Isaiah 53: 5

When the prophet Isaiah was given this prophecy in His spirit and he confirmed it in writing, it was a done deal between God and man. All that was left was the manifestation of the deal. In the New Testament we see this manifestation through the supernatural conception of the Virgin Mary and Jesus' suffering for us on the Cross of Calvary. Mary had no choice; the Creator of Heaven and Earth interrupted her life. Joseph was also warned by the Angel of God to simply accept being the surrogate father of Jesus.

Signs and wonders followed Jesus' teaching here on earth. The grave did not keep Him. In hell, He fought all the demons and took authority over death from Satan. That is why He said to His Disciples "In my father's house there are many mansions, if it were not so, I would have told you, I go to prepare a place for you." That is why I worship God. He is worthy of my praise. I love Him. Worship creates intimacy with God.

After we receive Christ in our hearts, we should desire to know Him through reading His Word, praying to Him, meditating on His Word and intimate Worship. His Word created us, so His Word cannot be separated from us. God created us in His own image. His Spirit is in us. The Word was God. When we read His Word we are made whole because His Word activates His Spirit in us. We were born again after we heard His Word being preached to us. Faith comes by hearing the Word of God. The Spirit of God is not active in people who are not born again, who have not accepted Jesus Christ into their hearts.

The sin of Adam separated us from God, which means the Spirit of God in us died and the sinful nature took control of our lives; that is why we need to be born again by accepting His Son Jesus Christ into our hearts, as the Lord of our lives. When we do this, Jesus Christ forgives our sins and reconciles us back to God. God's Spirit in us becomes alive again. Only Jesus Christ can make this happen because God sent Him to earth for this purpose, to become the final sacrifice for the atonement of our sins. That is why Jesus said: "I am the way, the truth and the life; no man comes to the Father except through me."

God created us to worship Him. When Jesus walked this earth He taught us how to pray: "Our Father, who art in heaven, hallowed be thy name, Thy kingdom come, Thy will be done on earth, as it is in heaven." The will of God is to be worshipped. God is being worshipped non-stop in heaven. We read this in Revelation 4: 10-11:

> *The four and twenty elders fall down before Him that sat on the throne, and worship Him that liveth for ever and ever, and cast their crowns before the throne, saying Thou art worthy, O Lord to receive glory and honour and power: for thou has created all things, and for thy pleasure they are and were created.*

CHAPTER 13

What Exactly Is Worship?

The meaning of worship as revealed to me is very broad. Worship is a declaration by the worshipper of how valuable, precious and worthy the one they worship is. It is an emotional and intimate act of love. The heart of the worshipper is totally consumed by the one they worship; they are completely drawn towards their lover. This intimate moment cannot be easily disrupted; in fact, it should never be disrupted. Disturbing it is like pouring ice-cold water onto the worshipper; it would be like piercing the heart of the worshipper.

Worship is an undisputed evidence of a love affair that exists between two people; it is a practical demonstration and display of one's innermost feelings for the lover. The worshipper displays their appreciation of the person they love. The worshipper is too involved to be ashamed of showing it, because it is a portrayal of their true image and feelings of adoration; therefore the worshipper is desperate to put the message across to their lover, so that their words involve their body language. Worship is serving and giving praise and honour to God, for who He is. God wants us to love Him back, to exalt Him.

This explains why the young man I saw in the February 2008 vision could not answer me when I asked him for directions. He was still consumed in intimacy with Christ, his lover; there was a longing in his eyes, a far-away look, a heavenward look that could not be disrupted by anything around him. He was still consumed in worship even though the session had ended and everyone had left the place of worship.

I will explain why I am referring to Christ as the young man's lover. There is an urgent call to every Believer for intimacy with Christ and intimacy can only be achieved through regular worship. Only worshippers will qualify as Brides to the Groom.

As a worshipper, king David appreciated the Word of God so much that he proclaimed this to God in Psalms. In Psalms 119: 105 he said: "Thy Word is a lamp unto my feet and a light unto my path." In Psalms 119: 11 he proclaimed: "Thy Word have I hid in mine heart that I might not sin against Thee." David valued God's Word so much that he determined to keep God's Word in his heart. The heart is like soil, whatever is put in it grows. That is why it was important for David to keep the Word of God in his heart, because he had had an experience at one time in his life where he had allowed his mind to entertain bad thoughts that led him into deep trouble (2 Samuel 11 & 12: 1-25). Through this nasty experience David realised the importance of renewing his mind by meditating on the Word of God until it became alive in his heart.

The enemy is determined to win a lot of God's people by showing them bad things so that he can use these things to play with our minds. He knows that if people look at something bad long enough, he can keep giving them the replay of it in their minds, meditating on his bad ideas until people act on them. Fear, sexual lust, greed, envy and jealousy are all sins that begin in the mind. This is why there is a lot going on these days on television and the internet. Things that encourage all kinds of sin are now found just by clicking a button. The enemy knows that the wages of sin is death. The enemy knows the Word of God even more than most Saints of God. That is the reason he puts Believers in a slumber, so that they do not take time to study God's Word. He knows what the Word of God says in Revelation 3: 15-16: "I know thy works, that thou art neither cold or hot: I would thou wert cold or hot. So then because thou art lukewarm, and neither cold nor hot, I will spue thee out of my mouth." Nobody wants to be half loved.

Once the Word of God becomes engraved in our hearts, it influences our thinking and our behaviour in a positive way. We begin to trust God. We begin to feel spiritually hungry when we do not hear from His Word. Our thought pattern begins to change; instead of selfishly focussing on our own needs, we begin to think of the needs of others. Above all, we begin to hear the voice of God from within us. We become drawn to Him more and more that we begin to enjoy worshipping Him.

God created us for His own pleasure. He expects and deserves to be worshipped by His own creation. In the Book of Exodus 2: 23 and Exodus 3, when God heard the cry of the children of Israel in Egypt because of the bondage they were in, God remembered His promise to Abraham, Isaac and Jacob and looked upon the children of Israel and respected them. God sent Moses to Pharaoh, to tell Pharaoh to release the children of Israel from their bondage.

> *And thou shalt say unto Pharaoh, thus says the Lord, Israel is my son, even my first-born: And I say unto thee, Let my son go, that he may serve me: and if thou refuse to let him go, behold, I will slay thy son, even thy firstborn.*
>
> *Exodus 4: 22–23*

God wants His people to serve Him, to give honour to Him and not to other gods that did not create His people, the invaders if you like. Pharaoh and his gods were invaders.

Abraham trusted and feared God. He obeyed God and left his own homeland to a place that God ordained for him. He experienced the full favour and goodness of God. He also experienced the love, protection and blessing of God in His life. Then God gave Abraham a dreadful assignment in Genesis 22: 2: "And He said, take now thy son, thine only son Isaac, whom thou lovest, and get thee into the land of Moriah; and offer him there for a burnt offering upon one of the mountains which I will tell thee of." Abraham did not question or argue with God or remind God of anything, he simply obeyed God. He knew God. He walked with God. He saw the dreadful assignment he was expected to carry out as a test of his faith and therefore he was determined to pass the test whatever the cost, because it was his God testing him. He believed in his heart that God would not let him kill his son. He obeyed God knowing that God was a good God. He trusted God as his Creator. His difficult situation gave him a reason to worship his Creator and to trust Him even more.

The land of Moriah was very far because it took Abraham three days to get there. Given the distance he had to travel and the assignment he was expected to carry out, Abraham had plenty of time to consider what he had been commanded to do by God. He probably hoped during his travels that God would intervene and stop him, but on the third day he actually saw the mount of Moriah and in his heart the moment of truth had arrived. Anyone in that kind of situation at that point would have had an increased heart rate and hence a heaviness in his body. They would have struggled to make those last few miles to the appointed place of sacrifice or even collapsed at that point.

As if walking those last difficult miles alone was not enough for Abraham, Isaac his son innocently asked him a very difficult question, as found in Genesis 22: 7–8:

And Isaac spake unto Abraham his father, and said, My father: and he said here am I, my son. And he said, Behold the fire and the wood: but where is the lamb for a burnt offering? And Abraham said, My son, God will provide himself a lamb for a burnt offering: so they went both of them together.

Even though Abraham had obeyed God and reached the place of sacrifice, he still had faith in God that He would not let him kill his son Isaac. I am sure he believed beyond any doubt that God would provide the lamb for the burnt offering and that Isaac's life would be spared. He knew that God was Love. He also knew that God was his Provider. Abraham's faith in God is also demonstrated by the way he answers his servants in Genesis 22: 5:

And Abraham said unto his young men, Abide ye here with the ass; and I and the lad will go yonder and worship, and come again to you.

He saw this test as a moment of worship. Anyone else at that point would have been on their knees begging God not to let that happen, but Abraham continued in faith with Isaac to the place of sacrifice. Abraham feared God in his heart and therefore he knew that obedience was better than sacrifice.

And they came to a place which God had told him of; and Abraham
built an altar there, and laid the wood in order, and bound Isaac his son,
and laid him on the altar upon the wood. And Abraham stretched forth
his hand, and took the knife to slay his son. And the Angel of the Lord
called unto him out of heaven, and said, Abraham, Abraham: and he
said, Here am I. And he said, lay not thine hand upon the lad, neither
do thou anything unto him: for now I know that thou fearest God, seeing
thou hast not withheld thy son, thine only son from me. And Abraham
lifted up his eyes, and looked, and behold behind him a ram caught in a
thicket by his horns: and Abraham went and took the ram, and offered
him up for a burnt offering in the stead of his son. And Abraham called
the name of that place Jehovah Jireh: as it is said to this day, In the mount
of the Lord it shall be seen.

Genesis 22: 9–14

He did not see God as a cruel God, because he knew that Jehovah was
his Provider. He therefore acted out of trust. He trusted God and God's
Angel showed up for Abraham at the last moment. God was impressed
by his faith in Him. He was impressed with his trust. God saw Abraham's
heart. Nothing is hidden before God. We cannot fool God. Abraham
feared God because he knew that God was Holy.

This is the most powerful and the most effective kind of worship,
because the Believer recognises that God deserves to be worshipped and
that their life circumstances do not change the greatness of God. He is
God in good times and in bad times; He is God in times of oversupply
or undersupply; He deserves to be worshipped for Who He is; He is a
Holy God, the Creator of heaven and earth and all that is in it. This
kind of worship reaches God and moves Him. Satan fears this kind
of worship because he knows that it is a dangerous weapon of mass
destruction to his camp, the worshipper's enemies. When a worshipper
in distress begins to sing and dance before the Lord, I believe that all
heaven watches in silence; this is when God's Angels of War position
themselves ready to take God's orders on what to do for the worshipper.
When a worshipper in distress begins to dance, it is because they know

that God is with them and promised that He would never leave nor forsake them.

From Abraham's example we therefore realise that a worshipper is obedient to the God they worship. The worshipper knows that God is a faithful God who keeps His promises. Numbers 23: 19 states: "God is not a man, that He should lie; neither the son of man, that He should repent; hath He said, and shall He not do it? Or hath He spoken, and shall He not make it good?" The worshipper fears the God they worship because He created them and they recognise that He knows them better and He controls their destiny. The worshipper also knows that God likes to be trusted and obeyed, for He rewards obedience. Isaiah 57: 13b: "but he that putteth his trust in Me shall possess the land, and shall inherit my holy mountain." The worshipper knows that God is a Holy God and a God of compassion.

For thus saith the high and lofty One that inhabiteth eternity, whose name is Holy; I dwell in the high and holy place, with him also that is of a contrite and humble spirit, to revive the spirit of the humble, and to revive the heart of the contrite ones.

Isaiah 57: 15

Worshipping God in hard times, times of trials and times of war is indeed the greatest weapon that we have been blessed with as Saints of God. It is also the evidence of our faith and trust in God. It is a sign of humility before God, acknowledging Him as the problem solver and the peace and joy giver, the worshipper's provider.

King David was a worshipper. As a small boy he trusted God so much that he refused to fear Goliath. He knew the God in whom he believed intimately because he had an early childhood experience of His presence and His goodness in his life. When his nation panicked at the sight of Goliath, the Philistine, David's anger arose. He demanded to be allowed to face the giant himself because he knew the greatness of his God and what He can do for those who put their trust in Him. In the Holy Bible we read:

And David said to Saul, Let no man's heart fail because of him; thy servant will go and fight with the Philistine. And Saul said to David, Thou are not able to go against this Philistine to fight with him: for thou art but a youth, and he a man of war from his youth. And David said unto Saul, Thy servant kept his father's sheep, and there came a lion, and a bear, and took a lamb out of the flock: And I went out after him, and smote him, and delivered it out of his mouth: and when he arose against me, I caught him by his beard, and smote him, and slew him. Thy servant slew both the lion and the bear: and this uncircumcised Philistine shall be as one of them, seeing he hath defiled the armies of the living God. David said moreover, The Lord that delivered me out of the paw of the lion, and out of the paw of the bear, He will deliver me out of the hand of this Philistine. And Saul said unto David, Go, and the Lord be with thee.

1 Samuel 17: 32–37

Experience is a great teacher. David's two experiences as a shepherd of his father's sheep had given him leadership skills as well as creating in him a heart full of courage and gratefulness. While looking after his father's sheep he had found himself in a life or death situation. He could have panicked and run for his life, leaving all his father's sheep behind. However, he refused to be a fearful shepherd and he chose courage. He realised his responsibility over the sheep and therefore would not let anything threaten his position as a shepherd. David did not wish to let his father down.

The Bible does not give us a full account of these two life or death experiences, but one would imagine that they had left David with no choice but to seek his creator's intervention. God intervened by empowering David with supernatural strength to overcome his adversaries, the lion and the bear. David must have instantly realised that the same God who created him also created the lion and the bear. Therefore David must have also instantly recalled that he was the one created in the image of God and not the lion or the bear, and that he had dominion over the animals. Therefore he trusted God to deliver him. God honoured David's trust by enabling him to kill these dangerous animals. David knew that his strength was from God. He adored God. He worshipped Him with a heart of gratefulness, a heart of thanksgiving. The Book of Psalms is full of David's heartfelt expressions to God. He believed in being real with God. He was not a pretender. God loves real people, not gossipers and selfish people. God likes people He can rely on.

A worshipper has great respect for other worshippers. A worshipper knows that no one can worship God in spirit and in truth unless they have had an encounter with God in their life. A worshipper recognises the power of God on others. Therefore, even if a Servant of God offends the worshipper, as happens sometimes, he will not revile the Servant of God but will leave the judgment to God. That is why when David served in King Saul's palace, and King Saul threatened to kill him out of jealousy, David preferred to run for his life. David feared God so much that he recognised that because of God's anointing on Saul, he had no right to fight him back or lay his hand on him, bearing in mind that David had killed a lion, a bear and the feared Philistine giant, Goliath. He ran from the anointed one of God. "Servants, be subject to your masters with all fear; not only to the good and gentle, but also to the froward" (1 Peter 2: 18).

However, a worshipper will not find it in their heart to revile anyone who offends them, be it a believer or a non-believer. This is because the fear of God is in the heart of a worshipper.

For this is thankworthy if a man of conscience toward God endure grief, suffering wrongfully. For what glory is it, if, when ye be buffeted for your faults, ye shall take it patiently? But if, when ye do well, and suffer for it, ye take it patiently, this is acceptable with God. For even hereunto were ye called: because Christ also suffered for us, leaving us an example, that ye should follow His steps: Who did not sin, neither was guile found in His mouth: Who when He was reviled, reviled not again; when He suffered, He threatened not; but committed Himself to Him that judgeth righteously.

1 Peter 2: 19–23

The worshipper also recognises the greatness of their God. That is why they worship Him in good times and in bad times, because His goodness and His greatness are not dependent on circumstances. Bad situations cannot stop the worshipper from worshipping God intimately, because it is then that the worshipper needs His presence most. God is touched by a sacrificial kind of worship, the worship that comes from a broken heart. God is moved by the sacrifices we make to Him. He identifies with this well, because He made a sacrifice for us when He sent His only begotten Son, Jesus Christ, to die for our sins on the cross of Calvary. The worshipper recognises that God is God always and that He changes not. The worshipper believes that, if God delivered Daniel from the mouth of the lions, surely nothing is impossible for God. He can deliver them too. He changes not. Therefore He is worthy of our praise and worship. God sees the heart of the worshipper, so it is the worship that comes from the heart that pleases God. The desire to worship God is rooted in the heart of the Believer in Christ. No circumstance can quench the desire to worship God.

As we desire to worship God more as individuals in our lives, the Holy Spirit will enable us to hear His voice, His guidance and direction in our lives. Jesus said in John 14: 14–16:

> If ye shall ask anything in My Name, I will do it. If ye love me, keep my commandments. And I will pray the Father, and He shall give you another Comforter, that he may abide with you forever.

So as we worship God, we demonstrate our love and humility to Him. He will enable us with the fullness of His favour. He will open our spiritual eyes and ears and enable us to understand God's purpose for our lives. He will empower us to accomplish His purpose for our lives here on earth, not for us to boast about it but all to His glory.

To be able to worship God in bad times, we need the grace of God. The apostle Paul highlighted the words of the Lord to him at a time when he was experiencing physical pain that the enemy had afflicted on him:

For this thing I besought the Lord thrice, that it might depart from me. And he said unto me, My grace is sufficient for thee: for My strength is made perfect in weakness. Most gladly therefore will I rather glory in my infirmities that the power of Christ may rest upon me.

2 Corinthians 12: 8–10

Paul recognised that nothing mattered much in his life but the glory of God. He recognised that the presence of God was valuable in his life. Paul knew without any doubt that God was a healer because he had experienced the healing touch of God in his life before, when he was a sinner himself and a persecutor of Saints of God, and the glory of the Lord appeared before him and his eyes were permanently blinded.

I have experienced moments of loneliness and physical pain like Paul, where I have felt that the enemy is really enjoying it and trying hard to use it to his advantage, to stop me from worshipping my God. But it is when I worship God in such difficult times that my victory comes. "And we know that all things work together for good to them that love God, to them who are the called according to His purpose" (Romans 8: 28). Therefore, I believe that God allows certain things or situations in our lives so that we are drawn closer to Him, to seek His face. He wants us to depend entirely on Him, not on ourselves. We can only be drawn closer to Him in prayer and in worship. He said in His Word: "Draw nigh unto me, and I will draw nigh unto you."

CHAPTER 14

The Consequences of Man's Traditions

G od is not interested in the traditions of man. God is not a part of man's traditions, whether in the West, in Africa, in Asia or any other part of the world. Traditions only reflect a lot of rebelliousness to God, in that they are not usually in line with the His Word, and they are oppressive to His people.

I recently heard a sermon by a great man of God, Dr Charles Stanley (InTouchMinistries.org), on sowing and reaping, in which he stated that it is important for people to know the history of their nation in order to understand where things went wrong, because we reap what we sow. On this, he quoted from three chapters in the Holy Bible:

Be not deceived; God is not mocked: for whatsoever a man soweth, that shall he also reap.

Galatians 6: 7

This I say then, Walk in the Spirit, and ye shall not fulfil the lust of the flesh. For the flesh lusteth against the Spirit, and the Spirit against the flesh: and these are contrary one to the other: so that ye cannot do the things that ye would. But if ye are led of the Spirit, ye are not under the law. Now the works of the flesh are manifest, which are these: Adultery, fornication, uncleanness, lasciviousness, idolatory, witchcraft, hatred, variance, emulations, wrath, strife, seditions, heresies, envyings, murders, drunkenness, revellings, and such like: of the which I tell you before, as I have also told you in time past, that they which do such things shall not inherit the kingdom of God.

Galatians 5: 16–21

Let this mind be in you, which was also in Christ Jesus: Who being in the form of God, thought it not robbery to be equal with God: But made Himself of no reputation, and took upon him the form of a servant, and was made in the likeness of men: And being found in fashion as a man, he humbled himself, and became obedient unto death, even the death of the cross. Wherefore God also hath highly exalted Him, and given Him a Name which is above every name: That at the Name of Jesus every knee should bow, of things in the heaven, and things in the earth, and things under the earth; And that every tongue should confess that Jesus Christ is Lord, to the glory of God the Father.

Philippians 2: 5–1

After I received Christ as my Lord and Saviour in 1979, the Lord navigated me on an journey and experience in my late teens that opened my eyes to many traditional evil practices that the enemy associated with culture, so that such practices were regarded simply as part of my nation's tradition, another deception by the enemy. This is how Satan blinded and deceived most African people, by making them worship their dead ancestors instead of worshipping God. In Africa witchdoctors and fortune tellers saw themselves as the help the people needed. In other parts of the world psychics and other similar mediums are very much esteemed. Most of these evil traditions affect even the born-again Saints among my nation, in that unless we are fully knowledgeable of the scriptures, we find ourselves falling into Satan's traps.

For example, in my Ndebele culture, a newborn baby is traditionally dedicated to the ancestors and all sorts of traditional rituals are performed on the baby in the belief that the baby needs protection from evil. Meanwhile, evil will be introduced into the young life against its knowledge. Many believers have failed to stand their ground against this ritualistic practice by their family members and out of the fear of threats associated with an "unprotected baby". I can give many examples involving such unbiblical traditional practices in relation to marital and family protection. These are what the Bible describes as the High Places, the Altars of Baal. Out of ignorance many Christians find themselves tangled in them. They say: "What you don't know won't hurt you." God in His Word tells us:

> *My people are destroyed for lack of knowledge, I will also reject thee, that thou shall be no priest to me: seeing thou hast forgotten the law of thy God, I will also forget thy children.*
>
> *Hosea 4: 6*

Today, the consequences of such ritualistic rebelliousness against Jehovah God, the Creator of heaven and earth, have been very severe and costly to most families and generations, not only in Africa but worldwide.

> *And thou shall not go aside from any of the words which I command thee this day, to the right hand, or to the left, to go after other gods to serve them. But it shall come to pass, if thou wilt not hearken unto the voice of the Lord thy God, to observe to do all His commandments and His statutes which I command thee this day; that all these curses shall come upon thee, and overtake thee.*
>
> *Deuteronomy 28: 14–15*

The curses are highlighted from verse 16 onwards, very dreadful curses even to read about, because some of them are so evident today in many families.

People and nations that reject the Gospel of the Lord Jesus Christ are open to the judgment of God in these last days as they were in the beginning. God has never changed. The only problem has been that people changed from being obedient to being disobedient to God. He silently watches His Servants being publicly rejected and humiliated all the time, but when His judgment comes upon such a nation, it is when they begin to question God's existence. They forget that for many years, they shut their ears from His voice and chose to live in sin. Today in Haiti, can the rich say they are better than the poor orphaned children they have been neglecting on their streets for so long?

What about my own country of birth, Zimbabwe?

Robert Mugabe rejected Christ as being a foreigner

Robert Mugabe's ZANU-PF party and government publicly declared their honour and gratitude to the spirit of their dead ancestor, Nehanda, as the one who had won them victory at their 1980 independence celebrations. Peace and unity across people of different ethnic backgrounds in Zimbabwe could have been achieved early enough if the Body of Christ had taken the upper hand in challenging the practice of idolatry, calling for the nation's repentance and asking God for forgiveness. Being silent was condoning traditional and cultural ways that were contrary to the Word of God. Therefore the Church was guilty of unbiblical ways of compromise. The Body of Christ is still guilty of this today as division continues within the church around the world based on man's traditions, especially concerning women.

From my own knowledge as I was still resident in Zimbabwe at the time, the Body of Christ in Zimbabwe did not speak out against Mugabe's demonic worship that suddenly became the pride of his new government in Zimbabwe, because the traditions of men were condoned in the Body of Christ among the African people. The Church became silent about public demonic and ancestral worship, because there was no unity in the Church due to political and racial hatred and unforgiveness since the war became intense.

The tribe one belongs to or the colour of one's skin is not a choice. It is not like a sinful habit or lifestyle that one can decide to change overnight, it is permanent. This is why racism and tribalism are very evil and the most dangerous tools that Satan uses to bring division and oppression to the earth. Being black is not a disability, as I have heard it called by some people. I am grateful to be black and I would never wish to be any other skin colour, God chose it for me for His purpose and for His glory and for sure I will glorify Him in my beautiful and perfect black skin.

It is dangerous for any person to be tribal or racially prejudiced towards other people, because there are good people and bad people in this world. God is a God of justice and good people should not be stigmatised based on their tribe, colour or ethnic background. As Believers in Christ, we should not be found with this kind of impurity in our hearts. However, we should never live in denial. Nobody is perfect. If we have prejudice in our heart, it's always advisable to admit it to God and ask Him to help overcome it. The human heart is deceitful, but God sees what is in it. We can deceive each other, but not God. We thank God for His grace and mercy; for the power of redemption through Jesus Christ, our Lord and Saviour.

We ought to allow God to change our mindset and remove the impurities within our hearts. Therefore, it is important to repent quickly; when we repent before God in humility, and confess our sinful and oppressive ways, God is able to deliver us from them. The power of the Holy Ghost can remove hatred and all evil from our hearts as believers, if we acknowledge that we have these weaknesses in our hearts and confess them to God. God is pure and Holy and therefore He wants us to be pure and holy too.

> *Christ hath redeemed us from the curse of the law, being made a curse for us: for it is written, Cursed is everyone that hangeth on a tree: that the blessing of Abraham might come on the Gentiles through Jesus Christ; that we might receive the promise of the Spirit through faith.*
>
> Galatians 3: 13–14)

Mugabe's evil ways and his rebelliousness against God by rejecting Jesus Christ and blaspheming Him as a "foreigner" are highlighted in many historical books, including Ian Smith's memoirs. Mugabe encouraged hatred and all kinds of evil to be committed on the Ndebele people and their party leader, Joshua Nkomo, until Nkomo left his home and country to seek refuge. The Ndebele people who had won seats in the new parliament of Zimbabwe were constantly shunned and ridiculed by members of Mugabe's party and the government and reduced to silence through fear of extinction through the atrocities and massacres by 5 Brigade.

The economy of the country deteriorated due to several years of drought, a decline in tourism and fuel shortage crises caused by government corruption. Mugabe and his wife used Air Zimbabwe as their taxi rank for shopping sprees abroad for their newly built multimillionaire palaces in a country full of starving, homeless orphans who sleep rough everywhere. There was a continuous misuse of public funds and resources by his government, the ruling elite, hence Mugabe's eye on diamonds and his military involvement in the problems of the Democratic Republic of Congo, to which all the country's fuel resources were channelled, followed by the illegal invasion of farms.

Recently many lives have perished nationwide in Zimbabwe from the cholera epidemic. Due to the deteriorated state of the economy, there was no medical intervention in place for thousands of poor people and not many doctors and nurses, as most had long left the country for greener pastures in neighbouring countries and abroad. Cholera was worsened by food shortages across the whole country. People were eating grass, leaves and even soil in some parts.

In the book of Exodus, God spoke to Moses to warn His people:

If thou will diligently hearken to the voice of the Lord thy God, and wilt do that which is right in His sight, and will give ear to His commandments, and keep all His statutes, I will put none of these diseases upon thee, which I have brought upon the Egyptians: for I am the Lord that healeth thee.

Exodus 15: 26

The God who appeared to Moses as the bush-consuming fire is still the same God today and for ever will be. He does not change. He spoke to our fathers and ancestors just as He spoke to Moses. He still speaks today. People in their rebelliousness choose what they want to believe.

In the same way, God gave the Apostle John the following revelation concerning future events:

And behold I come quickly; and my reward is with me, to give every man according as his work shall be.
I am Alpha and Omega, the beginning and the end, the first and the last.

Blessed are they that do His commandments, that they may have right to
the tree of life, and may enter in through the gates into the city.
For without are dogs, and sorcerers, and whoremongers, and murderers,
and idolaters, and whosoever loveth and maketh a lie.

Revelation 22: 12–15

Nothing takes God by surprise. He already knew that the white settlers of Africa would cheat the black people of their treasure, their resources and their natural habitat. We do not know exactly what God said to the white settlers, but He must have given them instructions on how to spread Christianity to the Africans without killing them. But African people confused the voice of God with the demonic spirits that usually manifested themselves during their traditional ancestral dances and worship, which Joshua Nkomo in his book refers to as the "African religion". He further states: "the Christian religion seeks life after death for the individual, while the African religion seeks rain, health and peace in the world for all mankind (1984: 15). It was clear that the Africans considered God's voice as the voice of their ancestors. When they spoke to Him they referred to Him as *Babamkhulu*, meaning "grandfather". This particular voice did not manifest through anybody. The shrine where the voice came from was not a human being, but a rock; just as God spoke from a mountain when He presented the Ten Commandments to Moses, or when He appeared as a burning bush and ordered Moses to remove his sandals. God always met His people at an appointed place to talk to them and to give them instructions for an assignment. They would have had to be loyal and obedient to God's voice and instructions to successfully accomplish their assignment.

God's audible voice manifests within the vicinity where the person would be. For example, in 1 Samuel 3 when Samuel was asleep as a child in the Temple, he heard God calling his name and each time he would wake up and run to Eli the priest, thinking that it was Eli calling him. "Now Samuel did not yet know the Lord, neither was the word of the Lord yet revealed to him" (1 Samuel 3: 7). Like Samuel, the word of the Lord was not yet revealed to the African people of Zimbabwe.

When the Lord called Samuel again the third time, Eli the priest perceived that the Lord had called the child.
Therefore Eli said to Samuel, Go, lie down: and it shall be if He calls you, that you shall say, Speak, LORD, for your servant hears. So Samuel went and lay down in his place.

1 Samuel 3: 8–9

In the same way that Eli had to teach Samuel to listen to the voice of God and know that it was God talking to him, it was not God's wish for the African people to remain ignorant of the voice of their God; therefore He was going to use the early white settlers to bring awareness to the Africans that He was not a voice of their ancestors, but that He was their God, their Creator and the Creator of heaven and earth. The white settlers already knew God and God wanted them to introduce Him to the Africans, their cousins. The fact that God referred to the white settlers as cousins to the Africans meant that the Africans and the white settlers were somehow connected and therefore were equally valuable to God. Cousins are not meant to dominate each other, they are meant to respect each other. The Africans were not lesser beings just because they did not wear trousers or own guns. God loved them as His people too. The Africans are a people of courage and like their cousins, the first white settlers, had certain transferable skills and knowledge to offer.

Another example of the dominance and disregard of African people by the white settlers was that of David Livingstone. In his explorations in Southern Africa, Livingstone discovered the huge waterfalls on the border between Zimbabwe and Zambia. He named it the Victoria Falls, but the truth is, the indigenous people of that area, who are known as the Tonga, already knew the falls and they already had a name for it, *Mosiwo Yatunya* meaning "The Smoke that Thunders". What Livingstone should have done is name the falls exactly as it was originally named by the Tonga, to be respectful to them. However, God knew all that would happen.

All God looked for was obedience to His voice, from both the Africans and the white settlers. God rewards obedience. It appears that both sides faltered. Disobedience has its consequences. We reap what we sow. I strongly believe that if the whole of Southern Africa had obeyed the voice of God during that time, it would still be the most prosperous part of the world.

However, God forgives when His people genuinely repent. That chance is still available, if both the whites and blacks in Zimbabwe could acknowledge their faults, confess to one another and forgive each other, God can still restore their land. They were originally supposed to live peacefully with each other, as cousins, which means they were supposed to mutually benefit from each other. We are told in 2 Chronicles 20: 20: "Believe in the Lord thy God, so shall you be established: believe in His prophets, so shall ye prosper." Being established means being set up for life, and to prosper is to progress positively in life without any hindrances, to be fruitful and successful in all you do.

After the nation of Zimbabwe achieved its independence from white rule in 1980, I saw the nation's rebelliousness being publicly declared on national television. The new government declared publicly that the spirit of Nehanda had fought for them and I watched on television the traditional dancers declaring their victory in dance with the full support of the new government. A street shrine was set up in honour of the spirit of Nehanda, fulfilling the scripture:

> And it came to pass after all thy wickedness (woe, woe unto thee! Saith the Lord God); That thou hast also built unto thee an eminent place, and hast made thee an high place [a pagan shrine] in every street.
>
> Ezekiel 16: 23–24

The Body of Christ in Zimbabwe, because of fear, became guilty of this sin as well because no one stood up publicly to oppose it. The new government crushed the voice of God by controlling every institution through lies and intimidation. Politicians took the upper hand in the rule of the nation. Therefore the Body of Christ remained silent. This was all due to the lie of the devil to the people of Southern Africa, which was that their ancestors were more important and that Christianity as a religion was for the whites only. Needless to say this lie cost the nation of

Zimbabwe their spiritual inheritance, and especially the Ndebele people of Matabeleland, as they are originally Jews, the remnant of King Solomon.

The consequences of the nation's rebelliousness have been witnessed for many years. Idolatry, witchcraft and sexual sins and corruption are on the increase, even in the church. God showed me visions of abuse of women by men in authority, and the neglect of orphans and widows. The sister I saw in my vision phoned me and told me about her struggles. She is pursuing the call of God in her life, but the challenges she has faced all relate to abusive men, pastors trying to take advantage of her as a widow, without any shame whatsoever. Their lukewarm spiritual lives have blinded them to what sin really is. These are men with respectable wives. Many are called, but few are chosen. The Body of Christ needs the Mercy and Grace of God.

Historically, it is proven that civilisation, cultural beliefs, traditions and rituals are factors that have hindered families and nations from worshipping God in honesty and in truth. African people, for example, were raised under a culture that believes that health and success are determined by their ancestors. Therefore they did everything to appease their dead ancestors by worshipping them. To this day, most satanic cults in Southern Africa deceive God's people by teaching them that Jesus is for the West, for the white people, and that they should value and worship their dead ancestors instead. As I write this book, there are people in Zimbabwe who are still trapped in one cult that rejects Jesus Christ, based on its traditional beliefs in ancestors. I trust God to deliver these and many others from this trap of the enemy soon.

Then one wonders exactly who these ancestors are that all these people so strongly believe in? How can anyone believe in an ancestor they never met? At least God knows me. He knew me before I even entered my mother's womb because He created me.

And why take the long and deadly route to blessing when Christ provided a shortcut for us through the Cross? Spiritual blindness cripples even highly educated people. They would rather stoop very low to visit a poor witchdoctor for consultation somewhere in a dark and dinghy hut in a rural area. People do not realise that only God can open their spiritual eyes to see and to know the truth. Wisdom and understanding only come from God. No educational institution can impart true wisdom or understanding. "The fear of the Lord is the beginning of wisdom; and the knowledge of the holy is understanding" (Proverbs 9: 10).

In the Old Testament we see a lot of evidence relating to the rebellious ways of God's people. Most nations rebelled against God and worshipped idols as their gods. Israel was God's chosen nation because their ancestors Abraham, Isaac and Jacob had acknowledged Him as their God. God is a God who keeps His promises. He promised Abraham that He would bless his seed, which is why He kept giving the Israelites chance after chance to repent. He honoured Abraham, his faithful servant, and would not go back on the promise He made to Him. However, this did not mean that God would condone the disobedience and rebelliousness of the seed of Abraham. He is a God of order, a God of principles and a holy God. Whenever the Israelites rebelled against God, He punished them by allowing them to be enslaved by other nations so much that their suffering would cause them to repent and seek the face of God again. Once God pardoned them and rescued them, they would soon forget and rebel again.

Dr Charles Stanley highlighted the importance of knowing our history as a nation, so that we know what went wrong, how we can avoid the same mistakes and the importance of repentance as individuals and as a nation.

> If my people who are called by name shall humble themselves and pray, and seek my face, and turn from their wicked ways, then will I hear from heaven, and will forgive their sin, and will heal their land.
>
> 2 Chronicles 7: 14

God does forgive sins. He is a God who is able to pardon us and give us a second chance to put things right with Him in our lives. He sacrificed His only begotten Son for this purpose, that through Him we may receive forgiveness from God.

My own experience of hardship created a worshipper in me. The battles I faced after I accepted the call of God for my life actually helped bring things into perspective as well as highlighting the groundwork I had to entrust to God for my ministry to take off. I learnt that worship does not only happen when things are going well for the Believer in Christ, but should actually happen more when all hell is breaking loose around the Believer. Most true worshippers are not controlled or discouraged by circumstances. When the enemy threw his best attack at me and my family, I realised that there was not much I could do myself except lift up my eyes, my hands and my voice to God in worship. I learnt to dance amid trouble. Jesus paid for our victory and nothing should ever be allowed hold us back. How we handle our circumstances is a matter of choice. My choice is to trust God, because He promised in his Word that He will fight my battles for me. So all I do is tell Satan that God is my defence, I fight no battle but God fights for me. All I do is claim the promises to me, based on His Word. I then praise and worship Him in expectation.

It was at this point of desperation in my life that I learnt to seek the presence of God through worship. It was then that nothing else mattered in my life but to touch God and feel His assuring presence so that I was not alone. I also believed in the promises of His Word that He would not leave nor forsake me, and that He would not allow me to be tempted beyond my strength. In my weakness and desperation I had only one option left as a Believer in Christ, to worship God.

Jesus warned the Samaritan woman at Jacob's well:

But the hour comes and now is, when the true worshippers shall worship the Father in spirit and in truth: for the Father seeks such to worship Him. God is a Spirit: and they that worship Him must worship Him in spirit and in truth.

John 4: 23–24

How else would I have learnt to be a true worshipper except through hardship? In hardship we have two choices, to hold on to God or to give up on God. I chose to hold on.

As well as that, God seemed to be leading me divinely to His people through dreams and visions. Some visions led me to people I had not spoken to or seen in ages. I had to track them down at all costs just to speak to them and convey the message I was sent with. I was led mainly to the Zimbabwean Saints of God. As I obeyed and acted, He kept leading me to more and more people. I found most of them facing severe challenges. "Worship God" was the message I carried.

I thank God that I obeyed Him when He sent me to His people, even though it was a challenging path for me, because these were people of God going through great economic hardship and hunger. It is not easy to speak to hungry people who have no food whatsoever when you have a refrigerator full of food in your part of the world.

The economic situation in Zimbabwe has been very challenging for the people there. I must say that God has been faithful to the Body of Christ in Zimbabwe in many ways. I could not help my friends there in any other way except share my own testimony with them. I gave them the very solution that the Lord taught me in my own predicament, to forget about my circumstances, lift up my hands and worship God in praise, song and dance and to focus on God not on my circumstances. I gave them the same scriptures that helped me to read every day from the Bible and to speak them and think or meditate on them from sunrise until sunset, but most of all to sing praises to God and worship God. I phoned them week after week, discouraging any negative talk. God is faithful to those who put their trust in Him.

When the enemy presents an ugly situation, I refuse it and I reject it in Jesus' Mighty Name. I speak life into myself. I believe what I speak because it is based on God's written word and I receive it by faith. I am blessed, I am not cursed and so are my children blessed because they are the generation of the upright. Therefore I declare that I am redeemed through Jesus Christ. Galatians 3: 13–14 says:

> Christ hath redeemed us from the curse of the law, being made a curse for us: for it is written, Cursed is everyone that hangeth on a tree: That the blessing of Abraham might come on the Gentiles through Jesus Christ; that we might receive the promise of the Spirit through faith.

The angel of the LORD encampeth round about them that fear Him and delivereth them.

Psalm 34: 7

No weapon that is formed against thee shall prosper; and every tongue that shall rise against thee in judgment thou shalt condemn. This is the heritage of the servants of the Lord, and their righteousness is of me, saith the Lord

Isaiah 54: 17

In acting on the revelations that God gives me, I have learnt that it is better to obey God's voice than to disobey Him out of fear of offending people. Therefore it is not wise to be afraid of making a mistake. A child would never learn to walk if getting hurt from falling would permanently put the child off trying again. God forgives our mistakes, but it is a must that we do not allow ourselves to be put off obeying Him because of them. It is not always easy to obey God when you have to pass on messages you do not even understand yourself, but God knows that the person He is sending you to will understand, because the message is meant for them not for you. Those who received me as a messenger were helped in many ways; but I would like to believe that through the mercy of God, those who rejected me as a messenger would also be helped.

There is no more fear in me. Satan's attacks on me were so severe that they removed all fear of evil in me. My suffering only increased my love for the Lord Jesus Christ.

As it is written, For thy sake we are killed all the daylong; we are accounted as sheep for the slaughter. Nay, in all things we are more than conquerors through Him that loved us. For I am persuaded, that neither death, nor life, nor angels, nor principalities, nor powers, nor things present, nor things to come, Nor height nor depth, nor any other creature, shall be able to separate us from the love of God, which is in Christ Jesus our Lord.

Romans 8: 36–39

Therefore I hate the devil but I do not fear him. "For God hath not given us the spirit of fear; but of power, and of love and of a sound mind" (2 Timothy 1: 7). I fear disobeying God because He created me and He is Love. His love rescued me. For there is no fear in love, but perfect love casts out fear. God's love for me is perfect because God is Love.

I feel great pain for those who allow themselves to be used by Satan to hate and cause pain on the innocent.

> *Recompense to no man evil for evil. Provide things honest in the sight of all men. If it be possible, as much as lieth in you, live peaceably with all men. Dearly beloved, avenge not yourselves, but rather give place unto wrath: for it is written, Vengeance is mine; I will repay, saith the Lord. Therefore if thine enemy hunger, feed him, if he thirst, give him drink: for in so doing thou shalt heap coals of fire on his head. Be not overcome of evil, but overcome evil with good.*
>
> Romans 12: 17–21

If those who worship the devil can work or dance all night, then as Believers in Christ we should have no problem worshipping Jehovah God, our Creator and the Creator of heaven and earth. He is our defence. He is our peace, our source of provision.

Satan's strategy in destroying families and relationships is to cause division. Those who fall for his traps blindly enter in a covenant with Satan. They become his agents in the fulfilment of his strategy. They need the grace and mercy of God to come out of that covenant.

What I have noticed is that most of them enjoy the evil they do. They like gossiping and holding grudges. They regard sin as nothing. You wonder what is bad to them. They are proud and their conversation is often focused on materialism, envy and jealousy. So, to be able to break the covenant they have with the devil, they will have to choose to fight for their deliverance. It will take courage for them to break off and turn to God for mercy.

With God all things are possible. It is a matter of choice. When you are up against flying souls, then you must know how to surrender to God, for the battle is not yours. You cannot fight the invisible forces with the natural mind, which is why such battles teach us how to surrender to God and to forgive our persecutors. The word of God says that we have what we say.

> *A man's belly shall be satisfied with the fruit of his mouth; and with the increase of his lips shall he be filled. Death and life are in the power of the tongue: and they that love it shall eat the fruit thereof.*
>
> Proverbs 18: 20–21

CHAPTER 15

How Do We Determine Our Level of Spiritual Maturity?

To advance to a higher level academically in theory or in practice, the system of this world was designed in such a way that people are expected to pass certain examinations, tests or assessments. Some tests may be hard while some may be easy. Therefore, to pass examinations would depend on how committed the student is to studying and the method of study he or she adapts to. Some methods of study may be too complicated, while some may make everything seem very easy.

What happens in the natural world is exactly the same as what happens in the invisible world, the spiritual world. In the invisible world, examinations are prepared for our spiritual development. Therefore, our development as human beings is twofold, natural and spiritual. This is because while we are born in the natural, we were not created by natural means, an invisible God created us. God is a Spirit. We therefore possess His Spirit in us. The Spirit of God is not active in the life of a non-believer. The non-believer needs to activate God's Spirit by acknowledging Jesus as their Lord and Saviour. Spiritual development can therefore only happen in a Christ-centred, saved and spirit-filled life.

I actually appreciate it when the Holy Spirit wakes me in the middle of the night because I know that He is working on my behalf and on behalf of others. So I pray and worship. I also remind myself that in heaven they do not go to sleep; they worship God all the time. This encourages me to join the heavenly hosts in worship. He created us for His own pleasure, to worship Him. Worshipping God brings healing to the worshipper; it brings hope and change in the life of the worshipper because it touches God. It is a sign of humility and trust in God.

When I was going through hardship a few years ago, I took heed to the words of wisdom that God gave me through His servant, my mentor. I learnt that the battles we face as believers are not only for our survival but that they are also developmental exercises, for our spiritual development. Therefore when we are faced with battles that seem beyond our strength, it is important that we assess them by their size and their purpose. However hot the battle the enemy may throw at us as God's people, we should always trust God because He still controls the thermostat.

God is bigger than any situation and He is able to turn around a 40-year battle in only 40 seconds! There is something to learn from each battle we face in this life. Unless we are able to humble ourselves before God and recognise that battles belong to Him not to us, we will keep struggling with the enemy. It is important to surrender our battles to God and to trust Him to teach us something with each battle. Some battles are trials from the enemy but some are tests from God. God only promotes us spiritually as we pass each test. This is because He is developing us to be like Christ Jesus. We should be able to assess the size of the battles we face, as some are only developmental exercises under controlled circumstances.

While certain situations may take us by surprise, we should remember that nothing takes God by surprise.

> *There hath no temptation taken you but such as is uncommon to man: but God is faithful, who will not suffer you to be tempted above that ye are able; but will with the temptation also make a way to escape, that ye may be able to bear it.*
>
> *1 Corinthians 10: 13)*

> *For this thing I besought the Lord thrice, that it might depart from me. And He said unto me, My grace is sufficient for thee: for my strength is made perfect in weakness.*
>
> *2 Corinthians 12: 9*

God was simply saying to Paul, put your trust in Me, for I am in control here, do not panic, rely on my strength, not on yours. The battle is not yours. In the Book of Psalms Chapter 50: 15 we are warned: "And call upon me in the day of trouble: I will deliver thee, and thou shalt glorify me." It is clear from this scripture that God wants us to rely on Him in hard times because He wants the glory to come to Him, not to us. He simply wants us to appreciate the fact that He is the one who delivers us from our troubles. He wants us to honour Him and to worship Him as our deliverer and not to steal His glory and make it our own.

We cannot remain as children of God. We have to develop to sons and daughters of God. Therefore trials and spiritual battles are meant to build our character to that of Christ. This is why we surrender our battles to God; we cannot fight Satan but God can. God is faithful to those who trust in Him.

> *The righteous cry, and the Lord heareth, and delivereth them out of all their troubles. The Lord is nigh unto them that are of a broken heart; and saveth such as be of a contrite spirit. Many are the afflictions of the righteous: but the Lord delivereth him out of them all.*
>
> *Psalm 34: 17–19*

So in battle times we should remind Satan whose we are and therefore declare that "Greater is He in me than he that is in the world" (1 John 4: 4b).

> *He makes the enemies of the righteous their footstool. He gives us victory over oppression. The Lord also will be a refuge for the oppressed, a refuge in times of trouble.*
>
> *Psalm 9: 9*

If as Saints of God we fail at first, we do not give up because failure is also part of our learning. "For a just man falleth seven times, and riseth up again: but the wicked shall fall into mischief" (Proverbs 24: 16).

We cannot fool God, He knows us better than we know ourselves. He knows when we are seeking our own glory. Not many people under the sun can say they have not been guilty of this at all. Most of us still struggle with this weakness, even as Believers. Quite often we are driven to achieve in order to be celebrated rather than to give glory to God, as He is the One who gives us power and creativity and skills and knowledge. Yet we turn round and say, "We worked hard to get to where we are today." Very often we hear comments like: "He has achieved well, he has done well for himself." It is true that a focused person will achieve their goals, but the glory is supposed to go where it is due, to God. We have listened to ceremonies where awards are given to those who have achieved in the film industry or music industry. What I have realised is that the award winners rarely start off by thanking God, they thank everybody who was involved in their achievement but God. Where God happens to be remembered, it is usually at the end. Are we too shy to declare our faith and love for Christ publicly?

In the secular world, we see a lot of celebrities being celebrated. People ignorantly idolise people who have achieved well or for their beauty. The media encourages it in a big way. Nothing much is reported on the national news about the progress of the Christian church in the world. When earthquakes or situations like that arise, the Church is always ready to rush in, while politicians argue about responsibility. To the politician, the Church only surfaces in bad times, like at funerals. Politicians are not very keen on seeking God for advice on issues that affect the world, instead trusting each other's ideas. The voice of God is not regarded as the ultimate one because of the sin of rebelliousness and idolatry.

It is acceptable in this world to be of any other religion but a Believer in Christ. There is great respect for people of other faiths, but not for those who believe in the Lord Jesus Christ. His name is even used as a swear word, yet no one in the world could use other faiths' gods as a swear word. Even school pupils feel safer to declare their faith in other beliefs or other gods. They keep their faith in Christ a secret for fear of being ridiculed.

And, behold, I come quickly; and my reward is with me, to give every man according to his work shall be. I am alpha and Omega, the beginning and the end, the first and the last.

Revelation 22:12-13.

The enemy used his religious hypocrites to ruin Christianity so that the world hated Christianity. But God is merciful. In His own time He rescues His chosen ones from Satan's hands. Jesus Christ did not die on the cross of Calvary for all to perish, but He died for the atonement of our sins. He became the final sacrifice for our sins. He took our sins upon Himself, conquered death, took the keys of hell in His hands and rose again on the third day. He is alive and is worthy of all praise. I worship Him because He deserves my worship. He forgave my sins and still forgives the sins of all who come to Him for forgiveness. The blood of Jesus is pure, blameless and powerful. It cleanses us from all unrighteousness and it protects us from all evil. The Prophet Isaiah prophesied about him in Isaiah 53: 5:

But He was wounded for our transgressions, He was bruised for our iniquities: the chastisement of our peace was upon Him; and with his stripes we are healed.

Only the willing and the obedient will eat the good of the land. The heirs of salvation are those who have been obedient to God in every respect, not just in the tithing and the sowing of money. God gives seeds to the sower. Only a seed sower can expect a harvest. There are Believers who have not held back when God asked them to sow or give, even when it was all they had. They sow in obedience to God's voice and command to them. They extend their hand to the needy out of compassion. They have the burden to see justice in the earth for the vulnerable and the poor and much more.

The economy of the world has been in the hands of sinners for decades, hence the Church's financial struggles to reach the poor with the gospel. However, it is now the Body of Christ that determines how long this continues to be the case. God is ready to transfer the wealth of the sinner into the hands of the heirs of Salvation for His kingdom's purpose, but the Church is not ready yet. The Church is causing a delay because there is no fear of God, no love and no holiness in the Church in this world.

CHAPTER 16

A Need for Unity

Following the vision of the call to every Believer to get intimate with Christ that I had on 11th October 2008, another vision came in the early hours of 12th October 2008 on the critical need for unity in the Body of Christ in this end time.

In this vision, I saw two identical black people standing on arms only. They seemed to be waiting patiently to be joined with the appropriate bodies. Their arms had multicoloured stripes running down them. Then further up on my right, there were many bodies of bulls without heads. The bodies were spinning round and round in search of the appropriate heads to be joined to. I noticed the colour of these bodies: some were black, some were white and some had black and white freckles. I looked back at the two people standing on their multicoloured striped arms and noticed that they were not a good choice for the bulls, which is why they were left out without bodies. The bodies were resentful of the two heads because their arms had orange, pink, red, yellow and white colours on them that did not match any of those bodies.

I then looked back to the two heads on arms and began to speak to them. I said, "It will be hard for you both to be chosen by any of those bodies." They smiled back at me and spoke very intelligently but with great humility. I would have never known how intelligent they were if I had not spoken to them. I then realised that it would be a great loss to those bodies if they did not pick these two heads. Remember, the two humble-looking heads were black in colour. They had very short typical African tribesman kind of hair. They looked very humble.

The Body of Christ is refusing to totally surrender to the will of God for the Church, before Christ comes. Unity in the Church is the will of God.

Within two weeks of these visions, on 24th October 2008, I was given another vision of a brother in Christ who had died in a car crash earlier that year. He was one of the people in the group I used to go out to minister with, in 1980–81 in Tsholotsho, as my father was the priest in charge of an Anglican parish there. We were all in our late teens or early 20s, born-again, and most but not all of us were from an Anglican Church background. It pleased my father when we made these weekend trips to minister at his rural parish and we often looked forward to it. A lot of people gave their lives to the Lord Jesus Christ just in time for Mugabe's North Korean-trained 5 Brigade to come and massacre them the following year. I thank God that my father was based in rural Tsholotsho as this enabled us to reach a few souls. This brother in the vision I was shown loved to worship the Lord. In the vision he was concerned about his neglected property and belongings.

As I was given this vision in daytime, I phoned his widow in Zimbabwe to find out if she was all right. She opened up to me and confirmed that what I had been shown was true: she was really struggling with her children. Just over a week after this, God sent me to a pastor in Zimbabwe about this widow's circumstances. The pastor was reluctant to assist this widow, as he believed that she was under a ministry that took care of its own members. I said to him, "But I was sent to you." He believed me but he did not wish to impose. After I established dialogue with the pastors of the ministry the widow was under, the pastor's wife wrote back to me distancing herself from the widow. She stated that she had only been more acquainted with the widow's late husband, not the widow. The widow and her late husband had been passengers when their pastor's car crashed, killing her husband. When I thought of the issues the widow had confided in me about, my heart was filled with pain. God healed my heart miraculously of that pain; it was like a knot in my heart and I give God the glory and all the praise for healing me. I was then reminded that some battles were learning grounds.

God showed me a lot of visions in October 2008. The visions were about the image and current position of the Body of Christ before His eyes. While I still pondered the meaning of all these dreadful visions,

He did not only reveal their meaning to me but also sent me to different pastors I knew in Zimbabwe, and he also showed me some I did not know. He showed me that some loved Him but were full of fear; others were too busy but He was not part of their business, they were not caring for the orphans, homeless, poor and the widows in their ministry and they expected a harvest, yet they were sowing sparingly, not sacrificially.

> But this I say, He which soweth sparingly shall reap also sparingly; and he which soweth bountifully shall reap also bountifully.
>
> 2 Corinthians 9: 6

I was shown that the fields were white and ready for harvest right there around them, but they were busy ministering abroad and in other parts of Africa, they were too proud and lazy to harvest the local fields; they were self-serving and self-righteous; others were deceitful; others preferred only to help those of their denomination; others were sexually abusive of women and impregnated young, homeless girls who did not even know how to raise the babies they were left with. The same pastor who did this was a very good preacher and I attended one of his services in the vision. He nearly raped me right after the service and I had to struggle to get out while his hands were tightened around me. I managed to break off and left him standing outside, still consumed by the lustful desire to abuse me. Some women from his church were outside and they saw this struggle. His shame was exposed.

There is no holiness in the Body of Christ in Zimbabwe due to disobedience, corruption, selfishness, hatred, division and rebelliousness. But God also showed me others who were isolated but loyal to Him, who were very poor but very intimate and trusting in Him, His true worshippers.

The busybodies in the vision were symbolic of some existing church denominations or ministries. I was shown that these ministries are very busy in what they are doing, but Christ, the Head of the Church, is not part of that. The simple reason is that they are too arrogant and too set in their own ways so that they cannot facilitate or welcome change. They are comfortable with the small membership of their churches. They have no interest in or love for other nationalities or people from a different ethnic background. They are comfortable among themselves and they are very selective of who they reach out to because of their arrogance and prejudice. They cannot expand their capacities for relationships and meet the needs of people from different ethnic backgrounds; they cannot prosper from where they are. Their work is not blessed. There is no fruitfulness in their work. They are basically rebellious ministries. They hate the poor because they don't like the burden of helping them.

God has financially empowered His faithful stewards around the earth to do His will on the earth, but the rest of the Body of Christ is holding them back. The fields are white but the reapers are few. Unless Believers declare the War Against Division in the Church (WADIC), there will be a critical delay in the supernatural transfer of wealth for the completion of God's work on the earth before Christ comes. God's Angels are positioned and ready, but God will not give them the order to do so because He cannot trust a divided church with the faithful stewardship of His wealth in this end time. He is the God of order.

The spirit of competition among churches is the one that inhibits God's people from the Truth. Some pastors are preaching without the anointing of the Holy Spirit and without love. How can the blind lead the blind? What can anyone do without the anointing of the Holy Ghost? You cannot stand before the pulpit to preach your own gospel to God's people without His anointing and without His love for His people.

These are pastors who are doing nothing but bringing pain and abuse into the House of God. They dislike challenges, therefore they will do everything possible to get rid of a challenge in their ministry. They see the poor as threats to their finances. Instead of looking to God as their source of provision, they look to the flock in their ministries. Therefore they are very kind to the rich but unapproachable to the poor. You wonder who they trust as their source of provision.

These are pastors who use their pulpits to criticise other pastors, in order to make themselves look good before their flock. These are intimidating pastors, who mark those who do not attend their service every

Sunday and call them "gospel prostitutes" for visiting other ministries. What is wrong with visiting another ministry? People should be free to test the spirits. They should be allowed to choose who their pastor should be. They cannot be pinned down to a church that has no power of the Holy Ghost, a church where gossip starts at the pulpit. God will not allow such pastors still to be hiding and deceiving His flock in this end time. If it is not the pastors who are allowing the spirit of division, it is the flock, the slanderous and the gossipers.

Through one of the jobs God led me to in Zimbabwe, I met a dear friend who one day opened her heart to me. She related to me how her first daughter was conceived, that she was sexually abused by her schoolteacher at the age of 15. The case was taken to court in Rhodesia, but the teacher had a very strong defence lawyer and the case got discharged. Her father was torn apart and so was her mother. Unfortunately the nasty experience created a distance between her and her mother, as her mother became hostile and unloving towards her. My dear friend later became born-again. She also went for fellowship at the same youth group that I went to, although I was not close to her at the time. There she met someone who wanted to marry her, but the youth leadership discouraged the young man on the grounds that my friend had a child and there were many young women without children at the youth group whom he could marry. Her boyfriend confided this to her. She was devastated. The leaders of the youth group did not know her story or even try to hear it from her. They completely ruled her out. As it was the leadership policy of the group to approve or disapprove, the man went on to marry someone else. A few years later she met someone else, but his mother queried the fact that she had a child; unfortunately she was going to have his son. He too went on to marry someone else. Now she was left with two fatherless children.

I also met a woman during my nurse training who was diagnosed as having long and enduring mental health problems. She came where I was, sat with me and began to open up to me about the emotional pain she had endured in this life. I realised that most of her pain was caused by people in the church where she used to go. She had shared her marital problems with people in her circle of church friends and they had despised her after that. She had discovered that her husband was having an affair with another man. When she opted for divorce and she approached her pastor about the problem, the pastor was very understanding and supportive to her and he blessed her. She went ahead and divorced, but it was the church folk who misjudged her and hurt her at a time of great distress in her life, when she needed their support and encouragement.

I believed her because she had been through a similar experience with church folk as I once did in my time of distress. Most church folk do not like hanging around with suffering poor people, yet the Word of God tells us to bear one another's burdens. However, they completely destroyed her. Now this woman is full of unforgiveness in her heart. She is one on the list of those known as "service users" in a mental health setting. She is on continuous prescription drugs, which means she takes medication for her emotional pain every day. She does not accept love from anybody. There are many like her, who hate themselves for what was done to them. Only the power of God can deliver such emotionally bruised people. Prescribed drugs are not the answer. God's people need a divine touch for their deliverance. Every pastor needs this Holy Ghost empowerment in these last terrible days, to bring deliverance to the oppressed.

Then there are others who run to their pastors for emotional support. They come to church to find love, only to be abused by the very pastors again. A friend of mine, a woman of God, lost her husband. She had already been called into the ministry when this happened and had been through a lot of financial challenges because after she left her career, they had to manage on one income and the children they were blessed with. As a widow, she then approached her pastor and opened her heart to him concerning the challenging needs she had been left to face. The following Sunday, and to her embarrassment, the pastor asked all the men at the service to stand up. He publicly addressed them in the area of provision for their families. He cautioned the men in his church never to leave their families unprovided for, because the church should not be left to carry the burdens of their widows.

As she related this to me, I thought, but what is the purpose of the Church if widows and orphans are resented in the church? I am sure that if she was borrowing from the church, she had a mindset of paying it back. If my friend and sister in Christ's experience got to me that way, what about the Lord Jesus Christ, how did He feel about this pastor, a servant whom He called? What is the Body of Christ here on earth doing about such pastors? Who are they answerable to? Who receives and manages issues of accountability in the Church?

Gone are the days when Believers would think of it as none of their business, because Jesus is coming for a spotless and blameless Church, a spotless Bride. Are you and I part of that church or do we still want to play safe and keep out of it? As His Body of Christ, we should not be still caught in a slumber of thinking that we still have time. Jesus is coming soon.

Before the judgment throne of God, we will all give an account of our contribution to this division. We may have contributed in a negative way by encouraging the division; or we may have contributed in a positive way by discouraging this division in the Church. What are we going to say before God on judgment day? What will be our defence? What are we doing about it?

So as a Body of Christ, we cannot afford to be hearing that one pastor somewhere is abusive to his junior pastors and to his flock and simply ignore it. The truth about disobeying God with tithes and offerings has not been clearly preached to God's people in many churches in Zimbabwe. People are poor because the truth has not been revealed to them and their pastors have been self-serving and selfish in many ways. The flock in most denominations get threatened into submission by being told that if you are a member of this church and you are not giving to this ministry, you cannot get the support of the ministry in your hard times, especially during a funeral or a wedding and other situations like that. This is a lie from the pits of hell.

This has been the experience of people in these self-serving churches. The truth of God's Word has been withheld from God's people because their pastors are also blind to the truth. In Matthew 15, Jesus challenged the Pharisees for being hypocrites by acting as if they knew the commandments better than the disciples of Jesus.

He said to His disciples, Every plant, which my heavenly Father hath
not planted, shall be rooted up. Let them alone: they be blind leaders of
the blind. And if the blind lead the blind, both shall fall into the ditch.

Matthew 15: 13–14

How can the blind lead the blind? Some church ministers have done so
much damage in their denominations that they simply need to sit down.
They use their own doctrine to enslave members of their congregations
so much that instead of comforting God's people in times of hardship,
they burden them even further through their man-made selfish policies.

Whatever people need to be taught in their churches should be
based on the Holy Scriptures, the written Word of God. They need to
be taught that there are consequences in disobeying God's Word. For
example, people need to know the reason for tithing 10 per cent of their
income to their church. The prophet of God, Malachai, clearly explains
the advantages and the disadvantages of tithing:

Bring ye all the tithes into the storehouse, that there may be meat in mine
house, and prove me now herewith, saith the Lord of hosts, if I will not
open you the windows of heaven, and pour you out a blessing, that there
shall not be room enough to receive it. And I will rebuke the devourer for
your sakes, and he shall not destroy the fruits of your ground; neither shall
your vine cast her fruit before the time in the field, saith the Lord of hosts.

Malachai 3: 10–1

People usually look for the right church by first visiting different ministries
or church denominations, so that they can decide wisely. People have a
right to choose where they feel there is adequate spiritual food for them.
Therefore pastors are not called into ministry to restrict their flock from
mingling with other ministries. We are not to dominate one another that
way. We do not own one another, but God does, and therefore pastors have
no right to abuse their authority in that respect. I once heard a great woman
of God preach and make reference to Ephesians 4: 30: "Do not grieve the
Holy Spirit; if your flock are not well fed they will find food elsewhere."

Such selfish and controlling pastors affect the whole Body of Christ before the eyes of God. People do not like being controlled as if they are in prison. God wants order in His house. One of Dr Mike Murdock's wisdom principles states: "God's only obsession is order" (wisdomonline. com). Judgment must begin in the house of God.

I strongly believe that the united and collective Body of Believers in Christ will be able to move this mountain of division in the church. God is watching us. Psalm 121 states that He neither sleeps nor slumbers. He is a Spirit but He gave us the bodies to perform His plan here on earth. Are we willing to be the vessels that honour Him and His purpose for the earth in these last days?

As a Church, we have to be violent in repossessing the land in this end time. I mean that, we have to be relentless in taking it. We cannot afford to give up. Yes, there will be challenges.

> *Because of your unbelief: for verily I say unto you, If ye have faith as a grain of mustard seed, ye shall say unto this mountain, Remove hence to yonder place; and it shall remove; nothing shall be impossible unto you.*
>
> *Matthew 17: 20*

How is this going to happen? Every Believer in Christ will have to be proactive and relentless in activating the Word of God and His principles and revelations to us. Identifying the strongholds that have hindered unity in the collective Body of Christ is our responsibility. This is only possible through prayer, pulling down the strongholds, and through hours of worship. This is our violence.

> *(For the weapons of our warfare are not carnal, but mighty through God to the pulling down of strong holds;) Casting down imaginations, and every high thing that exalteth itself against the knowledge of God, and bringing into captivity every thought to the obedience of Christ; And having in a readiness to revenge all disobedience, when your obedience is fulfilled.*
>
> *2 Cor. 10: 4–6*

My own experience as I began to spend intimate moments in worshipping God was that He began to reveal to me a lot of things about the needs of other people, mostly Zimbabwean Believers in Christ I already knew, even pastors and what was going on in their ministries. He began to send me to them. As I obeyed God in this, I was horrified with my discoveries.

I discovered that there was no love or fear of God but that a lot of selfishness and pride was associated with most of the ministries I was sent to in Zimbabwe in 2008. I was either told off or ignored. I could discern that it was a question of: "How could someone so familiar like me be sent to men and women who have been walking with God for so many years? Who was this new-comer to be sent to them?" But I was only a messenger. God uses whom He chooses. I certainly did not choose to be used by God, He chose me long before I even knew Him.

So it is not about how long you have been in ministry. God hates pride. Some pastors are sitting on the throne. They like being acknowledged and respected. Jesus washed the feet of His disciples, teaching them the spirit of servanthood, that the greatest among them shall be the least.

God looks for humble and willing vessels. Most of such vessels are still out there in the world of sin; they are yet to be reached with the Word of God; they are yet to be born-again. If we sincerely love God, we will humble ourselves before Him in obedience and with His love that changed us from our own rebellious ways, we will in turn bring these lost vessels back to Him. We will reach the unreachable and touch the untouchable.

Jesus told the story of the prodigal son, how he could not wait for his rich father to die in order for him to get his hands on his inheritance and enjoy a rich lifestyle. So he asked his father to give him his share of the inheritance. His father did. We are told that the young man then left to a far-away country where his riches made him very popular with friends and young women. As expected, he wasted all his inheritance on women and when he finally had nothing left, all the friends and women deserted him. A mighty famine hit that land and he became so poor that he found himself a job to feed the swine in the fields of that country, but the hunger drove him to eat swine food.

However, having learnt a great lesson in his life, a lesson of greed, immaturity, selfishness and experiencing poverty, he repented of his mistake and considered going back to his rich father. And when he came to himself, he said:

How many hired servants of my father's have bread enough and to spare, and I perish with hunger! I will arise and go to my father, and will say unto him, Father, I have sinned against heaven, and before thee, And am no more worthy to be called thy son: make me as one of thy hired servants.

Luke 15: 17–19

He humbled himself in his heart and resolved to lower his standards and ask his father to accept him back as a servant. He received mercy and honour from his father because he humbly repented of his sinful life. A humble heart realises that salvation is not the doing of a man, but is by the Grace of God. It is also humility to recognise that none of us called ourselves into the ministry, but Jesus is the one who called us. Humility in God is the key.

It is no secret what God wants done. This is not a war against the visible, it is a war against the invisible.

We cannot fight a spiritual battle using natural ways and weapons. Satan is the invisible force behind this battle, and as the man of God Dr Charles Stanley puts it in one of his sermons:

Satan loves to divide the Church because he knows that so many people will be affected by it. His ultimate goal is to destroy the Body of Christ and everything that can bring glory to God, including you and me. This man of God further says that's why we should love and encourage and uphold one another as Saints of God. God hates pride.

InTouchMinistries.org

In 2007 I wrote a 45-page testimony on my own wilderness experience, where I found myself up against the invisible forces of darkness that were out to destroy my family and me. As the battle ensued for months without end, God's promises of hope and deliverance still remained unchanged, but it was entirely up to me to access His promises by obeying His Word and trusting Him. To maintain my sanity, I had to remove my eyes from my circumstances and focus on God through prayer, praise and worship. This is how the war eventually ended. As the battle against Satan and his cohorts was too great for me, the only way forward for me was to realise that my God was greater than Satan, and therefore I surrendered the invisible battle to the Most High God, who is the first Cause of Everything, the Creator of Heaven and Earth.

CHAPTER 17

Can We Learn from the Tower of Babel?

I t took me many years to discover that Iraq is the original home of Abraham and the place where God confused the languages of His people after they planned to unite and build the Tower of Babel. I found it interesting to learn that in Iraq people were all united, but their unity was motivated by the fear of being scattered abroad, of being divided. God never said to His people that He would scatter them abroad, but Satan brought that fear of division to God's people and used it to separate them. However, man was still sinful because the second Adam, Jesus Christ, had not yet paid the price to reconcile man to God. In Babel, sin still ruled in the hearts of the people.

Fear is a result of sin; the sin of doubting God's love and promises to us, as well as the sin of rebelliousness against God. Satan always uses what we fear most as a weapon against us. But he is a liar. Thank God for Jesus: in all things we are more than conquerors through Christ who loved us. For there is no fear in love, but perfect love casts out fear. With God before us who can be against us? Greater is He in me than He that is in the world. Satan divided God's people through fear, but God's love will bring us back together again. I believe that unity will happen before Christ comes, and it will begin in the Church.

For decades, Satan has been fighting the Body of Christ without much resistance at all. This cannot be allowed to continue any longer because there is no time to waste. Jesus is coming soon. God's faithful sowers and stewards, the just, are all ready to receive the supernatural wealth transfer from God's Angels, but the Church is holding back this process. The Church must resist Satan's longstanding war against the Saints of God.

Why has the body of Christ been divided for so long?

The Church has tolerated this spirit of division for far too long. How can the Groom marry a disintegrated Bride? How can Christ be coming for a divided church? He did not suffer the shameful and painful death of the cross for His Body here on earth to be still so divided by way of race, colour, status, tribe or church denominations.

How are the poor around the world going to be reached and assisted if there is no unity in the collective Body of Christ? The battle against division in the Church is a critical one before the coming of Christ. Once the collective Body of Christ wins this war, this victory will enable the Gospel to reach the uttermost parts of the earth and for the souls that are won to remain in Christ. The mutual networking of the collective Body of Christ will enable the stewardship of the sinners' wealth around the world. The unreachable of this world will be reached, thus benefiting the poor and isolated, the orphans, homeless and lonely, widows, single mothers and children, who will be removed from prostituting themselves for livelihood. There will be justice for the poor.

I recently listened to a television programme where Dr Mike Murdock taught on Wisdom Principles. He said, "The invisible has got power than the visible, because what you see is produced by the invisible" (Wisdomonline.com).

I realised that racism was created by the invisible, Satan, the deceiver of mankind. He succeeded in dividing people by their colour and by their ethnic or tribal background. Over decades and to this day, many lives have been shattered or lost due to the evil of racism. Black people and other nationalities refused to believe in Christ and preferred to rebel against God because they could not reconcile Christianity and the unfairness of racial segregation and oppression. This was Satan's strategy to discourage the black man from connecting with his Creator. He did not waste time in entering the hearts of those missionaries that were sent to introduce God to the Africans. He quickly showed them the treasure in gold, silver and diamonds. He blinded the white settlers and missionaries to the hidden treasure that was in a black man.

The Black Man is the greatest dancer and worshipper the world has ever seen. The passion in dance and the powerful voice of a black man in worship are comparable to none. Satan did not want God to be worshipped by the black man because he knew that the power of the Holy Spirit was going to bring spiritual change on a larger scale. However, the power of God is ready to bring about a great turnaround in a way the world has never seen before. The Glory of God will be seen.

At the Name of Jesus every knee should bow, of things in heaven, and things in earth, and things under the earth. And that every tongue should confess that Jesus Christ is Lord, to the glory of God the Father.
Philippians 2: 10-1

It is important to visualise our victory against division in the Body of Christ. The desire for unity has to begin within the mind and heart of each believer. In the book of John, Jesus spoke to them:

But there are some of you that believe not. For Jesus knew from the beginning who they were that believed not, and who should betray him. And he said, Therefore said I unto you, that no man can come unto me, except it were given unto him of my father. From that time many of His disciples went back, and walked no more with Him. Then said Jesus unto the twelve, Will ye also go away? Then Simon Peter answered Him, Lord, to whom shall we go? Thou hast the words of eternal life. And we believe and are sure that thou art Christ, the son of the living God. Jesus answered them, Have I not chosen you twelve, and one of you is a devil? Jesus spake of Judas Iscariot the son of Simon: for he it was that should betray him, being one of the twelve.
John 6: 64-71

The very weapons that the enemy has used to divide the church are the very strongholds that should be bound and pulled down. Earlier on, I mentioned that what the enemy meant for harm in my life, God turned it around for my good. I became a worshipper in my place of trouble, right in the wilderness. I believe that what the enemy meant for harm for the Collective Body of Christ, God is ready to turn around for His Glory.

Quality time spent in praise and worship is the key to intimacy with God for every Believer in Christ. If the devil's drummers can drum to him all night, what is holding us back from worshipping the Living God and the Creator of Heaven and Earth throughout the night? This will only be achieved if the Body of Christ unites in agreement according to Matthew 18: 19, in this war against Satan, the enemy of unity. To mention a few of Satan's weapons that I identified and those that were revealed to me:

- disobedience to God in the area of giving and tithing
- laziness in praying
- laziness in reading the Word of God
- lack of love in interceding for other people
- jealousy
- envy
- competition
- gossip
- slander
- criticism
- misjudging
- greed
- selfishness
- racial and tribal prejudice
- hatred
- covetousness (selfish desires).

It is important for the Body of Christ to realise that just as God uses people to fulfil His plan on earth, so does Satan; he uses people we know and have fellowship with in church to destroy the work of God through the strategies listed above and many more. In Zimbabwe he has destroyed some ministries through pastors fighting for positions when doors of opportunity open up for the church leadership, some even resorting to witchcraft. Those who have been walking with God for decades are swift to grab them from those that, according to them, are undeserving of such opportunities, but God is now bringing justice in His kingdom right here on earth and therefore Judgment must begin in the house of God.

The Body of Christ in Zimbabwe has been economically tested beyond imagination in that since Robert Mugabe's demolition campaign in 2005, pastors were left to face the homeless people, orphans and widows affected by the 5 Brigade massacres in Matabeleland, HIV orphans and the drought that followed the farm evasions. In 2008, most people lived on water and leaves or soil. Pastors were not exempt from this test and therefore while I am assigned to highlight certain issues of concern in the Body of Christ, I must warn the reader that we cannot afford to laugh at some of the issues highlighted here. The shaking is happening around the earth, so let us pray for those who stumble in difficult times, including ourselves, as we do not know how the shaking will affect our part of the world. We cannot afford to watch Satan winning God's people. Jesus paid a price with his own blood for us all. Let us therefore not forget that Gospel truth, boldness, humility, love and compassion cannot be separated.

On this note, I would like to highlight a vision I had on 16th August 2009. I was in a big church which looked like an old Anglican Church, but the people inside were not Anglicans. I had my first daughter with me. It was as if people were waiting for someone, a pastor. Then suddenly, a well-known young black American pastor arrived dressed casually and there was an atmosphere of urgency about him. He announced that he would make an effort to speak to all people and to answer their questions and then leave quickly once he had done this. He spoke to everyone around, but when it was my turn he vanished suddenly from behind me and I could not tell which way he had gone. He was raptured and I had remained with the pretending, demon-possessed folk. It was terrible being left to discover the mess in that church. I had had a very important question to ask him concerning my daughter. It was as if I was left deliberately to work it out. After most people were gone, I realised that a lot of filthy things were now back inside the church. Then as I was on my way out (I can't remember the person or people I was with), ahead of us I could see a movement of people and these were supposed to be statues. When other people looked at them, they pretended to be statues. I realised that they were all ghosts, demons in the church. Behind us, I saw rats and garbage all over the floor of the church where the people had been.

It is in the interest of every pastor of a church denomination to ensure that the war against division in the Church is declared in their respective ministries. Why are most pastors afraid of losing church members to other churches? I once heard one woman of God rebuking this very spirit that some pastors have in a sermon. She said, "If you are feeding your sheep properly, you have nothing to worry about because your sheep will remain." How far from the truth can this be? If the preaching is not helping God's people, they should be free to go where the preaching is good. Jesus called us to serve each other, not to control and dominate each other or those we are called to serve.

Cooperation among pastors of all church denominations is of utmost importance to achieve unity. Humility will bring about cooperation. The willing denominations might have to start coming together in prayer locally, as God shows us how. I say willing, because you cannot force a donkey to walk once it decides to be stubborn. Willingness among the pastors of church denominations is utterly crucial. "If you are willing and obedient, you shall eat the good of the land" (Psalm 1: 19). If the old are unwilling and too stuck to their old ways, God will empower our children to fight division in the Church.

The unity God's people had in building the Tower of Babel was driven by fear. They feared being separated and scattered abroad. Everything they feared happened to them. God has not given us the spirit of fear, but of power, of love and of a sound mind. You see, God's principles applied then and they still apply today, because He is the same God, He has not changed. Therefore, they were scattered abroad and their languages were confounded so that they could not all understand each other. But God is now calling for unity again among His people, so that they can build His kingdom and not the Tower of Babel. The unity that God is calling for now among His people is not driven by fear, it is driven by love. Fear is from Satan, love is from God.

In the final part of the vision that is the main subject of this book, I saw a pastor testifying about the overwhelming love and appreciation his congregation showed him. They cared for their man of God. There was unity of purpose in that congregation.

During the building of the Tower of Babel, the people were not born again; they were still sinners. Christ was not the foundation of what they were building or the head of their unity. Some denominations are very busy doing their own thing without the anointing of the Holy Spirit. They are busy seeking their own Glory. Where Christ is acknowledged as the Head, there is Wisdom and the Glory goes to Him. Where Christ is, there is no fear, no competition, no jealousy, no envy, no selfishness, no greed, no racial segregation or oppression, but only love. This love is from God. It is sacrificial love. He sacrificed His only Son for us, Jesus Christ. As we appreciate God's Grace and His Mercy for us, we appreciate and embrace the suffering of Christ. With Christ in the centre of what we do, there is love and therefore unity will be achieved in the Body of Christ. "For God hath not given us the spirit of fear, but of power, and of love, and of a sound mind" (2 Timothy 1:7).

Where there is praise and worship, the Glory of God will be there. The Glory of God is the presence of the Holy Spirit. He dwells in the praises of His people. The Holy Spirit comes upon the humble in Christ, the selfless and kingdom-driven hearts.

My own battle against the invisible world of darkness taught me how to get into a spiritual fight without giving up. I learnt that Satan and his henchmen were relentless. God opened my spiritual ears and I could hear the demonic drumming and their voices in the middle of the night. I could also hear the familiar voices of my adversaries leaving my window and flying out in the early hours of the morning. How could I sleep having been given such a revelation? I had to be relentless too.

The automatic light behind my house used to come on at any slight movement, yet it failed to pick those flying souls that left my window flying in the air. This is how I found out then that the battle was in the atmosphere.

The Word of God clearly states that Satan is the God of the air. This is how I knew that I would have to target the atmosphere and pull down those satanic strongholds. Satan's agents were fighting me from every angle. Even female psychics in the West were sending me letter after letter with their pictures on the outside of the envelope. I began to write on the envelope warfare scriptures and "Return to sender" without opening the letters. I would even receive telephone calls from Satan's agents promising me large amounts of money. I learnt to speak back the Word of God and to claim the scriptures relating to the sinner's wealth as well as claiming the restoration of all the devil stole from me, according to Joel 2: 25. I targeted the atmosphere morning, afternoon and night, binding the hindering strongholds and pulling them down to the pits of hell in Jesus' Mighty Name. It worked! They stopped bothering me. All the enemy wants is to get you tired and to give up. He knows that when you get tired, you will stop praying and pulling down the strongholds.

> For though we walk in the flesh, we do not war after the flesh: For the weapons of our warfare are not carnal, but mighty through God to the pulling down of the strongholds; Casting down imaginations and every high thing that exalteth itself against the knowledge of God, and bringing into captivity every thought to the obedience of Christ.
>
> 2 Corinthians 10: 3, 4, 5

God is able to perform that which He has promised to those who put their trust in Him.

I remembered in the book of Daniel Chapter 10 that a hindering stronghold that he did not even know about was the one holding back the revelation to the vision he did not understand. Remember that Daniel was a young man who was gifted in the interpretation of dreams. When he failed to interpret his own dream, he became tormented in his spirit to the extent that he failed to eat for 21 days. He had no joy. But the Angel of God delivered his answer to him finally and explained to Daniel that His revelation had been delayed due to a war that was going on. The Angel had wrestled against the spirit of Persia that intended to hinder Daniel's answer from reaching him.

As we unite in this war, we all have to play our part in discerning and discouraging the spirit of division among us. Judgment must begin in God's house. It is very important to remember that not all anointed believers are holy. Let us look at King Saul for an example.

In 1 Samuel 28 we read about king Saul's rebelliousness to God. King Saul would have never disguised himself in the middle of the night to visit and to consult the witch of Endor if he was still holy. He had been holy once, but he had opened a door to Satan in his life, a door of fear, envy and jealousy. Saul feared David more than God because of his jealousy over the favour of God on David. He was anointed, but his unrepentant heart led him further and further into rebelliousness against God, thus losing the presence of God in his life.

The Apostle Paul wrote:

This know also, that in the last days perilous times shall come. For men shall be lovers of their own selves, covetous, boasters, proud, blasphemers, disobedient to parents, unthankful, unholy. Without natural affection, truce breakers, false accusers, incontinent [no self-control], fierce, despisers of those that are good; Traitors, heady, high-minded, lovers of pleasures more than lovers of God; Having a form of godliness, but denying the power thereof: from such turn away. For this sort are they which creep into houses, and lead captive silly women laden with sins, led away with divers lusts, Ever learning, and never able to come to the knowledge of the truth. Now as Jannes and Jambres withstood Moses, so do these also resist the truth: men of corrupt minds reprobate concerning the faith. But they shall proceed no further: for their folly shall be manifest unto all men, as theirs also was.

2 Timothy 3: 1–9

But evil men and seducers shall wax worse and worse, deceiving and being deceived.

2 Timothy 3: 13

It is dangerous for Saints of God to abuse the power of God on our lives. Most of us today are anointed and rebellious men and women of God. We have taken the anointing for granted and forgotten what it took for us to have it. We have no fear of God in our talk. Careless talk, especially criticism, is the first sign of disobedience. Such Believers are the very people who bring pain and division in the Body of Christ. We know the Word but the fear of God is far from our hearts. We manipulate the scriptures to bring judgment and condemnation and all kinds of pain to God's people. We see ourselves as "holier than thou". We look down on others and we are quick to compare and criticise the servants of God. We speak amiss even with new converts or those who are yet to be saved. There is no watch before our mouths and the door of our lips is not guarded.

The Holy Spirit creates a worshipper. Worship creates intimacy with God. Once this intimacy with God and every Believer in Christ is restored in the Church, repentance will be possible. Judgment will begin in the house of God. Repentance will lead to forgiveness of one another.

In the worship vision, it was not the women I saw on their knees being taught how to worship, there were only men in that place. Satan first visited the woman in the garden of Eden and deceived her. If Adam had loved God more than Eve, the temptation would never have reached his heart. A friend of mine once said, "Love is a matter of the heart." What we love is rooted in our hearts. What is rooted in the heart is always manifested by actions. This is how the saying came about that "Actions talk louder than words". The fact that Adam received the apple from Eve is clear evidence of what was rooted in his heart.

Adam was the first one to be created in God's own image. God empowered him with the gift of naming everything that He had created. God trusted Adam and He loved him and cared for him, because when God saw that Adam was lonely He blessed him with Eve. Then Adam's heart got captivated by Eve, it got turned away from God to the blessing. Whenever God manifests a blessing in the lives of His people, be it a car, a house, clothes or money, we soon forget how long we prayed for it to come and we begin to love and be captivated by the gift so much that we even slow down our prayer life or stop praying altogether. We simply forget that God is our source of provision.

God wants to see His men worshipping Him. He wants the first love between Him and the man restored. This is because He wants to restore men's dominion over Satan. This is Grace. God is Love. Man hurt Him much, yet He still provides a way of reconciliation and restoration for man to commune with Him once again. God knows that Satan is the enemy of our soul. Unless as a collective Body of Christ men are ready to fight Satan's divisive ways and remove all stumbling blocks, God cannot do it for them.

In the last few years, God has been giving His people the kingdom revelation in preparation for the end time. The revelation of taking dominion back from Satan is a critical one, because Jesus overcame Satan for this very reason, to restore men back to God. He became the final sacrifice for the atonement of men's sins. All that God is expecting from us is obedience to Him. He is the one giving these revelations to His people. His Will has to be done on earth at this critical time before His Son comes. "Believe in the Lord your God, so shall ye be established; believe in His prophets, so shall ye prosper" (2 Chronicles 20: 20).

Early in 2008, God gave me a vision in which I could hear the happy voice of someone I knew in my early years as a believer in Christ. In the vision, this brother's voice was worshipping and praising, but I could not see him. He was not far from me, yet I could not see him. When I woke up, God led me to find this brother in Zimbabwe and to pass to him that "He is Jehovah Jireh, the Lord my Provider; He will provide." I managed to get his mobile phone number. This was a period of great hardship in Zimbabwe; people were literally dropping dead on the street from hunger. I had not spoken to the man in years, but I used to hear of his difficulties after his wife died and left him with their two little children. After I had sent him the message, I endeavoured to speak to him and I was amazed to hear what he said: "My sister, I am invisible to the world but I am very joyful inside of me. Since I got made redundant, I have not been anywhere in the public eye and my life has not been easy, but I am very joyful and I have been expecting something from God. So when I got your message, I knew God was speaking to me." He further said that the Lord was leading him to write a book of what He was revealing to him. It was a message about the kingdom, its meaning today.

> And I will restore to you the years that the locust hath eaten, the cankerworm, and the caterpillar, and the palmerworm, my great army which I sent among you. And ye shall eat in plenty, and be satisfied, and praise the name of the Lord your God, that hath dealt wondrously with you: and my people shall never be ashamed.
>
> *Joel 2: 25–26*

CHAPTER 18

The Legacy of Disobeying
the Voice of God

We can see the legacy of disobeying God in the history of Zimbabwe, from the Zulu King Lobengula of Matabeleland to Joshua Nkomo and his friends who heard the warning voice of God but kept it a secret that God said they should not fight their cousins. God further told them that they would only get back their land after 30 years and after much bloodshed. If our fathers had listened to the voice of God, the Matabeleland holocaust would not have happened. God is a fair and just God. He always forewarns His people of the danger of disobeying Him, but His people choose to oppose Him. From the Garden of Eden to this day, God's instructions and warnings to His people have always been clear. He never made it a secret that there would be consequences of disobedience. God wrote His laws so that Moses could read them out to His people. His people failed to keep His laws. He then sacrificed His own Son, Jesus; the Creator of Heaven and Earth became flesh and was born of a slave girl, the virgin woman Mary.

However, God's Judgment Day is not far off. The books will be opened. I believe that each one of us will give an account of our life here on earth and I also believe that each person's judgment will take as long as God decides. No stone will be left unturned. What is even more touching is that every soul who ever lived on earth will be present on Judgment Day; there will be no absentees.

I heard Pastor Brenda Ray preach on the "Woman of Substance". She said, "Time was made to govern the earth – God does not live in time – He lives in eternity" (KICC TV).

Foolish people do not realise when they are in positions of authority that God is a Holy God and that He is the determiner of each and every person's destiny. When I worked as a legal secretary in Zimbabwe, I used to type what is called a Rescission of Judgment. This document only works in the system of the world, not in the Kingdom system. Jesus is the ultimate judge and His judgement cannot be annulled because it is final.

> *And I saw a great white throne, and Him that sat on it, from whose face the earth and the heaven fled away; and there was found no place for them. And I saw the dead, small and great, stand before God; and the books were opened; and another book was opened, which is the book of life; and the dead were judged out of those things which were written in the books, according to their works. And the sea gave up the dead which were in it; and death and hell delivered up the dead which were in them; and they were judged every man according to their works. And death and hell were cast into the lake of fire. This is the second death. And whosoever was not found written in the book of life was cast into the lake of fire.*
>
> *Revelations 20: 1 –15*

The voice of God should have the upper hand in the decisions that affect the nations of this world

Politicians should understand that wisdom and understanding only come directly from God. The wisdom of man is folly.

Counselling politicians is the responsibility of church leaders and politicians should be submissive to the church leadership. The judgment of God is the consequence of ignoring His voice and undermining His servants. God is no respector of persons.

Politicians' error in ignoring the voice of God continues in most parts of the world. Many detrimental political decisions could have been avoided if the Body of Christ had the upper hand in decision making. Today Britain and the rest of the Western world are congested with African people and those from other Third World countries seeking refuge because of postcolonial errors.

Most Third World leaders were politically empowered prematurely; they were not emotionally ready when they came into office. They were still messed up and angry. So what could you expect? How could abused African politicians possibly be entrusted with the welfare of their subjects? The transition from revolutionary fighter to the president of a nation is just too drastic. They needed special counselling, emotional and spiritual healing before taking their positions in Parliament. This is where the Church was supposed to come in, but the Church was messed up too. God likes to transform our mindset first before manifesting His blessing in our lives. New wine cannot be contained in old wine skins.

I believe that the healing process can still be achieved if the Collective Body of Saints of God could take the upper hand in making restitution in the political affairs of this world quickly, before Christ comes. With God all things are possible.

Jesus paid a blood price for all people, even for those yet to be born. He is the King of kings, the Lord of Lords. He is the Bright Morning Star, the Lily of the Valley, the Lion of Judah, He is the Master, the Saviour, the soon and coming King. God is gracious; He is a vindicator and a restorer.

The Bible is full of historical examples of exactly what is still happening today. This is why the Bible is an up-to-date bestseller that will never be compared to any other book. Self-serving crooks, betrayers, liars and haters like King Saul still exist in the Church today. If you don't come across them here on earth, you will see them on Judgment Day. This is why Paul wrote that judgement must begin in the house of God, so that God does not judge us; but many of us would rather leave it for the Judgment Day. It is foolishness to fail to judge ourselves as individuals and as the Body of Christ and to prefer to be judged by God. Yes, there are faults within us that we may miss due to lack of God's wisdom, but some faults are so obvious that the Holy Spirit reveals them to us as soon as we make them, although we choose to ignore His conviction. If an anointed person tells a lie, he or she knows that she is telling a lie. God is pure and holy. We turn a deaf ear instead of falling onto our knees and repenting before God. If we leave it to God after He gave us the Holy

Spirit to convict us, counsel us and help us to conquer the enemy of our soul, then it will be very sad for us on Judgment Day.

It was not Mugabe who began the struggle against racial segregation and oppression in Rhodesia, yet he has been seen as one who suffered for the country. He was a teacher all those years before his friends invited him to be the secretary of the party. He was much younger than our fathers who began the struggle.

Just before he retired, my father was an Anglican priest-incharge of a parish in rural Tsholotsho. As always my father had the poor in his heart. As the Mission had borehole water, my father grew vegetables and maize to help the poor, as it was a season of drought. My father saw at first hand the victims of war, especially the young girls who were raped by soldiers and left with fatherless babies. This burden for the poor led to his vision to build an orphanage and old people's home back in the early 1980s.

Before my father identified the area where he could build it and commenced planning for it, Mugabe's 5 Brigade visited him. They accused him of feeding the dissidents, thoroughly beat him and left him for almost dead, but God kept him alive. There was no media coverage of this, even though the Anglican Church he served and represented all his lifetime knew about it. In contrast, the Roman Catholic Church was not silent or afraid to speak out against the atrocities in Matabeleland, unlike the Anglican Church.

Considering that we live decades after the end of slavery, the system of the Western world has continued to oppress black people through its various institutions, and the Western Christian Church remains silent. There is a lot of hypocrisy in the Body of Christ. The Church is trying to manipulate God by focusing more on the evil done by Adolf Hitler's regime to the Jews; but the Church is not yet repentant of its racist attitude towards God's black African people, hence the evil that continues to be done to them.

Zimbabwean people did not get any help from Britain, Europe or America during the liberation struggle against Ian Smith's racist regime. This is the reason Mugabe's propaganda always works with his supporters, because he uses this very experience to stir up anger. However, it was

Nkomo who began the struggle of seeking the support of nations around the world, not Mugabe. Mugabe was Nkomo's party secretary and once he had learnt enough from Nkomo, he and others broke off to start their own evil-driven party. Mugabe had everything dished out to him on a silver platter; even the very ZANLA forces that helped him into power were originally under the late Josiah Tongogara's leadership and command, who got killed in a car crash just in time for Mugabe to take over as leader and chief commander. His qualifying criteria for leading the ZANLA forces were his political knowledge, his eloquence in English and his drive for revenge.

The morning after signing the Lancaster Agreement in December 1979, Peter Carrington and Margaret Thatcher took off to Tanzania with Mugabe and his delegates as their strategy for a peaceful settlement in a former British colony. They freely offered power to Mugabe three months before the 1980 presidential elections were due, in a secret location in Tanzania. They were hoping that this would remain their secret, but they failed to notice that Julius Nyerere was an African leader who had other African confidants. Nkomo's meeting with Mugabe that morning became a failure. He and Ian Smith died without knowing this truth.

Nkomo also states in his biography (1984) that President Julius Nyerere of Tanzania telephoned him and reported that "the elections are not free and fair". But after it was announced that Mugabe had won, Nyerere agreed that the elections were free and fair.

Nyerere was tormented by the detrimental secret he knew and therefore he telephoned Nkomo in his endeavour to cover up his guilt for hosting Thatcher, Carrington and Mugabe's secret meeting in his country. To preserve relations with Britain and Mugabe, he decided to support Mugabe's victory. If he was in Tanzania during the elections, how could he tell if the elections in Zimbabwe were free and fair?

Ian Smith also confirms his meeting with Nkomo after the elections:

At 8.30 p.m. on 18 March, Nkomo arrived. He was deeply concerned at the way things had turned out. Apart from the fact that the elections had obviously been rigged, intimidation and thuggery were continuing and

Muzorewa's and his supporters were getting their heads bashed in every day. The British, Nkomo noted, were condoning this as they had with the election result. Nkomo revealed that, when Mugabe visited Mozambique and Tanzania shortly before the election, he had carried a message with him from the local British team to Machel and Nyerere, assuring them that the election would go the right way, and from then onwards there had been no criticism from those quarters – a complete volte face. (1997: 351)

Both Smith and Nkomo suspected that Britain had known about Mugabe coming into power before the elections were even held. They knew about the campaign of intimidation that the ZANLA forces were perpetrating among the villagers and communities in the Eastern District. None of the other parties was able to campaign freely in that area. The Governor Lord Soames and the British Foreign Minister could not bring Mugabe to discipline his ZANLA forces. They did not want Nkomo to win the elections because they hated his boldness about the land issue. This had been Nkomo's priority and reason for war and he did not make it a secret, yet Mugabe lied about his reason for fighting because he wanted the support of the British to kick-start him into power before he revealed his brutal side.

Racism and division in the Christian Church

Racism in the Christian Church is the reason for continued silence on issues relating to Zimbabwe and other African countries. The issue of racism has not been addressed properly in the Church because the Church is supporting it and the Church is refusing to repent. Sadly, most of those who grew up in racial oppression have not totally forgiven or surrendered to God and the oppressor has not totally repented from the ways of oppression. This is the reason we have white-only and black-only churches in the world today.

When Mugabe's 5 Brigade and his CIOs began to victimise, intimidate and kill the Ndebele people, our white bosses knew, yet there was no media coverage of the massacres or any intervention for us in Matabeleland. Almost ten years later, white farmers at the mercy of the same henchmen received media coverage and an open hand of welcome from the British government and other Western countries. Are we not God's people too? Unlike the white Zimbabweans who had the West for refuge, Zimbabwe was our only home, so thousands perished in silence. Mass graves and terror were witnessed everywhere in Matabeleland. People were buried alive and whole families burnt alive.

When the young people of Matabeleland flocked to Britain for refuge, immigration sent them back immediately or threw them into prison as soon as they arrived, followed by a long process of processing asylum applications. As a result, most young black Zimbabweans have been deprived of acquiring any useful skills or education.

What would Jesus do about the racial division in His Body if He walked this earth today? Jesus would visit the oppressed and sit among them and listen to them, comfort them and heal their wounds. The religious Pharisees and Sadducees (the media of today) would also be there to see what Jesus was up to, in order to criticise or catch Him out. Jesus took a risk with the woman at the well. If He had not ignored the racial barriers and the stigma of being caught talking to a Samaritan woman, the woman at the well would have never experienced true deliverance from her unworthiness and low self-image. She would have never found hope in the community that despised her. Jesus risked everything because He knew that He was the answer to her lack of self-worth and her need for deliverance from her pain. Is it not true that God's hidden treasure of abundance is right within the stigmatised, the forsaken and the alienated?

We have a choice to make as believers, to take up our cross and follow Jesus, pursue the destiny He has for us, or to pursue our own desires. To be able to break racial barriers between us, we have to follow the example of Jesus, an example of love and humility. On our own we cannot do it, because the enemy uses the pride of the flesh to hinder us from fulfilling God's purpose for our lives; but the Bible tells us that God resists a proud heart.

When Jesus came to this earth, he clarified the reason for His coming, to do the will of His Father, to teach us the kingdom way of life, to show us how to live with each other and how to please God with our lives by doing His will here on earth. This is a choice we have to make. God does not force us to love Him and honour Him. He has given us the will to choose.

Diversity should be celebrated. It is God's gift to us His people. We should not feel threatened by it. Differences in people are to be celebrated as well. They should be seen as opportunities for learning, as discovery zones. There is a lot that God has for us here on earth that we still have not discovered because we have allowed barriers of all kinds to limit us. God is not a boring God, He is the God of all creation, so diversity belongs to Him. If we fail to celebrate our differences here on earth, we will miss out on God. God will ask us on Judgement Day why we did not value and appreciate our differences, His creation. It's a case of taking a risk.

I have quoted insights from Joshua Nkomo's book, *Nkomo: The Story of My Life*. If I had judged it by its cover, I would not have taken an interest in buying it and reading it. Most of us are guilty of judging certain things and people by their appearance and therefore we do not take an interest in getting to know about them. Sometimes we can only know the truth if we endeavour to do our own research instead of always relying on the biased research of others. We need to ask God to reveal to us the hidden treasure in people of different ethnic backgrounds and especially unattractive ones. There is a reason such people exist on the earth.

CHAPTER 19

How Can We Divorce
Religion from Politics?

P olitics and religion cannot be separated because the policies made by politicians, whether good or bad, affect everyone, even those yet to be born. To this effect I would like to highlight the following issues to which the Church continues to turn a blind eye.

In the 1950s, when black people in Rhodesia and South Africa decided to go to war in retaliation against racial segregation and oppression and against white minority rule, Ian Smith's government, Britain and the Western world referred to them as "terrorists". Could it be that the colonialists were also terrorists in the way they visited and settled in Africa? If they were not terrorists, then how did black African children end up as slaves in the West? Africans were simply terrorised.

If as a Body of Believers in Christ, we are able to acknowledge that 2000 years ago Jesus died for us to have eternal life, we should not feel offended when issues that took place 200 years ago are highlighted because they are still going on. Mistakes are learning curves and we cannot keep ignoring the issue of racism.

Failing to accept our wrongs as born-again believers in Christ is sinful to God, because we are refusing to change. It is due to pride that we cannot accept our faults and repent of them. If we continue to discriminate and hate other people for their tribe, language or colour, we are not repentant and we cannot count ourselves pure before God. We cannot therefore ignore issues of division that have not been dealt with. Communication breaks evil barriers of suspicion, hatred and unforgiveness. Someone once said that silence is a negative way of communication, it sends the wrong signal.

If we do not ask God to reveal His secrets to us, we will miss out. The Prophet Isaiah wrote:

Who hath believed our report? And to whom is the arm of the Lord revealed? For He shall grow up before him as a tender plant, and as a root out of a dry ground: He hath no form nor comeliness; and when we shall see Him, there is no beauty that we should desire Him. He is despised and rejected of men; a man of sorrows and acquainted with grief: and we hid as it were our faces from Him; he was despised, and we esteemed Him not.

Isaiah 53: 1–4

How many today would lift our hands to worship Jesus if we really knew what He looked like when He walked the earth? Do we really love Him? We might easily think of ourselves as smarter than the Pharisees and Sadducees. The reality is that they actually saw Him grow from a little boy in a carpenter's home. There was nothing glamorous about Jesus. It is therefore important to realise that you and I could have been in the position of Pharisees and the Sadducees. We could not have done better than them. We are all guilty of denying Him with our unbelief and we all crucified Him.

Joshua Nkomo and my parents were still children when the white settlers demolished their homes and forced them out of their land, destroying everything they owned, including the year's crop, food and grain from the cellars that they had harvested. Was this not terrorism? These memories are still vivid in our parents' minds, but because they are black, nobody has taken time to listen to their experience. "Ye shall know the truth and the truth shall make you free" (John 8: 32).

Robert Moffat and his friends, the white settlers, found themselves exactly in the position of the Pharisees and Sadducees when they saw the African black people. They forgot that God sent them to preach to the black man and saw black people as savages who deserved to be gunned down. That is the reason the Missionaries supported slavery, because they did not see a black person as anything worth considering. It is also the reason the Missionaries handled the gospel of the Lord Jesus Christ like a lottery, in that they only made the gospel available to the upper-class white colonialists, pushing most black people into the Islamic religion. Justice was not done for the Lord Jesus in that His Gospel was used to oppress His people even more.

This is one of the reasons some ignorant religions are hateful of Christ. Jesus loves them and He is still crying for His people. He came to earth for all and took the sins of the world upon Himself on the cross, so that nobody ever had to pay for their own sins or commit suicide. Jesus died for every soul because He created all nations.

CHAPTER 20

The Need for Holiness and Integrity in the Church

H as the Body of Christ in the Western world seriously considered the reasons behind the attacks in New York on 11th September 2001? As Saints of God, it is very important that our assessment and judgment of situations are not prejudiced by the world's standards, because God is a God of justice; He is no respecter of persons. He is also a God of recompense. We cannot manipulate God as a nation or His Church because He is Holy. We must therefore consider consulting the Holy Spirit for a deeper revelation. If we sow hatred and division, we will reap the same.

I had an experience of what I mean here in 2005. I had finished my placement shift for the day and rushed to one of the university computer rooms to check my emails, when I found a disturbing email from my deaf brother in Zimbabwe. He told me that the cottage he was staying in could be demolished at any time, as President Mugabe had ordered that all such cottages and houses that were outside planning permission be demolished. This was another move of revenge by Mugabe because the nation had not voted for him in 2000. He had become very unpopular even in Mashonaland. Therefore, as expected, he resolved to demonstrate to the people of Zimbabwe that he still had power over them. My brother did not know where he would stay with his wife and two little children. When I got home that afternoon, I threw myself before God and cried about the situation in Zimbabwe.

As I asked God how long the suffering of the poor people of Zimbabwe at the hands of Mugabe was going to take, He led me to the book of Ezekiel. As I read chapter by chapter in desperation for an answer, it revealed to me that the people of Zimbabwe are a rebellious people and that unless they repent from their ways of idolatry and compromise, Mugabe will continue ruling them. It was basically not up to God, it was up to the people of Zimbabwe to take a step towards their own freedom by obeying God's commands. There was sin in the land. I was shocked at this revelation and embarrassed before God. This was the last thing I had expected to hear when I threw myself on the floor crying for my brother's situation.

I remembered Abraham pleading with God for his cousin Lot who lived in a land that God was about to destroy because of its rebellious lifestyle. Every kind of sin was found in Sodom and Gomorrah. God saw what I did not see. Certain things became clear as they were revealed to me in the spirit. The people I thought were innocent victims, it turned out that most of them were not. They had been compromising and were rebellious to God; they did not know that God had been watching. The money I had been sending to some of my relatives in Zimbabwe was not being used in a holy manner.

The worst thing that brings the punishment of God on a nation is when the Body of Christ compromises itself by either ignoring such wicked and detrimental ways or adapting to the rebellious ways, systems and traditions of the world that are not biblical. For example, as hard times in Zimbabwe got worse, most people who had relations and friends abroad were able to get foreign currency and resell it locally at whatever value they chose; apparently most Believers in Christ in Zimbabwe got involved in this corrupt practice, which they call "money burning".

When I found out what this meant, I was really disappointed. It is a corrupt practice and very destructive to the economy of the land. It is also a selfish, greedy practice that widens the gap between the rich and poor, enslaving and crippling the poor even more. What about those poor people who do not know anyone abroad? What did it mean for them? How could God accept our corrupted and defiled tithe and offering? Is He not a Holy God? Does He not care about the poor?

Throughout 2007 I was shown visions of desperate widows, single mothers and orphans being neglected and sleeping rough. Then in 2008 I was sent to a few pastors in Zimbabwe, but they did not listen to the message I carried. They challenged me. They had been walking with God for years, therefore who was I to be delivering such messages to them? Others simply ignored me. I must admit that it was very painful for me, but God healed me and showed me that it was not I being rejected but Him.

When God sends me to people it is very scary, but who am I to choose how God uses me? I really feel sorry for those pastors I have been sent to in the past who ignored me, and I pray that the Mercy of God be with them.

Therefore it was revealed to me that the deteriorating circumstances of Zimbabwe were fuelled and propelled by the lack of integrity and compassion in the Church there. Nevertheless, there was a small number of the Holy remnant there who never bowed down to idolatry or ate the bread of corruption. It is this holy remnant, the apple of God's eye, that has touched God and God is about to move on their behalf. He is a God of justice and He revealed to me that He is bringing justice on the earth. God further revealed that the justice system is about to change, because the current justice system on earth does not reflect the one in heaven, it is wicked and corrupt. God is taking over complete control of the justice system.

In October 2008 God gave me the name of the Justice Minister of Zimbabwe. I had never heard of it or seen the man before. God sent me twice to him concerning issues of injustice, one that was done to me, and the other related to the humiliating abuse of unsuspecting, innocent and respectable women by a top security man in Zimbabwe. I used a reputable courier to send this mail to him, but to this day I have not received any response.

Hard times are meant to be opportunities to experience God, the supernatural provision of God, but instead of challenging God to perform His Word in our lives, we give up too easily. I felt humbled before God at these revelations and more so when my journey of discovery began and I discovered I did not even know most people as well as I thought I did. "Ye shall know the truth and the truth shall make you free" (John 8: 32).

God allows certain things to happen so that we can learn from them and grow in our spiritual understanding and maturity. It is then that we seek refuge in God and seek His opinion through discernment and through His Word, and rely totally on Him for guidance and direction through prayer.

Jesus did not save us to remain as children of God, He wants us to develop to sons and daughters of God. If we are joint heirs with Him then we must allow God to develop our spiritual lives so that we are able to take dominion in His Kingdom. He also allows painful experiences to enable us to search our hearts and souls so that we may repent and correct our ways. He is the Creator of all and He only rewards humility and obedience. He resists the proud heart.

I believe that 11th September 2001 is one such experience. When God shows us why things happened the way they did, we need to humble ourselves before Him and realise that if we do not repent from our ways of compromise as the Body of Christ, these painful events will be presented over and over again until we realise that our spiritual maturity requires repentance from our rebellious ways and disobedience to God and learn that vengeance belongs to God only.

It is important to remember that the way we react to God's revelations will either prosper us or give us another similar experience for our learning. Therefore as we repent, asking God for forgiveness and guidance, we are taking the important steps towards spiritual maturity and prosperity.

If my people, which are called by my name, shall humble themselves, and pray, and seek my face and turn from their wicked ways; then will I hear from heaven, and will forgive their sin and will heal their land.

2 Chronicles 7:14

The Western Church needs to take the upper hand in dealing with God's revelations, remembering that God is no respecter of persons and He never forgets when injustice has been done.

It is therefore important to note that some of the men and women of God in the Western Church got carried away in hatred towards the people of the Islamic religion since 11th September, regarding them as "terrorists" because of the pain the nation has suffered. The Western Christian Church should be careful that its support for Israel is genuine and not a manipulation of God for His favour. God cannot be manipulated; He is a God of Justice. Some damages are correctable, but some require God's Mercy and His Grace.

I am therefore under the unction of the Holy Spirit to bring some of these issues to the awareness of the Body of Christ worldwide. God wants certain fundamental issues dealt with relating to Western policy towards the Third World, particularly towards His ex-colonised, oppressed and robbed African people.

For example, those controlling and monopolising the wealth in this world are still dragging their feet on Third World debt cancellation. But who is behind the International Monetary Fund that robbed and further ties Africa into a debt it never owed? God loves the black man and He wants to recompense him. Yes, He is a God of Justice.

CHAPTER 21

There Is Black Oppression in Every British System

Black people are oppressed throughout the Western political system in that their problems are not given fair attention. For instance, the health care system abuses the Mental Health Act by keeping black people, and especially men, oppressed through inappropriate health diagnoses. It is a well-known fact that many black people are diagnosed as schizophrenic and therefore put on psychiatric prescription drugs for life, deliberately ruining their chances of employment and progression.

During my community placement as a student in mental health nursing, I had the opportunity to visit a black client in his late 40s in the community. He lived alone and he had been diagnosed with schizophrenia. The man lived in such terrible, slum-like conditions I had never seen anything like it. I never thought there were people living like that in Britain. The man would have been better off in Africa where there is fresh air and warmth. This was wintertime and the man actually slept on his settee in the little living room because he needed the gas fire to keep him warm; the house had no central heating. I made several attempts to get the Housing Association responsible to go to look at this dump, but my efforts were fruitless. The reason given by the surveyor was that the property was too crowded inside for him to sort it out.

How could a person be expected to be normal in those conditions? I only managed to sort out his bank account for his benefit to go into, which he was very pleased about. Unfortunately my mentor on that placement removed me from that case, as it was not under her caseload. According to her I was supposed to focus on her clients. I had started on the case with a different mentor who had to go on maternity leave a few weeks after I started. This was a blessing for me because she was very kind and caring for her patients. She had taught me everything I needed to learn before she left. I visited all her clients with her and she observed my skills in giving injections. By the time she left I had learnt almost everything I needed to concerning care delivery. She entrusted me to follow up this black man's case and ensure that I put pressure on the Housing Association, because it was reluctant to sort out this black man's situation. Unfortunately I do not know what became of it or if she found any progress when she came back from her maternity leave. I was not happy with the attitude of the male nurse who took over the case.

The other example I would like to give as evidence of the neglect and oppression of black people with mental health problems is one that occurred in 2009. I had made friends with this particular young woman, whom I had met in February 2007 at the hospital where she was admitted; her bed was next to my daughter's bed. I noticed that she never had any visitors. She told me that she had been admitted before Christmas 2006 as she had been found unwell on the street. She had been homeless since she came from America, where she had fallen out with her adopted white family as they had not been keen on her since their mother had died. Their mother had adopted her at a young age. She had actually been raised in an English family but they moved to America. Now she is known in the mental health service as one without a family.

I decided to give her my telephone number just in case she needed someone to talk to. It is not right for a human being to have no one in a world so full of people just because we do not want to commit ourselves to other people's problems. We only love people who have no mental health issues. Jesus loves the ones with mental health issues as well.

She rang me from the rehabilitation centre where she lived and asked if she could come to ours for Christmas, which she did. I felt blessed, because the previous Christmas she had turned me down at the last minute.

Then she rang me stranded early in 2009. She had been discharged from the rehabilitation unit in February when she had planned to visit New York. That visit did not go well and she decided to come back within two weeks. On her arrival she headed for the only place she knew, the rehab centre where she had been staying all along. She found that she had no room there and she was denied entry. When she rang me she was still there, I could hear a male voice in the background and it was still daylight, about 4 p.m. I had insisted on the phone that she should remain there because it was too far for me to travel to her at that short notice. I thought she was relapsing, I did not believe that she had been to New York at all. It was too much to take for me in such a short space of time, because the last time I had spoken to her she was still at the rehab centre and she had not indicated that she would be visiting New York so soon. To me, she was not fit enough to have been left to visit New York on her own. Her mobile phone battery was almost running out, so she did not stay long on the phone. Then she phoned again some hours later and said she was on the train to nowhere. I told her to go to the hospital and check herself in, as it was late.

Meanwhile, I phoned the rehab centre and asked for the full story. Everything the woman had said to me turned out to be correct. I then told the nurse there that she would be sleeping on the streets if the crisis team was not contacted. She said she had tried to contact the crisis team, but the man she spoke to did not seem keen to help. I asked for the crisis team's number. The nurse on duty told me that he was fully aware of the woman's situation, but if she took a taxi all the way from the airport surely she must have a lot of money. I told him that she is a vulnerable person. She told me that she had no cash left. The male nurse told me that he was going home and that if I was her friend I should be the one accommodating her for the night. I said that if I had known the story as I understand it now, definitely I would have let her come to my house. I challenged him from a professional point of view and reminded him what the crisis team represented. When he realised I was a knowledgeable person, he began to wake up. I said to him, given the time that had been wasted between her arrival at the rehab centre and the contact they made with the crisis team, surely something should have been done for her. I asked him to contact the police for help so that she did not sleep on the street. He refused. He said, "What will I say to the police? You should ring them yourself because she is your friend."

It does not make sense for a professional to be employed as a mental health nurse and as part of the community mental health crisis team yet to refuse to fulfil his duties in a crisis. All he needed to say to me was that he would do something about the crisis, instead of telling me that his shift was finished and he was going home while a woman in the system was spending the night on the street with her luggage.

My friend phoned me in the morning. Her social worker had the keys to the flat she had been discharged to before she left for New York and she could not get into the flat without the keys, which is why she had rung me for help the previous night. I advised her to contact the police and tell them everything she had told me.

After I finished speaking to her, I received a call from the crisis team, from a different male professional. He was very concerned about the previous night's events. The way forward was all I was concerned about myself. He asked me to describe the woman's appearance, which I did. I also informed him that I had advised her to contact the police for help. I gave him her mobile number. Later on, the crisis team rang me and told me not to worry because the police had picked her up and put her in a bed and breakfast. The man apologised for his unhelpfulness and thanked me for being so helpful. I appreciated his humility in calling me and apologising.

In the morning I tried to ring the social worker to explain that the woman was back from New York and needed her flat keys. I then established that she had been removed from the system and her records closed once she had been discharged the previous month. Any caring doctor would have left room for her just in case her visit to New York did not go well. I could not believe how quickly her name had been removed from the whole system. This incident made me think how many black people end up on the street just because the system has failed them.

Many of the young black men and women who flood mental health units are kept under control by way of drugs. The side effects of most of these drugs are not very helpful, as most of them cause panic attacks, involuntary muscle spasms, psychosis due to serious hallucinations and further depressive moods.

With black people being more vulnerable to being diagnosed with a psychological problem by their GP, their chances of employment are reduced because employers shun them once they find out they have visited a psychiatrist. Their approach to policies relating discrimination at work is negative. A survey conducted by *Mind* in 1996 revealed that 34 per cent of people with mental health problems had been forced to resign from jobs, while 69 per cent had been put off from applying for jobs for fear of unfair treatment. Unemployment is inevitable once a person is diagnosed with a mental illness. If they apply for a job, the approach of the Occupational Health Department would be negative; as a result, people don't apply or they lie about their health condition.

Rejection by the wider community is frightening and sinister once someone is known to have mental problems. The *Mind* survey also revealed that 47 per cent of people with mental illness had been harassed in public; 11 per cent had been physically attacked and forced to move home because of harassment.

During my training, I sat in a hospital ward review where a female psychiatrist perhaps forgot I was there when (after a black female patient diagnosed with bipolar disorder left the room) she threatened to increase a certain drug "just so she could fix her by keeping her sedated". The psychiatrist did not make it a secret that she hated the black patient. All the woman had boldly expressed was her desire for a particular drug to be decreased and her request to be discharged. I discovered that it was a case of "Who is the boss around here?"

The Mental Health Foundation (MHF) survey reveals that even though GPs were perceived as the first point of contact by their patients, they were blamed for having attributed physical health problems to symptoms of mental illness. Many general practitioners are prejudiced towards black people and therefore oppress them by failing to understand their problems. They do not give black patients enough time even to express their feelings, as the GP would be looking at the clock and then quickly diagnosing them as depressed in order to flood them with addictive anti-depressants.

I have in the past experienced being asked "How can I help you?" the minute I enter the GP's door and before I could close the door or even sit down. At that point I did not know whether to continue or to leave without even bothering to tell the doctor how I felt. I thank God He stopped me from putting my trust in medication. I refuse to visit a GP on my own account. I wrote my husband a letter and told him that whatever in life happened to my body, I should never be taken to the hospital and if I die, I do not want any post mortem on my body. I should be buried in peace, no cremation, but burial only. Jehovah is my healer. I will not give glory to medication, where it involves my own health. I respect doctors and nurses but I fear God.

In February 2010, I found myself in Accident and Emergency with my first daughter. After one young, unconfident doctor failed to find a vein to take a blood test, she disappeared for another hour while I stood there watching my daughter in pain from the migraine and epileptic seizures. Realising that no help was forthcoming, I asked to use their phone to ask my husband to come and collect us, since the ambulance had brought us in. The senior doctor came to try to take blood samples, but failed as well. We were sent for a head scan and then to a ward, where I spent the night and the next day trying to calm her down. As it was now the second night, we were transferred again to another ward where things got even worse.

The nursing staff in this ward were very unkind. I was too tired to spend the second night sitting up. There was still no medical intervention. One of the night nurses gave me the extension for the ward in case I needed to phone them to check on my daughter that night, but she reassured me that my daughter would be looked after. I went home to sleep. First thing in the morning, just after 7 a.m., I rang the ward. I was put through to the nurse who was looking after my daughter. She reassured me that she would give her breakfast and that the doctors' round would be around 9 a.m. I felt the need to get there on time for the doctors' round as I had to speak on her behalf. I got to the hospital just after 10 a.m. The morning staff had tried to feed her but had quickly given up, so I found her bowl of breakfast cold and dry.

She was sitting on the bed with her hand on her head, with tears and swollen eyes from the migraine and the progressive seizures. The minute she saw me she became upset. She pointed at a beaker next to the jar of water. I gave it to her and she drank it all in a short space of time. That meant she was desperate for water, but there had been nobody to help her. I felt bad for having slept at home. I approached the ward doctor for a painkiller. I then asked the tea lady for fresh cereal and hot milk to feed my daughter, but she only had cold milk. The nurses refused to allow me to use the microwave. I offered to heat the milk myself and to take full responsibility for it, but I was ignored. I was refused hot water as well for the same reason, health and safety. I mentioned that the nurses from the ward we were transferred from were able to give us hot milk or hot water at our request. They all walked away from me as if I was causing trouble for them. The tea lady was very sympathetic and kept shaking her head. She offered cold milk and said it was better to try that than nothing. I tried it but my daughter refused because she does not like cold breakfast. However, I thanked the lady for her kindness. She repeated to me that she could have done it for me but she was not allowed to.

The Asian doctor who had been watching my desperate quest for hot milk to feed my daughter saw how they all ignored me and when I requested something to stop my daughter's pain, he mentioned that I could actually report the matter to PALS if I wished to. He agreed to give me his name in support and wrote it down for me. I had to wait for lunchtime. Even though I had been given a food menu to choose from, when lunchtime came the nurse asked me to come and choose from what was left. This happened again later on with the evening meal. I wondered why I had been given the menu to choose my daughter's meals if I had to make do with what was left after all the patients in the ward had been given their meals.

Whenever I sought some kind of assistance, the nurses were unapproachable. I had to endeavour to clean my daughter up on my own because she had not been cleaned since the day before. At least in the other ward the nurses were very kind, they did everything possible to ensure my daughter's comfort. They even offered me tea. She was still in the same dirty sheets I had left her in the night before. Her incontinence pad had not been changed all day since I arrived at 10 a.m. because no one looked at me when I tried to approach them for help. She had not been washed either. So I cleaned her up and used the nappy I had brought from home. Around 4.30 p.m. after pacing up and down the ward, I felt very distressed and like a prisoner. I made up my mind to discharge my daughter myself and take her home with me.

There had been no medical intervention since Saturday night, and this was now Monday afternoon. The results of the urine tests were going to take another 2–3 days. The nice doctor had managed to take blood samples that afternoon. The results would find us at home. I decided to ring my husband and asked him to come and collect us. What was the point of keeping my daughter in a place like this when she could have hot food at home? When my husband came to pick us up at 5 p.m., the afternoon tea lady came round with the tea trolley. She offered tea to the patients, but I opted for hot water instead for my daughter. Then my husband asked for a cup of tea and she gave it to him and left. I took it that it was because he was white like her. I had not been given any tea since I had arrived in the ward at 10 a.m.

During the three years of my training in the same hospital a few years ago, I could never have treated patients like that. Staff attitudes were very bad towards me. I once said during my training that unless attitudes towards people like me changed in the British education system, I did not see how these young white nursing students would be able to nurse someone like me. During group work, your opinion was never regarded and you could even see while you spoke that the others were not interested. They were not even keen to know us; they felt comfortable in their own groups of friendships. If as black students our white colleagues treated us as invisible people, how would they notice a black patient in a ward? I knew this was going to be a problem and God sent me to that hospital to remind me so that I could put it in this book. Most lecturers were aware of the separation between white and black students, but they failed to encourage us to get to know each other. They were tired of asylum seekers. I was seen as one too, even though I have citizenship; it is only a piece of paper as long as I am dark skinned.

From my observation, especially on my management placement at the hospital where I worked alongside black nurses, there was less appreciation of their input in the workplace, as a result of which most black nurses I worked with had no intention of applying for higher positions. They felt safe being in lower positions because of the lack of respect they experienced from the junior staff. White healthcare assistants are given more respect than black professional nurses.

In nursing homes, I discovered that most qualified nurses and other professionals from India, Saudi Arabia, the Philippines and Africa are working at the level of a health care assistant and their rota is not very flexible. They are simply enslaved in their jobs in the West. Nursing home managers are mostly racist and oppressive. As a student, I also experienced abuse by a white health care assistant in one nursing home, but when I took the matter to the nurse manager, she quickly came to the defence of her member of staff by stating to me that she had been under a lot of stress since her dog died.

It is not just in the medical system. UK statistics show that the chances of a black man being stopped by the police on the street are very high, thus restricting black people's joy and freedom, making them angry so that their emotions of anger are not seen as a cry for help but as a further excuse for oppression. These problems are documented in the educational literature, but the practice is not changing. Why bother lecturing about it in universities if nothing changes?

In 1994 I undertook an English course at a college near my house. I was appalled when the anthology being studied by my English group contained a poem called the "Big Fat Black Woman". Being the only black student in class, I was asked by the tutor whether I had any comment. I did not have a comment because I was disgusted that an educational institution could actually encourage racism in its corridors. As if this was not enough, the college sneaked behind my back and contacted the local council to investigate my immigration status. The next thing I received was an urgent letter from the council summoning me to their offices with my passport. Did I look like someone who had been illegally smuggled into Britain on a cargo airline? As if this was not enough, my Zulu middle name became a laughing stock within the college staff offices. When I went in to have my college ID photo taken, the member of staff said to me she was eagerly waiting to see the face behind this name.

The prison system in the UK is full of men and women from Zimbabwe and South Africa who came here to seek help. Foreigners cover most agency work in nursing homes and hospitals, but they are very miserable and unappreciated. I have worked with them.

Many Believers in Christ who have residence in the UK visit the prisons to pray for the inmates and the stories that they hear reflect the cruelty of the unrepentant oppressor. For example, how can a black young woman who ran from Zimbabwe leaving her children and a baby behind be locked up in prison for years while her asylum case awaits a hearing? Is it not obvious that the baby and children back in Zimbabwe would need food to eat? Why should it be an issue for Zimbabweans to come to Britain for refuge or economic reasons? If a mother is locked up in prison because her case is in a queue while she earns no income to send back home to her children, is Britain's immigration system not committing murder to foreign Zimbabweans along with Mugabe?

What are equal opportunities?

The British government's legislation clearly defines the purpose of equal opportunities. It states that equal opportunities are about the elimination of discrimination in our society. They are about the effective use of human resources and positive action measures to ensure that employment opportunities and service provisions are bias free and made readily available to people from the target groups.

The legislation further states that equal opportunities involve the breakdown and removal of discriminatory structures, biased policies and prejudicial practices in organisations. It seeks to replace processes that perpetuate inequality with better and more effective ways of working which would provide equal access for all in services and employment opportunities.

The equal opportunities legislation includes:

- Sex Discrimination Act 1975 & 1986
- Race Relations Act 1976
- Equal Pay Act 1970 & 1989 amendments
- Employment Protection (Consolidation) Act 1978 & 1980 amendments
- Disabled Persons (Employment) Act 1944 & 1958
- Disability Discrimination Act 1995

Given the experiences of most black people in the UK, including myself, the equal opportunities legislation has not been effectively enforced. Black people who try to raise a voice against the unfair practices that they have been subjected to are usually fobbed off with the allegation that they are "playing the race card". This attitude further oppresses black people especially students in Britain, in that it pushes them into "suffering in silence", as it was the case where I was.

When I registered for an Access to Higher Education course in September 2000, I did not anticipate the problems that ensued. The course was meant to be a year, but all the black students were disqualified from applying for university because they had not measured up or met all the criteria to gain the required credits. Surprisingly, almost all the white students were given the credits to move on. Things were made even harder for the black students this time around. We were given a new micro-biology module that was pretty intensive for Access to Higher Education; in fact the module was not necessary at that level as far as I was concerned since I had been to university. As if that was not enough, at the end of the two-year Access course we were given a timed written biology exam. Other favourable students were given the same exam but unsupervised. They were allowed to write the exam in the college library using textbooks! I found out because one came to tell me how easy it was and she was allowed to use the textbook in the library. When the time came for the exam auditors, I realised that I had not passed again because part of my psychology work had not been assessed. The same tutor who allowed others to write from the library had been sitting on my work for months ensuring that I did not make it. After two years of doing a course that should have been completed the previous year, I was given a credit certificate but not a full certificate for entry into higher education.

This time I refused to accept the failure. I had been driving a long way for two years to get to the college and my wasted time. I endeavoured to settle the problem in court. I did not even have to get to court, because once the course coordinator realised that I was angry and I knew that after all others had had the liberty of writing the last biology essay exam in the college library, using textbooks, she did not waste time but posted me my full certificate. This is how I ended up at university on a three-year nursing course, facing another battle on a different level.

Before I joined this college there was an article in the newspaper about a court battle between two black brothers and the same college. They were hoping to study law as a subject and therefore they represented themselves in court against the injustice that had been done to them. The Judge treated them as "trouble makers" and their case was thrown out of the window. My experience with the same college would prove the judge on that case wrong. However, if the British justice system was not designed to cater for black people, then submitting a case in court is a waste of time for black people.

The A-level English tutor who emotionally abused my second daughter told me quite frankly that even if I took the matter to court I would not win. I suppose he was telling me the facts that he knew. She had even attempted suicide because her tutor had been determined to frustrate her. I had to engage the Racial Equality Council on the case. The solicitor I saw was very open with me; he told me that on a previous similar case he had warned the head teacher of my daughter's school to change his attitude because he did not like his way of handling matters. In my daughter's situation the same head teacher had taken sides with the tutor against me. The tutor lied about me and forgot that my husband had been by my side when I confronted him about my daughter's situation during a parents' evening. The head teacher quickly wrote me a letter and summoned me to apologise for insulting the tutor, threatening me that the tutor was taking advice from his union on the matter. I am the one who had been insulted on parents' evening for asking a question regarding my daughter's treatment and the head teacher was provoking and infuriating me even more. All he should have done if he really cared was to ask me to explain my side of the story, instead of concluding that I had been verbally abusive to the tutor.

I patiently sat down and replied to his letter. He did not know that he was confronting the daughter of a "well-known letter writer". He then tried to pick every little thing out of my letter that he could use against me. Having worked as a legal secretary all those years in Rhodesia and Zimbabwe, I knew my boundaries very well. He threw another reply back at me. It was now like a battle between him and me. Although as a head teacher I would have expected him to handle the matter in a rational manner, he totally believed what he had been told and therefore pinned me down on having insulted the tutor by calling him a racist. If I never called real racists in Rhodesia racists, how could I have been so foolish as to publicly call a tutor a racist at parents' evening, in an institution and a country completely dominated by white people?

A meeting was arranged with the school governor, the solicitor for the tutor's union and all my daughter's English tutors. As I had consulted the Racial Equality Council, it was also ready for the meeting. As the time of the meeting drew closer, the head teacher did what he knew would work for him: he decided to ring my husband at work to talk him out of attending the meeting with me. He actually offered my husband a separate meeting with him. My husband turned his offer down and insisted that he would be attending at the same time as me. When my husband rang me about the phone call from the head teacher I could not believe it. I quickly informed the Racial Equality Council about it and this was used against the head teacher.

The head teacher wanted to divide and rule my home. My husband at one point was actually shaking with fury at the meeting as he asked the tutor a question. The tutor gave himself away during the meeting with his careless words again. He openly displayed his big bully side.

My daughter had had a good educational experience at the same school before this tutor joined the school from another borough. Almost all her teachers liked her and she had been a happy child until she progressed to A levels. At the time, the abuse destroyed her self-esteem and confidence and her friends did not understand why she had to go through that. She suddenly changed and became introverted. This was not my daughter any more. My first daughter, who went to a special school at the time, was getting a lot of support from her school. Her confidence was skyrocketing while the one who had been born confident was being deliberately put down and damaged by her A-level tutor. God intervened quickly here, otherwise I would have lost my daughter to suicide at age 16.

All her hair began to drop out, leaving no sign of hair follicles. The hospital diagnosed the condition as alopecia and that it was caused by stress. How could a 16 year old be stressed? At school she wore headscarves to cover her baldness. I had to remove my own hair in solidarity. When she wore a headscarf at school she was seen as trying to show off or to stand out. They did not know that she was completely bald. So I asked them at that meeting if they thought it was fashionable for my daughter to be wearing a headscarf at school.

To cut a long story short, the head teacher was compelled to write a letter of apology to me. The Racial Equality Council's job is not very easy in Britain. My representative was not white; he was of a Middle Eastern background and he was very rational compared to my daughter's white tutor and the head teacher. The solicitor had recommended that if the head teacher failed to answer the questions I had about my daughter's abuse during the meeting, he would then intervene.

The definition of prejudice, according to Hayes (1994), is "when a person holds a certain attitude or mental set towards a particular target, this has usually become fixed, there is a reluctance to change even when presented with alternative possibilities or ritual explanations." God will vindicate His people because nobody chooses their skin colour. The black skin colour is perfect before God's eyes. He created us; we are fearfully and wonderfully made.

The education system in Britain is like a battlefield as far as black people are concerned. The system was designed to ensure that black people do not get far in education. The system was designed to oppress black people and keep them in the lower stratum of society. The equal opportunities legislation deliberately fails to specify anything relating to the education system. I believe this was deliberately omitted, as the education system is the strongest weapon Britain has against black people. The tutors in Britain are just like the Rhodesians. If you want a British taste of Rhodesia as a black person, then enrol yourself for education in Britain and you will certainly know where Rhodesians originally came from.

Many black nursing students from Zimbabwe were failed because of their placement mentors who did not like them. Most university tutors went along with that. White students do not have a similar experience. They do meet problems from those who may be jealous of them, but their problems are different and they receive a lot of sympathy in their placements, while black students are treated almost as part of the workforce.

The following was my niece's experience in London. Since she was a hospitality student, the university placed her in a reputable hotel in London. A white French hotel supervisor actually spat in my niece's face. She phoned me upset, but when I told her to phone her university tutor it appeared as though she was not aware she could actually do that. She had previously rung me reporting abuse by a white French man at her placement. He had been giving her a hard time for quite some time and others around her had noticed it. The alternative solution to her circumstances that her black hotel manager offered her were not very good. She therefore chose to put her head down and endure the situation just to finish her placement and go back to her university. Needless to say, the French man got away with abuse towards a black student. He is bound to continue abusing those who are placed there next. Zimbabweans and other black African students do not feel secure enough to report abuse, therefore they soldier on.

"Putting your head down" is a coping strategy that black people use in Britain in order to achieve their goals. Racism is definitely brewing in some of these professions. This is a painful story that could only be told by a black person.

The problem with human beings is that we only see as far as our immediate circumstances; it takes us a while to see the bigger picture of where God is taking us. The worst thing about spiritual blindness is that it prohibits us from seeing what has been there for us all along. The process of spiritual development requires discipline and obedience, just as the body's muscles are developed through hard work and discipline.

It has taken me many years to see clearly. Life is a journey of discovery. We only discover what God already created before we were even born and that makes God who He is, a Holy God. He is worthy of our honour and praise. I thank God for navigating me through difficult places over the years.

Attitudes that are motivated by racial or tribal hatred cannot be changed in any other way except through Christ. Jesus Christ is the answer for the whole world. If Western Christians are prejudiced towards black people and foreigners of other ethnic descent, no man can change them except God. God created us all, He knows each one of us and He knows our destiny. He is the ultimate judge and His justice system is pure.

CHAPTER 22

The Family and the Man

The Family is God's order here on earth. God's original plan for the family is found in Genesis 1: 27 and Genesis 2: 21-25.

In Ephesians 5, the Word of God states that the man is the head of his wife and she must submit to her husband in everything. For a man to be in authority, his confidence should be in God, not in himself. A man without confidence in God will regard himself as the master of his life. This is the reason we have chaos in the world today, because when the devil attacks the self-confident man, everything around him crumbles. Our confidence should only be in God's Word, so that when the devil comes against us, we are able to remind him of the Word of God.

Is Jesus not a good role model in this? God also created Satan. This is why when he tempted Jesus in the wilderness; Jesus used the written scripture to fight back. Jesus said, A servant is not greater than his Master. We cannot fight the devil with our logical mind because he is cleverer than us, but he is not cleverer than the creator of Heaven and Earth, our God.

God wants to restore every man's dignity (black or white) and confidence in these last days. The enemy has, since the fall of the first Adam, diminished the dignity and rightful status of a man here on earth. God is a God of order. He likes order, and the family is His way of restoring order here on earth. The destruction of the male has led to the destruction of the family, God's order here on earth. The enemy has succeeded in putting an inferiority complex and the fear of failure in the hearts of men to such an extent that for years now the rate of suicide has been increasing among men.

To regain their courage, most men then resorted to destructive habits that further destroyed their lives, such as smoking cigarettes, weed, dangerous drug abuse and alcohol abuse. All these evil and dangerous habits happen for the sake of gaining confidence.

Due to the inferiority complex that men have suffered, they have used the weaker sex, the female, as their punch bag or door mat. A woman only respects a man of integrity. A woman is not foolish. This is the reason we have women today who have seen or suffered the consequences of men's failure and inferiority, and therefore they are no longer interested in marriage. This is another deception of Satan, the enemy of our soul.

This is also due to watching violent movies encouraging gun crimes, sexual sins like men raping their wives, sexual abuse of girls and women by the drug addicts and men with diminished self-confidence, pornography encouraging more child abductions for the sex trade, gambling, theft, burglaries, increased criminal activities such as drug trafficking, murder – you name it, Satan has been turning the earth into pure hell right before our eyes, using men.

In its endeavour to solve such problems, the justice system of this earth further worsens things in that it locks up all these men in prison, leaving women to raise children single-handed. Not all women and mothers who are left by their spouses in this manner are able to cope on their own. Therefore some resort to inappropriate survival ways such as theft, thus increasing the number of children in the state care system. Children in foster care grow up with a lot of anger in them. They become self-haters. Their anger leads them to all kinds of criminal activities from a young age, especially boys. This was never the will of God for the family. It is out of God's order. Dr Mike Murdock states in one of his wisdom principles, that God's only obsession is order (wisdom-online.com).

How has the black man coped as a husband and father?

The black man's dignity has been the most violated under the sun; hence the need for him to be a father to his children and a good husband to his wife. Most black men have under difficult circumstances been good husbands and fathers of great families, where you find good manners and respect in the children they raise. My father was one such man. He taught us respect. He showed us how to pray. My father hated poverty. He always brought poor orphans home to live with us. We would wake up in the morning with a strange child in our blankets. There was no time for an introduction, we had to include the child in our lives and by the grace of God the child would tell us his story, but we never asked any questions.

In 1991, my father set up and registered an orphanage and old people's home in Matabeleland. His younger brother, my uncle, is a builder. He tried his best but he is now quite old and my father struggled with the funding, as a result of which the home was not completed. He visited me in 1998 in the UK, but his heart was always in the completion of his orphanage home. At the time he hinted that he would like my husband and myself to manage the orphanage. I did not answer him because I did not want anything to do with it, so I kept quiet because I did not wish to hurt him. I never knew that God's call was on my life at the time. I simply did not want anything to do with Zimbabwe. All I wanted was to be left in peace.

My husband then tried to help my father find funding for his orphanage and old people's home. His endeavours to get help from a UK organisation that helps charities were unsuccessful. In 1990, when my father began the work on the orphanage, the HIV situation in Zimbabwe among children on the streets was showing signs of further deterioration. My father was already 69 years of age and on a pension as a retired and part-time Anglican priest. It was quite upsetting for my father to see the deterioration of the economy of Zimbabwe and hence the increasing plight of the orphans and widows and the homeless.

The black Anglican priests were expected by their superiors to build schools from scratch, without any resources or help whatsoever from the bishops. Once an area got established and we settled in well and began to know the local village people, my father would be moved again by the bishop to start afresh elsewhere. This cycle continued. His family was growing too, so we had to be separated from our older siblings, as they had to live in a boarding school far away.

In *The Challenge for Africa: A New Vision* (William Heinemann, 2009; reprinted by permission of The Random House Group Ltd), the winner of the Nobel Peace Prize, Wangari Maathai, states:

> *As in other regions of the world, the base of African society is the family. Since the earliest days of slavery, through colonialism and beyond, virtually the entire economic system of sub-Saharan Africa has depended on uprooting the African man and forcing him explicitly or by default to seek employment away from his home. Men have gone to work on commercial farms they didn't own; they have gone down mines and into quarries often at considerable distances from their families. (2009: 275)*

The servant and slave mentality that the black man suffered historically is not something to be taken lightly. It does not help the African continent much that after it was robbed of its black children as well as its riches, it has been kept financially indebted to the Western world. Where is the compassion of the Western Body of Christ in all this? Where is the indication of regret and repentance over the slave trade and the colonisation of Africa if Africa continues to suffer poverty and indebtedness to those nations that benefited and were enriched by African manpower and resources? The cancellation of Third World debt is long overdue.

Our African black fathers were robbed of their dignity to the extent that they still feel intimidated by the West. This is why African leaders and people who suffered at the hands of brutal colonialists are finding it hard to forgive. My mother once related to me the pain she went through when she watched as a child all her parents' harvest of grain for the year being bulldozed to the ground by the white settlers. They were forced out of their homes and land and pushed to dry, arid parts of the country that were not easy to cultivate and where all the wild, dangerous animals of Africa were found.

Why has the enemy succeeded in keeping the Church divided for so long?

White Christians where I fellowshipped used to testify about having a "humbling experience" on holiday in Mauritius where they enjoyed mixing with the local people and spending time in their villages. The experience they described was exactly what our rural life was like as black Africans in Zimbabwe. We could not understand why our white brothers and sisters preferred to go all the way to Mauritius to get a humbling experience when it was right on their doorstep! Most of these Saints of God have never been to our rural homes to experience how we live. What was the difference between the Mauritian people and us? They still have not learnt the local languages of the African people. In the Western World we see a similar situation, where there is still a great distance in relationship between the black Saints of God and the white Saints of God. There are still black- or white-only church denominations and communities several years after slavery was abolished. One would assume that by now unity could have been achieved in the Western Church, but it is not the case.

The average black man is always quick to forgive because he realises that he should appreciate the little amount of change that has taken place so far. The black man also recognises that lack of forgiveness will get him nowhere.

On the other hand, the oppressor is still finding it hard to accept a black person. The arrogance of the oppressor has over a long period caused him to disassociate himself from black people, hence the emotional pain caused to the black man that God has been watching.

In South Africa Nelson Mandela was quick to forgive after being locked up like a bird in Robin Island for over 20 years, but there is still racism in South Africa to this day. This is the reason behind most African leaders' deliberate retaliation. They are still emotionally wounded and they were never apologised to when they took over power. Grudges can only be removed through divine intervention. It can only be the work of the Holy Spirit if the hearts are repentant or ready to forgive, but the black African man has never been apologised to sincerely or respected as an equal being, even in the West. Settlements were reached but the dialogue was incomplete in that hypocrisy ruled the hearts of the oppressor even after the end of minority rule, especially in Zimbabwe and South Africa.

My father had a lot of stories of racial abuse he experienced as a young boy. However, I found that my parents prefer to withhold such stories from us. They do not want us to know much of what happened to them. My parents are both alive, but I have never felt easy asking about their lives because I know that the pain is still there.

My father would sometimes make a joke of his experiences. He told the story of when he required a birth certificate for school. He and his father had to travel for many miles on foot to the District Commissioner (DC). On their travels they passed sleeping lions, but when they arrived at the DC, a young white officer sent them back without the birth certificate because, as my father says, his father was too exhausted when they arrived there and he forgot to salute the young white officer. They were ordered to go back and come again another day when they would remember to salute him. There is no respect in that. The African culture, unlike the western culture, respects the older person. Even as siblings we were raised to respect each other.

I personally experienced a subtle racial battle in Zimbabwe from 1981 to 1992. I call it subtle because independence was already declared but my employer was still racist. In 1981 I had my first job as a legal secretary in a legal firm. I was the only black girl and they found it hard to share the same toilet as me, so they held a meeting to try to suggest that I use the public toilets outside the office. As I was already born-again, I laughed this away because I found it interesting that I was regarded as dirty. I had never experienced racism before as schools used to be separated by ethnicity. I never mixed with white people, so for me it was a new experience. What I found frustrating was the fact that I was the least paid for the same job as others. This never changed much for those who remained under the employment of a white boss. I could not understand how even those bosses that were born-again remained silent and unrepentant on this particular issue. I moved from the legal sector to the commercial industry and I found the same challenge. I would train young white girls fresh from college and still earn half of their income.

In the early 1990s, people in Bulawayo had a meeting with Joshua Nkomo about the suffering that was still happening at the hands of white employers in industry. In his reply, Nkomo said, "Start your own factories, and stop moaning about factories that don't belong to you." People got angry with him for saying this and saw him as abandoning and betraying them; but they were also all aware of the fact that he had his fair share of problems from the ruling party at the time, as described in his book. The news was dreadful to watch on television, as Parliament was always making fun of Nkomo and his cabinet ministers, booing them every time they tried to speak. This was now black on black. Meanwhile, the white Rhodesians capitalised on this situation. Most of them sold their homes and took all the money out of the country, which I would have also done if I were white. It was a very dreadful time and a very shameful time. We were now stuck under the brutal leadership of Robert Mugabe. Nkomo was going through a lot of frustration himself as far as the economy of the country was concerned, because this had been his target area of change that he had fought for all those years. The slow progress in Mugabe's government was not going down well at the time. Mugabe had not come to power with the same economic strategy for Zimbabwe as Nkomo.

What Nkomo said to the people was very true, but people did not know how to be free from racial oppression and servanthood, they were too used to bowing to the oppressor. However, I did not believe that starting our own factories was the solution as far as racism was concerned, because the international marketing of our raw material for imports and exports was very much in the control of our white cousins. Those are the positions they would not let any black person have. They did not mind Africans in the human resources department, or on the production side of manufacturing, but not in the areas of import and export and marketing.

Would white- and black-only factories be a solution to the problem? The answer is no. Unity of purpose is the only solution. As far as the Body of Christ around the world is concerned, the reality of the coming of the Lord Jesus Christ should strike home. I still believe that the white person as the oppressor of the black man is still holding the key to the solution for racism. The key is repentance and humility before God. The black man's dignity has been injured long enough. He may be a good preacher, but he is still black.

My childhood memories are distorted because of the suffering of our black parents and later in the 1970s the armed struggle to end racial segregation and oppression. I remember the footsteps I used to hear time and again of people running from police whistles, dogs chasing black people and gunfire. I was always curious to open the door and see, but we had to remain inside. I remember as a child in the late 1960s when we lived in Tshabalala Township in Bulawayo, I saw a police van stop and the white policemen with a huge dog forcing every black man into the van street by street. My father was pushed into the back of the police van that was crammed with black men. There was desolation about the coming times, the kind of desolation I saw three times in a vision in 1998. I remember later on that day in Tshabalala Township seeing my father coming back home having been released because he was an Anglican priest, but I was left to wonder about the rest of the men from the neighbourhood who were in the van. This was the kind of dominance and unfair treatment that forced black people into a revolutionary war.

The Western Christian community cannot ignore the issues of racism because God wants restitution in the Church. We have not heard or seen any actions of repentance in the Western Christian community at all. The racism problem is right before the eyes of the Western Christians. Their church denominations are still either black or white. There are still well known racist Christian communities and churches in the West that do not welcome black people. They do not even have to say to you that you are not welcome because their body language says it all. My 2½-year-old daughter used to tell me each time I picked her up from the toddler group that was run by the Anglican Church near me that "nobody spoke to me, nobody spoke to me". I used to believe her because each time I dropped her off nobody would really speak to me. I let her go twice and I stopped taking her for fear of damaging her emotions.

The white Christian clergy has known for many years that there is racism in their societies, but they remain silent because they support it. This is the reason change has been delayed. Even though legislation on equal opportunities was passed many years ago, the attitude of prejudice the Western Christian world holds towards black people is fixed. There is a reluctance to change. The leader of the British National Party (BNP) declared on television that only white people should remain in Britain and that Britain is a Christian country and will not tolerate certain religions like Islam. What he does not realise is that Jesus was kind to people of other religious beliefs; He did not hate them. He died for them too on the cross. Real Christians, who know the Christ that I know, will not resolve religious differences in such a hateful manner. The BNP leader is a typical Anglo-Christian descendant who ruined the gospel of the Lord Jesus Christ by spreading oppression, discrimination, division and hatred in Third World countries and hence the slave trade. After bringing the stolen African children to do all the dirty jobs in the West, suddenly the stolen children must disappear from Britain. Black British people, the generation of the stolen slave children, do not even know their original identity or which part of Africa their ancestors came from. They cannot speak a single African language. Where in Africa are they supposed to go?

I discovered that in the West black people were lied to, in that they were told that it was their parents who sold them into slavery. The truth of the terror of slavery was hidden from them. They were not told that slaves were children stolen from their back yards by the Arab and Portuguese traders. This was terrorism. Every other thing is a lie. Black villages were terrorised in that respect, in the same way as Mugabe is doing among the Ndebele/Zulu people of Zimbabwe. They were seized from their neighbourhoods never to go back to their parents again. This is the truth that was hidden from the surviving slave generations in the West.

My research on the history of Southern Africa shows that Christianity was like a lottery, in that it was only offered to those of a lighter skin colour, not to black people. Black people were not allowed to mix with their lighter-skinned brothers and sisters; they were forcefully removed from their black mothers to live in a society of their own and they were referred to as "coloured people". Ian Smith used the coloured people as the property of the state because they had white blood in them. The coloured men were forced to be in the military, they had no choice. They were raised to despise the black side of their families. Smith separated them totally from their black families, and most of them emerged to look for their black families after independence. The education system was also divided in colour. Rhodesia had white schools, coloured schools and black schools. It worked to our advantage but to the white people's disadvantage, because they never got to learn our language while we got to learn theirs.

The oppressor then granted that people of a darker skin should only be encouraged to worship Allah. The Moslem religion was actually encouraged and assisted by the oppressor, the Anglo-Catholic Christian Church. Satan used the racist missionary to divide God's people by way of religion. Christianity was offered to the middle and upper class, while the rest of the slaves and servants were pushed into the Moslem religion.

If the Anglo-Catholic missionaries encouraged the oppressed into Islam, when God actually sent them to introduce Him to His black people, was this not disobedience to God and the greatest mistake that the Anglo-Catholic missionary ever made? We reap what we sow. "Ye shall know the truth, and the truth shall make you free" (John 8: 32).

The damaging effects of racism in the Church are still very fresh among those from Southern Africa and especially black men. Black people in Africa and around the world need emotional healing as well as spiritual restoration. Jesus Christ was not properly introduced to the black man. The work of the Cross of Calvary was therefore defied by the West, in that Jesus was portrayed as a white man and one who only died for whites. This is what most bitter African people still say today. However, that is not what Jesus suffered for; He suffered and died for all nations.

When God kept sending me to His black pastors in Zimbabwe, I could not get through to them. I felt rejected and I thought it was perhaps because my husband is white, or I was perceived as unworthy to be sent to them. Apart from discerning the division in the Body of Christ among those I was sent to concerning the poor widows and orphans, I discerned a division and selfishness in the leadership. I also discerned a lack of love and commitment to the poor, the orphans and widows. But how can they give what they have never received?

The people in Matabeleland need to be reached with the gospel message of forgiveness, but it has been hard to reach the devastated families with the gospel of Jesus Christ with Mugabe still in power, as they are still very bitter. Some lost every family member, some have no limbs, girls were raped and left with babies whose fathers they do not even know, it is chaotic. Why did Britain do this to us in Matabeleland? Why did they hate Nkomo so much that they assigned a ruthless dog over us? God told Nkomo that he would have his land after 30 years, but the 30 years have long elapsed and Nkomo is long dead and Mugabe is completing his "clean-up" strategy without any interference from those who gave him rulership over us.

Our fathers did not suffer in vain. With God on our side, we will rebuild Matabeleland.

CHAPTER 23

The Way Forward

The Body of Christ has to rise up and take dominion in the earth. It is now the time for the Saints of the Lord to take control of the affairs of the kingdom of God on earth. We cannot be sitting back and letting the enemy ruin and delay the work of God any longer. Holiness in the Body of Christ will enable us to find the spiritual empowerment we require for change to happen. Jesus is coming soon. He wants to empower more and more people to reach the uttermost parts of the earth with the gospel of Jesus Christ. Television ministry is great and we thank God for it, but the spirit of boldness and the love of God will enable us to reach God's people with the presence of God.

Jesus paid the sacrificial price of death on the cross for the sins of the whole world, not just for one particular group of people. He already paid for us to be reconciled back to God. There is no other way to God except through the Lamb of God, our Lord and Saviour, Jesus Christ.

God wants men to worship Him

The challenge is that even born-again men in the church today find it hard to lift up their hands and worship God. They find it hard to dance and praise God. They are very conscious of themselves. They think that worshipping and dancing before God is a sign of weakness for a man. They do not realise that the opposite is the truth. The devil lied to them! He made them hard-hearted and foolishly arrogant, because he knew that when a man loves God he does exploits for the glory of God.

Don't get me wrong, I love men and I am married to one whom I love very much. But God wants us to open up to Him and trust Him as our

Father. He wants us to be able to run to Him like little children running to their father.

> *And they brought young children to him, that He should touch them: and His disciples rebuked those that brought them. But when Jesus saw it, he was much displeased, and said unto them, "Suffer the little children to come unto me, and forbid them not: for of such is the kingdom of God. Verily I say unto you, Whosoever shall not receive the kingdom of God as a little child, he shall not enter therein."*
>
> (Mark 10: 13–15)

The heart of a child is quick to repent. Children are quick to forgive and to forget. That is why they still go back to the one who slapped them a few minutes ago. That is why children should never be abused in any way. Jesus said, "Whosoever shall offend one of these little ones that believe in me, it is better for him that a millstone were hanged about his neck, and he were cast into the sea" (Matthew 9: 42).

Therefore, God is calling to everyone for intimacy, especially His male beings of every colour. Women have no problem with expressing themselves. Why do most men find it hard to open up about their feelings? There is pride in it because they do not want to feel vulnerable by letting go. They do not want to surrender totally to God; they like to take control of every area of their lives. God hates pride. The reason most young or old male human beings cannot show respect and affectionate love to women in their lives is simply because they lack intimacy with God, their Creator. God wants to see Men worshipping Him more and more.

Dr Miles Munroe has been preaching on this subject for a few years now. He states that a man must know his self-image so that he does not lend himself in debt trying to salvage his self-image, "the first beginning man". He states that the original male is a cultivator.

I believe that the reason in my vision I was shown only black men on their knees is because God wants to bring something beautiful out of the robbed and abused African people, but the African man is still set in his detrimental traditional ways. The mindset of the black man needs to be renewed in many aspects. I love and respect my African brothers, but only the truth will make us all free.

Traditionally, most African boys were raised with the idea that they are superior to girls. This was due to the fact that they carried the family name from generation to generation, as well as looked after their parents in their old age. Therefore, a male child would be esteemed and valued from an early age by both parents. Being born a girl was a disadvantage, in that girls were regarded as strangers in their own home. The stigma associated with being a girl was that you would increase and expand the name of people you were going to be married to. Parents of girls therefore did not invest in them in terms of education, as girls were supposed to learn how to run a home and care for everyone in their home from an early age. It was the girl's duty to ensure that there was hot water boiling for everyone's bath and breakfast in the morning. The sweeping of the yard was done in the early hours of the morning before others woke up. Boys were expected to open the stables for the livestock, milk the cows and bring the milk home for the girls to cook. They were therefore excluded from domestic chores such as fetching firewood, washing dirty laundry, cleaning the home, cooking or looking after the children.

A man traditionally married for his mother, not for himself. His wife was expected to work like a slave for the whole family. She was not expected to get exhausted. She was expected to function like a machine. Everyone would bring their dirty laundry to her and relax while the new bride did all the dirty laundry, cleaned the home inside out, and cooked for everyone. I watched with disbelief when I witnessed this traditional practice happening before my eyes not very long ago. No one could think of such a thing still happening in this day and age, but it is still happening right there among my own people.

Perhaps there may be other cultures that may identify with this kind of prejudice towards women. It does not impress God at all. He did not create women to be abused in this manner. Genesis 1 and 2 highlight the completion of the creation. Genesis 3 highlights the fall of man from sin and the consequences of the fall. Jesus then pays a special blood price for the redemption of mankind from the curse of sin and hence our restoration to our God (Galatians 3: 13–14). Any practice that abuses and enslaves another human being is cursed.

As a result of these abusive traditional and cultural beliefs, most African black men turn out to be very lazy and irresponsible husbands, never mind how educated they may be. They behave in a burdensome way to their wives, like grown babies. It is acceptable in African society for a married man to be promiscuous, but not for the woman; 90 per cent of wives in Africa do not trust their husbands at all. If you said you trusted your husband, they would laugh at you because they have probably seen him somewhere with another woman in his car or in a movie house or drinking place. Therefore because of such long-standing cultural traditions, born-again black men face a lot of challenges. The enemy brings them down through this iniquity of tradition and rebellion against God.

Another example is interference from his own mother and family. It is not the culture of Africans to wait for an invitation or to warn those they may wish to visit of their plans. They just turn up. Once the mother or sister of the man turns up and finds her son or her brother tending to his crying baby while the baby's mother catches up with her sleep, there would be great interference in the marriage because he would be told off for being under petticoat government. It would then be up to the man to take a stand and declare that he was now married and he would not have his mother or sister running his home. In most cases, even if he spoke out, the battle would end up involving the invisible forces, black magic. When a man takes a stand alongside his wife, the angry and jealous mother will do everything possible to prove to him that she gave birth to him and she has a right to control his life or even end it.

A friend of mine came from work in the evening only to be told by her maid that her mother-in-law had come in during the day and completely emptied the kitchen of all food and groceries she had for the month. Her mother-in-law ensured that her son's income came to her, and as a result of her interference my friend never knew where her husband's income went, hence their family's needs. She was too embarrassed to confide in anyone else about her mother-in-law's interference in her marriage. She could not trust anyone to keep it quiet. As a result she has, since her marriage over 20 years ago, carried the financial burden of raising and educating her family single-handedly.

Paul wrote that wives should submit to their own husbands in everything, but it is God's will for husbands to love and protect their wives. If a born-again husband allows his family members to turn his wife into their doormat, as is the case in most African marriages, then he is accountable to God. The word of God commands all wives:

Wives, submit yourselves unto your own husbands as unto the Lord. For the husband is the head of the wife, even as Christ is the Head of the church: and he is the saviour of the body. Therefore as the church is subject unto Christ, so let the wives be to their own husbands in everything. Husbands, love your wives, even as Christ also loved the church, and gave himself for it; That He might sanctify and cleanse it with the washing of water by the Word. That He might present it to Himself a glorious church, not having spot, or wrinkle, or any such thing; but that it should be holy and without blemish. So ought men to love their wives as their own bodies. He that loveth his wife loveth himself.

Ephesians 5: 28

So if born-again husbands fail to protect their wives from this enslaving African tradition, they will face the judgment of God. It would be better to quickly judge ourselves and repent from our unbiblical ways and traditions. The original will of God for us is written in Genesis 1 and 2. Once Adam and Eve sinned against God, the Spirit of God in Adam became inactive because he became a rebel. It was the beginning of men's rebellion from God. This is why God wants to restore His Church, but it is up to the Church to repent from their old unbiblical ways if God has to come in. God cannot restore where there is still disobedience and rebelliousness. Man's traditions are rebellious to God.

God wants to forgive, bless and restore His men. It is important for the man to be spiritually the leader in a home as this is God's order in a marriage. When a husband is spiritually dead, things get out of order in a marriage. Although a lot of women take up the leadership role of praying and teaching the ways of God to the children, it can be too burdensome for a wife who has sons only. Her sons need to see their father taking up the role of a spiritual model in the marriage. This is important for their future. The world today is full of boys who grow up without praying and worshipping fathers. God wants the man to reconnect with Him spiritually. If God as a spirit is not acknowledged in the life of a man, then a man who is not spiritually connected with God is an incomplete man.

Satan always uses those close to us to bring pain, division and misery in the life of a Believer. If he uses your own family members who you dearly love, you really have to tighten your belt and remember whose you are. Just because you have been born in a certain family does not mean you have to bow down to them.

> *But ye are a chosen generation, a royal priesthood, an holy nation, a peculiar people; that ye should shew forth the praises of him who hath called you out of darkness into his marvellous light.*
>
> *1 Peter 2: 9*

This is why God told Abraham to leave his people and dwell afar from them. God did not say take Lot with you. God wanted Abraham to enjoy his blessings without any interference from those who would take him for granted. God wanted an upright man that He could trust as a friend again; a man He could prove His goodness and lovingkindness to; a man of courage and obedience; a man who feared his God; a man who would give Him a reason to redeem man from his sins through His only Son, Jesus Christ. Abraham proved to be that man. He loved and obeyed God even before the Ten Commandments were introduced. He simply believed God for His Word. Today we want to know the catch first before we can take the step of obedience. We don't find it in our hearts to tithe or give obediently. It is like music in our ears when we read or hear about the promises of God.

As in Abraham and his cousin Lot's case, it is always the close people or family members who take men and women of God for granted. This is why it is very important for God's Servants to be sensitive to the leading of the Holy Spirit in the area of relationships. Some relationships delay the manifestation of the purpose of God in the life of those He has called. Therefore hanging around with wrong people can delay the progress of fulfilling the purpose of God in one's life. This has been the case in my situation. To be able to know who your enemies are is your first breakthrough towards fulfilling your purpose. The battle towards this discovery has been achieved through serious divine intervention.

Men in general, of whatever nationality, have too much time on their hands compared to women. That is why they have hobbies like planning evil terror attacks, gangs, engaging in extra-marital affairs, watching pornography and "men-only" drinking places, where you will find "acceptable female patrons". Hobbies should be carefully considered because they are satanic strategies to steal and turn the heart of the man from worshipping and spending quality time with His Creator. Most men spend a fortune on hobbies but fail to obey God in tithing and giving to the needs of the Church. This is rebelliousness.

Women sacrifice and settle for low-paid work just to provide for themselves and to gain better qualifications. Men give up easily. Such men are a liability to their wives. This is why lazy African black men have done nothing but bring trouble and health problems to their wives at home. They channel their energy in entertaining themselves through selfish habits such as promiscuity, visiting drinking houses and spending nights out with other women thus causing worry and misery to their hard-working wives and mothers of their children. Not to mention the number of orphans who walk the streets of Africa today due to the unfair and selfish cultural habits of men.

I have noticed that even in the body of Christ in Africa, men do not rebuke each other unto righteousness. When my ex-husband began to backslide, other male believers gossiped and laughed about it, instead of approaching him and quickly challenging him back to the Lord. I thought perhaps it was because we were all still in our early 20s at the time and were not experienced in issues concerning those who were stumbling. He definitely needed help because he rebelled even more into sin when he noticed that a particular Christian brother was giving him the cold shoulder at church. The fact that he told me about it means he knew why the brother was ignoring him and it caused him to give up. If that brother had channelled his anger in openly rebuking my ex-husband, I believe his anger would have been justified. It was not just anger, it was pride, the "holier than thou" attitude that the Pharisees had. Who knows, perhaps that brother could have been the one that would have won him back to the Lord quickly, as he was only in his early stages of backsliding. I had been trying hard to separate him from a friend who was drinking alcohol.

After my first marriage ended in my late 20s, I was waiting for the bus one day when a hypocrite of a "brother in Christ" who was a preacher as well came to me and expressed how sorry he used to feel for me because he used to see my ex-husband visiting a brothel all the time. I asked him why he hadn't told me. He said he thought I knew. He waited until I was divorced before coming to me about it. That is compassion at its best. I respect my former husband more than I respect Believers who failed to intervene when they saw him stumbling. There are witches and wizards that are professing Christians. They see things that could endanger your life but prefer not to interfere. We are supposed to be one as the Body of Believers. If something hurts your sister in Christ, it should hurt you as well. If you find yourself laughing and gossiping about something that causes pain to a Believer, you are a witch or a wizard.

Open rebuke is better than secret love. Faithful are the wounds of a friend; but the kisses of an enemy are deceitful.

Proverbs 27: 5, 6

Polygamy: A traditional excuse for promiscuity and sexual immorality

Sticking to one woman is a rare occurrence among African people because polygamy was part of their tradition and culture; decades ago, women did not mind sharing one husband because of his riches. I do not know how they tolerated it, but it seemed to work for most families. Even the women seemed to get along very well. My father had one wife and so did his father. None of my father's brothers had more than one wife.

Most African men use the long-standing tradition of polygamy as an excuse for promiscuity. This is simply rebellion against the Word of God. Satan is the enemy of our soul and we need to appreciate and embrace the Grace of redemption through Jesus Christ. We cannot allow traditional and cultural habits to undermine the suffering that Jesus endured on the Cross of Calvary for mankind. The penalty for rejecting the sacrificial price Jesus paid for our redemption from sin is very high, eternal damnation.

Silly African men use the case of Abraham in the Bible to excuse themselves for going after women all the time. What they fail to realise is that Abraham did not initiate the idea, his wife Sarah did. Even then, it was not normal because even though Sarah did it in faith, it caused her maid to dishonour her. It is important to realise that the enemy always plays with the mind. Even though Sara's maid dishonoured her, God still blessed her son Ishmael, because it was not his fault that he was born. God is a God of justice.

When God promises us something, it is important to follow His instructions carefully so that we do not end up causing problems for ourselves. This was the case with Sarah. She was told that she would have a son, but she looked at herself and doubted God. Most of us have been silently guilty of doing the same. We are fortunate today that our own weaknesses are not documented for the world to read. Jesus said remove the log in your own eye before you can remove the spec in somebody else's.

As a result, Sarah decided to help God without first asking Him if it was proper for her maid to bear Abraham's child. I am sure that in the same way that God had visited her before, He would have heard her and answered her. The mistake would have been stopped quickly, but she used her own mind to work how this was supposed to happen. God never ordained that a man should sleep with two women while they were both alive.

If it were God ordained and proper for women to accept sharing a man, God would have taken two ribs out of Adam to create two Eves; but the Bible tells us of only one rib that was taken from the man to create his helper, the woman, not his sex machine, punch bag or family slave.

The Lord Jesus came as the second Adam to restore man's heart back to God. Is the sacrifice God made for us all not enough for us to turn away from our sinful habits and let God be God in our lives? Tradition is a curse of iniquity. God hates traditions of men. It is the very curse of tradition that causes some Church denominations to disapprove of female preachers of the gospel. In the Book of Genesis when God created Adam and Eve, He never said that Eve was lower than Adam. God can use whom He chooses to use. If God did not approve of using women in His work, He would never have had women like Hannah the mother of a great prophet of God, Samuel who God used to anoint Saul and thereafter to anoint David. What about Rahab who assisted in saving the nation of Israel in their time of need; the prophetess Deborah who sang praise unto the Lord God of Israel; Esther who saved Israel from Haman's hateful plan of extinction; Ruth's bravery, love and humility; Elizabeth, the mother of John the Baptist; Mary, the mother of our Lord and Saviour Jesus Christ, a brave young slave girl, a virgin whose life was interrupted by God but humbly welcomed the challenge without any protest or disobedience to God.

Finally, apart from the first Adam, is there a man on this earth that was not carried in a woman's belly? Only the devil and his angels can stand up and say they were never born of a woman. So any man that abuses, despises and disrespects a woman is devilish and satanic.

The abomination in high places

Homosexuality is an acquired habit and a curse. It is found among religious priests as well, and it represents the lie and deception of the devil. It is Satan's strategy to destroy the Church and the order of God for humanity on earth, the family. It is also Satan's strategy to defy God's way of increasing us on earth, sexual intercourse between a man and a woman. Homosexuality focuses on the lust of the flesh and it is a sinful habit of rebelliousness against God, as is sex between man and animals. Sexual greed and the lustful nature of a man are due to the fall of Adam. For this sin to be found among priests is evidence of what Jesus warned His disciples, "Ye shall know them by their works." The reason we have heard or seen all this abomination in the church is due to the pride of the fallen man, who keeps running further and further from God, deliberately avoiding Him.

Young black African women trapped in prostitution

On 1 November 2009 at 4.50 a.m. I was woken up to record the following vision.

We stopped the car somewhere near what looked like an open marketplace. It was after hours for the market still to be open, but I could see people there and I was glad that it was still open. I left my husband in the car and rushed to pick what I wanted as I had already spotted it, but as I kept getting closer it was different from what it looked like from a distance.

As I got closer to what I thought was an open market for vegetables and things like that, it was actually something else. My upper body was suddenly all exposed and I had to run with my hands covering my chest area. I was so full of shame as there were men everywhere. I could hear a man commenting as he saw me. To my shock, what I thought was an open market was actually a huge cage full of young girls and women. They were all locked up in open cages like birds. It was a prostitute area and the cage was fully packed. I realised that they were used to being exposed and they were not bothered much about covering themselves like I was, but they had no choice; most of them were very miserable. Others were behaving very badly, dancing alone in a silly manner as if they were drugged or drunk. They all seemed to be trapped there. I kept going round looking but there was no food market, just the girls and young women in cages. A few were walking around outside as if guarding the place.

I decided to leave the area, as I did not feel safe at all there. Then I walked up the road. I noticed two people behind me pushing something like a huge wheelchair, but it was not a wheelchair. It was a woman my age or younger, but she had many marks on her face. Her face looked very unhealthy. She looked unhappy or very jealous of me. She passed a sarcastic comment about why I was looking at her. I was looking at her because the girl she was walking with suddenly disappeared with the man who was waiting on the side of the street. It was actually the scream that came from the area they disappeared to that made me stop and look behind me. The other woman did not seem bothered about the screaming girl. I ran to look, but I only saw a little girl dressed in pink on the other side of the pathway. She continued screaming, looking at something between where she was and where I was. She cried as if in shock and she kept bending down as she screamed. There was a man sitting down like a tramp between where she was and where I was and along a little narrow passageway. He seemed to be doing something weird or pulling something from his mouth like a head of an animal, like a goat. There was blood everywhere as if a slaughter or a delivery had just happened. I felt very uncomfortable with the scenario. I decided to go before taking a closer look, as I did not wish to see much of it.

It all seemed demonic, from the naked girls to the two who disappeared on the side of the pavement into the same area where this crying voice was coming from. It was demonic. It was abomination going on and it was a place in Africa. Then I was woken up to write it down. As I wrote it down, I realised that I had actually witnessed something similar in real life.

In about 1999, my family went on holiday to Belgium and Holland. As we arrived at Brussels immigration from the Eurotunnel, armed police ordered my children and me to stand on one side because I did not have a visa in my Zimbabwean passport. I had not really thought about it. We waited for them to finish the whole queue of people from the tunnel, after which they took us into their office for questioning. They had to make a decision to put a visa in my passport themselves, which I was very grateful for because my youngest daughter was sobbing non-stop by then. She did not wish to go back on the Eurotunnel again.

After a few days in Brussels we proceeded to Holland, where we spent a day in Amsterdam. We stumbled into the red light area, where the whole street was full of prostitutes in broad daylight. We had wanted to go for a walk along the river. I was not happy because the experience ruined my holiday.

We wanted food or drinks, I cannot remember now, but we headed for what we thought was a normal restaurant or pub where we saw a lot of men sitting around the tables outside. We were hoping to sit there as well, only to find that these men were actually enjoying a parade of black girls in underwear. The pub had large glass windows meant just for that purpose, to parade the young women. I stood there looking at these men and what they were cheering. But there was silence when we got there as they could see the anger and shock on my face. Inside the building was the owner of the business, a white woman sitting at the reception desk. The prostitutes were all black. They also looked at me and I could see they were unhappy with what they were doing. Their faces were miserable. I saw a cry for help. I did not like this at all, I felt very angry at all these men sitting there drinking and waiting so that after they are drunk they end up with those girls.

We left that place. All the way down the street were half-dressed, miserable and lonely looking black girls standing in apartment windows, waiting. I stopped to look further down and I could see a white man guarding the area. My 6-year old daughter actually pointed to an apartment further up, showing me more, so we stopped to look, where a girl in a white bra looked in our direction.

I did not like what I saw in Amsterdam. Those girls were definitely in prison. I do not think they even go anywhere. I wonder if they benefit from what they do or only the business owners benefit. Even when we went into the busy area where people seem to be all enjoying their lives, I could not forget about those girls. I hated Holland so much that I could not wait to leave.

After I was reminded of the sin in Amsterdam by my vision, I researched on the internet about it. I found out that most of these black girls were sex traded from Nigeria. They are lied to by the people who coerce them into leaving their country. They believe that they are going for an education and that everything is arranged for them. Once they are there they are told that they cannot leave until they have paid all the costs of bringing them to the West. They are ten times more; so high that it would take a lifetime to settle the bill. This is how they are trapped. In Nigeria their families never hear from them again. Research revealed that the trade also involves witchcraft from Nigeria and black men are involved in it, working in association with white madams at each end.

I realised when I spoke to people after I witnessed the caged black girls in Amsterdam that most people in the UK know about it and they say it has been that way for years. People are not aware that some of those came as little girls and are stuck. There is a difference between a free prostitute and a caged one. A freelance prostitute has a chance of finding refuge or information to liberate herself from her bondage, whatever is making her choose prostitution for a lifestyle. It is obvious that white prostitutes are also there, but they are not in the public eye in glass windows with only nylon bikinis and bras like those young black women.

What I see here is an unrepentant attitude in the West as far as the rights of a black skin are concerned. Every young African person comes to the West hoping for an education and a better life than the one they leave behind. If young black African women are publicly imprisoned in the Western world for white men's sexual pleasure, then the slave trade is still there but in a subtle way.

But God will deliver His people from bondage in the same way that He delivered Israel from Pharaoh's captivity. If God opened the Red Sea for the Israelites to escape the bondage of Pharaoh in Egypt, He will open a pathway for the freedom of the encaged sexual slaves to escape the captivity of the white madams, the legalised brothel owners and the Pharaohs of today.

An oppressed man is bound to be an oppressor

An oppressed man knows nothing but the pain of oppression. So how can African leaders who suffered such great humiliating oppression from

Western colonialists be able to treat their subjects with love and respect? They cannot give what they never received. As a result of their own struggle to gain independence and liberation from the Western oppressor, they became hard-hearted and unforgiving. As if this was not enough, instead of being freely compensated for their long-suffering, deprivation and oppression by the West, African leaders were treated as borrowers. As a result, the West continues to exploit Africa and watches in silence as black African leaders oppress their own subjects.

I watched the news in the early 1990s when a campaigner for the Ogoni people of Nigeria came to Britain to seek help from the British government; it was the late Ken Saro Wiwa. He was of an Ogoni tribe and was raised in an Anglican Church home. He was the founder of the Movement of the Survival of the Ogoni People (MOSOP), whose hometown in the Niger Delta has been used for crude oil extraction for over 50 years. British immigration refused him asylum and it was resolved that he should be sent back to Nigeria. This happened and he was executed.

Ken Saro Wiwa had been campaigning over the oil issue in Nigeria. The oil fields in his village area were not properly managed, as a result of which the villagers were unable to cultivate their land due to the damage created by the leaking oil to their land and hence the danger and threat to the Ogoni people's lives from the randomly burning oil fields. The Nigerian government then was benefiting from the oil trade with the West, despite the plight of its own people. Even though Nigeria had long been liberated from colonial oppression, the effects of oppression are still being reaped.

God Himself is now ready to empower the Africans to rise and preserve what is left. The battle for Africa is no longer a quest for guns and all kinds of manmade ammunition; it is a battle for the supernatural power of God. The African man has to be willing to receive this empowerment from God. "If ye are willing and obedient, ye shall eat the good of the land" (Isaiah 1: 19). God alone can enable the African man to achieve change. God alone can bring healing and restoration to the broken hearts and lives of the African people. With God before us, who can be against us?

African Believers in the Western world have been shown that life can be better for God's people in the Third World. It is time for the Body of Christ to reject the oppression and injustice of the Western world. It is time for the Believers and followers of Jesus Christ in the West to campaign against Third World debt, which must be cancelled. It is time to give back to Africa what was stolen from it. Africa needs its dignity back.

If My people, which are called by My name, shall humble themselves, and pray, and seek my face, and turn from their wicked ways; the I will hear from heaven, and will forgive their sin, and will heal their land. (2 Chronicles 7: 14)

The black man's contribution to western wealth goes without recognition

It should sincerely be appreciated that the riches of the West were very much the work of the black slaves. The slave child cultivated, watered and harvested the cotton fields and sugar plantations of America that earned the country's revenue and riches, putting the West in good stead economically. Although many black slaves perished in the gold mines of Southern Africa, the gold they mined was not for their benefit, it was for the oppressor's benefit?

In Zimbabwe (then Rhodesia) and South Africa, many Anglo-American companies that mined products like cement, coal and asbestos left a lot of African people with uncompensated respiratory problems, resulting in great suffering and loss of life to this day. Asbestos was used in Rhodesia for hospital and building purposes, for the roofing of most low-cost houses that are still occupied by mainly the poor today. Entire communities in South Africa where asbestos was mined are still affected today. Residential homes were built around the quarry. Children play in the dust and the wind in the area is always causing this dangerous dust to fly everywhere. In Bulawayo, for example, you can see the mopane trees in that area all covered in cement dust, yet the workers' compound is also situated in the mining vicinity.

I observed on BBC television before her unfortunate death that the late Diana, Princess of Wales bravely visited the parts of Africa where postcolonial Western-sponsored banditry and unrest had resulted in landmines and other explosives that were left buried in the ground and no efforts were ever made to remove such life-threatening traps. The innocent victims have endured the consequences of this evil. The late Princess of Wales was seen on television touching and feeling the pain of the children whose limbs had been lost while at play. She highlighted the unfairness of supplying landmines and such explosives to Africa and how thousands were left buried by those who planted them, totally disregarding the deadliness of the environment they were creating for the future innocent generations of poor African countries.

How soon will the supernatural wealth transfer occur in the earth?

The decision is up to the Church. Jesus is coming soon!

God never stopped empowering his Saints financially. A few holy ones have always been empowered. More faithful stewards are required for this purpose. Not every Believer is an heir of Salvation. It is only those who have been faithful and obedient to Him. God wants to empower the Church at large for His word to be completed in these last days, but this requires unity in the Church. His Grace still abounds, but how much time we have is not known to anyone except God.

According to Matthew 5: 14, we are the light of the world. Only the risen Christ in us would make us shine in a dark world. Without Him, the Holy Spirit cannot reside in us, and therefore it would be impossible to be the light in the darkness.

The Holy Spirit is the One who empowers us to bring change in our lives. He cannot operate where there is division. This is why I related earlier on the vision I saw about the bodies of bulls that were turning round and round on the same spot without any heads. These were church denominations where commotion of all kind is rife; Christ is not part of these proud and headless ministries.

For the power of the Holy Spirit to intervene in this end time of challenge and war against division in the Church, we all have to acknowledge before God as the Body of Saints of God that we are all guilty of the sins of the Church. We all have to kick pride out of our lives and repent before God in one accord and in humility.

> *If my people, which are called by my name, shall humble themselves, and pray, and seek my face and turn from their wicked ways; then will I hear from heaven, and will forgive their sin, and will heal their land.*
>
> 2 Chronicles 7: 14

Lack of repentance, pride, rebelliousness, division and jealousy are what caused Satan to be demoted and dumped from his position in Heaven to earth. He rebelled against God when he should have repented. He influenced part of God's angels to rebel against God, thus causing division in heaven. Satan wanted to ruin and steal God's worship and turn the angels of worship to himself, because he wanted to be like God.

The reason for the prolonged physical bondage of the people in Zimbabwe is due mainly to the Church's rebelliousness and compromise, even by some pastors or ministers. If they repent from their ways, God will deliver them from their Goliath. It took only a little faithful boy, David, and a few stones to bring Goliath down.

To the Christian Church in Zimbabwe

The government of Zimbabwe is a reflection and image of the Church and the family in Zimbabwe. There is a serious parallel in the three areas I have highlighted in Zimbabwe as it was revealed to me. The evil of neglect and hatred that happens in the government of Zimbabwe is also happening in the Church and in the families there. There is a merciless satanic stronghold of division and mortality that needs to be identified and pulled down.

God rewards obedience to Him and integrity. Shortcuts do not work. Anything that comes easy goes easy. Zimbabwe came easy for Robert Mugabe; he never suffered for it like Joshua Nkomo or Josiah Tongagara, the original ZANLA Commander whom Mugabe killed in Mozambique. Everything was given to him on a silver platter; that is why he has easily destroyed such a beautiful country of such a hardworking people.

Most Christians in Zimbabwe are so used to begging that when they are asked to tithe and sow seeds to the work of God, they get depressed. They are so impatient that even those who sow want to reap the following day. They cannot wait for their seeds to germinate and bring increase to them. Instead of watering the seeds with prayer and praise to God in their waiting, they kill the seeds they sow by complaining about the delay in their harvest. The sowing and reaping principle here on earth is parallel to the spiritual one. There is always a season of watering and cultivating in between the period of sowing and reaping. Most Zimbabwean believers do not know this principle, yet most of us were raised by peasant farmers. We lived and survived on the harvest of our hard work. We should know better. What makes us think when we sow seeds in our churches we should get a harvest the next day? Impatience is a sign of a lack of faith in God. God only rewards those who trust Him, those who wait. My God is a patient God. He is still patiently waiting for rebellious people to turn from their sin and come back to Him with a repentant heart. He will forgive them because they are His creation.

Some of you say you are holy and yet you hide a lot of filth within your homes and in the management of your church ministries and you say God cannot see. You are very proud of the way your ministries appear on the outside. You are so used to your ways of compromise that they are just a normal way of life now to you. But they are not normal ways before the eyes of God. You say in your hearts that no one can see. But you hurt your flock and carry on as if you did nothing and you have made it your habit to hurt those who do good unto you, just as most family members are in the habit of doing. When your flock come to you for help and you see their weaknesses, you abuse them even further and you condemn them when you should be encouraging and comforting them, just as it also happens in most families. The oppression of God's vulnerable people around you is not anything you are concerned about.

Most Christians, like family members in Zimbabwe, only keep demanding from their relatives in the diaspora, yet they do not really love, care or pray for them; they only want to keep receiving financial help from them. They are selfish users. They only contact you for the money you work hard for, while they spend their time in gossip, witchcraft, lies and selfishness. They say nobody sees it. Are their ways of compromise hidden from God?

Some so-called pastors open churches in Britain just for the benefit of getting tithe in pound sterling. They pursue their subordinate pastors in the diaspora, demanding from them and emptying their churches of all the tithes and offerings. The donations they get for the poor in Zimbabwe are channelled into their own personal use. They then wonder why there is so much suffering in Zimbabwe.

The Body of Christ in Zimbabwe has the answer to these questions! God cannot oppose Himself where there is rebelliousness because the devil knows the truth of God's principles. If God opposed Himself and condoned what His Servants do, how would He explain this to Satan? The problem of Zimbabwe is not with Mugabe's government, but with the Church that is corrupt.

The young orphaned girls and women are in prostitution around you, being abused for their poverty while you pass them by and do not want anything to do with it. You thrive by undermining other people, being triumphant over their weaknesses, yet you say in your hearts you are the Servants of the Lord. You want your flock to honour you but you do not want to honour God in your ways. Your hidden ways of compromise deny Him. God is not part of your ministries. Jesus is not the head of your denominations.

He will raise Himself worshippers from the orphans, from the widows and from the very prostitutes that you pass by on your streets. If He cannot be worshipped in purity in your denominations, a voice of worship shall arise from the homeless on the street and under your bridges. The homeless orphans will worship Him in purity. Jehovah will raise Himself worshippers from nothing, who will worship Him in Spirit and in Truth. He will hear their voice of worship and tend to their needs. They will drink from the wells they did not dig and they will occupy the houses they did not build.

> *Thou givest thy mouth to evil, and thy tongue frameth deceit. Thou sittest and speakest against thy brother; thou slanderest thy own mother's son. These things hast thou done, and I kept silence; thou thoughtest that I was altogether such an one as thyself: but I will reprove thee, and set them in order before thine eyes. Now consider this, ye that forget God, lest I tear you in pieces, and there be none to deliver. Whoso offereth praise glorifieth me: and to him that ordereth his conversation aright will I shew the salvation of God.*
>
> *Psalm 50: 19–23*

God has not failed to save the people of Zimbabwe from Robert Mugabe and his henchmen. God is able to change the 30-year problem in 30 seconds if the people of Zimbabwe repented from their sinful ways, especially the black Zimbabweans. If God is not well represented in the Church then forget it. God cannot oppose Himself. He cannot restore where there is compromise, pride, hatred, greed, selfishness, witchcraft and all kinds of filth.

Selfishness, hatred, pride and greed are on the increase in most families, including the Body of Christ in Zimbabwe. Most black Zimbabwean Christians are writhing with sins of abomination including witchcraft, the abuse of the poor, disrespect for widows and women of all ages, and neglect of the homeless and orphans due to lack of love and compassion. In one second the restoration of the nation of Zimbabwe would commence if the Body of Christ totally humbled itself before God in repentance, but most normally do so with one eye closed and the other one open, or with feet astride just in case it does not work so they could always go back to their old ways. God cannot be fooled; He cannot be mocked; He cannot be bribed.

In an African news report, the Christian Church in the capital city of Harare was turned into a war zone. Members of St Paul's Cathedral were physically involved in fighting leading to church boycotts by some members, while others continued to risk their lives by attending services. The report stated that a great division occurred due to a political divide in the church leadership.

Jesus' warning to his disciples was that "you shall know them by their works". Some denominations continue to be influenced by Satan in rejecting the Grace of God through our Lord Jesus Christ, therefore proving that their foundation was never based on the Living Word of God but on unbiblical doctrine. "Except the Lord build the house, they labour in vain that build it: unless the LORD keep the city, the watchman wakes but in vain" (Psalms 127:1).

Restoring the black man is also God's focus in this end time

Wangari Maathai, the author of *The Challenge for Africa: New Vision*, states that the African man should be re-introduced to the family. She also highlights the consequences suffered due to the separation of the man from his family by the oppressor, the colonialists. Wangari's detailed account of the consequences suffered by the African family is an inner cry that every African family has had to endure decade after decade. We thank God for raising people like Wangari, who are able to get painful issues out of their system and document them for future African generations. She has managed in her book to paint a true picture that almost every African can truly identify with. I have never been to Kenya, but her detailed account is identical to the Zimbabwean issues. This only makes me realise how similar African culture is. It is only the languages that separate us.

The book calls for action by all concerned. This is not the time to be reading such books and doing nothing about the writer's inner cries. It is time for change. It is time for the African man to rise up and drop the slave and beggar's mentality and take the initiative for change for the future generations of Africa.

The true Jesus should be re-introduced to the black man, the true liberating Gospel of our Lord Jesus Christ, not the Anglo- Catholic enslaving Gospel that came with constitutions that robbed and enslaved the whole continent of Africa, reducing the Black Man to powerlessness, slavery and begging. The Romans behind Anglo-Catholic Christianity are the ones who misrepresented Jesus Christ to the Third World nations. They preached the Gospel of the Virgin Mary as the important figure and the mediator between man and God, a myth that does not exist in the Holy Bible. They caused Jesus to be rejected by the souls He died for. Jesus already paid a blood price for every soul on the earth today. Yet those that God entrusted with the preaching of His Gospel hid the true gospel from His people.

The Anglo-Catholic Church prays to the dead Virgin Mary and they also pray for the dead Saints. This is not biblical; where do they get this scripture? The Word is against consulting the dead or speaking to the dead on behalf of the living. Only the rebellious man does this. King Saul did it after God rejected him. He visited the Witch of Endor in his desperation to speak to his spiritual mentor, Samuel the prophet of God. Samuel was not alive, but Saul asked the witch to raise his soul so that he could consult him. The witch did it and Samuel was not amused to be disturbed from his peaceful sleep. Even Jesus said let the dead bury the dead, because he was putting the message across to the ignorant people that they should really be concerned about the living not the dead. Some people go out of their way just to put a beautiful costly tombstone on a grave.

We cannot choose to keep rejecting Christ because of the way He was introduced to us by the oppressor, the Anglo-Catholic missionary. When God sent the missionary to preach to His African people, He did not say the missionary should also enslave and oppress them. This was disobedience on the part of the missionary. Disobedience has its consequences.

We should therefore open our eyes and ask ourselves why they are not following the teachings of the Holy Bible. Why do they prefer their church doctrine of praying by way of catechisms and through the Virgin Mary? We have a choice to make: to remain blind to the truth or to open our eyes and see who is behind Christianity as a religion.

Terrorism is the Goliath that is symbolic of the rebelliousness of the Christian Church and its failure to represent the true Gospel of Jesus the Christ that was entrusted to it. "God is no respecter of persons" (Acts 10: 34)

The Lord Jesus has been deeply wounded by this. He did not die for His Gospel to be diluted and belittled. Esteeming marriage between two men or homosexuality (Sodom and Gomorrah's sin), the removal of God's teachings about acceptable ways of compromise as in sex before marriage or living together outside marriage, fornication and adultery, all in the name of freedom of choice and political correctness, have been seen as abomination in high places by God. Other examples are condoning the oppression of black people in the systems of the West; condoning the oppression of poor women by sex traders in the West; condoning ways that undermine the importance of the God-ordained order of the family; separating children from their biological families through the social care system and thereafter failing to mentor them spiritually and in accordance with Holy scriptures, that the Christian Church has done; rigging elections and causing ethnic cleansing in Africa and nation to rise against nation; condoning abomination by letting politicians run the affairs of the world with total disregard for the Creator of Heaven and Earth.

If my people which are called by my name shall humble themselves, and pray, and seek my face and turn from their wicked ways; then will I hear from heaven, and will forgive their sin, and will heal their land.

II Chronicles 7: 14

Jesus did not come to this earth to introduce religion. He came to introduce the Kingdom. God has anointed His men around the world to preach the message of the Kingdom in these end times. As Dr Myles Munroe of the Bahamas clarifies, Jesus came to establish the Kingdom of Sons, not a kingdom of servants. King Jesus died to protect His subjects;

servants die to protect their kingdom. He further states that religion is man trying to reach God, but the Kingdom is God trying to reach man. "From that time Jesus began to preach, and say, Repent for the Kingdom of heaven is at hand" (Matthew 4: 17).

CHAPTER 24

To All the Saints Around the World

I n this book there has been a lot of discussion on the liberation war
that took place in Zimbabwe from the 1960s to the 1980s. It has
spoken about the missionaries, the oppressors, the terrorists, war
rebels and dissidents. It has also highlighted the effects of these on the
innocent victims of war. It has put forward disobedience to the voice of
God as the reason for the war, the strategies that were employed in this
war and the hope the war was meant to bring to those who started it.
It has then stressed the consequences of disobeying God's voice, such
as confusion among the fighters, including the betrayal of Nkomo by
Mugabe, the discouragements, its futility and the little that was achieved.
We have seen how there are ongoing massacres in Matabeleland and how
the Zimbabweans and other Africans have been scattered abroad due to
the legacy of Western colonisation.

This proves beyond any doubt that God never created us to dominate
each other. Nothing works outside the original plan and manual of God
for humanity. All these are consequences of disobeying the original voice
of God by taking vengeance into our own hands against the offender, yet
vengeance belongs to God.

Can the United Body of Believers in Christ around the world learn
something from this mistake? After all has been said and done, God still
has the ultimate voice and a plan and purpose for this end time we are in.

There is a parallel between what we read in this book and the end-
time war we are about to enter as born-again Believers in Christ. However,
we are now entering a different kind of war. It is a Holy War Against
Division in the Church (WADIC). The Saints as the Army of God against
the oppressor of mankind, (Satan and his henchmen) have declared this
war. This war requires certain skills, without which one cannot qualify

to be a positive part of it, but would be an enemy to one's brothers and sisters. Such a person would be a dissident, a rebel, a sell-out and a terrorist informer.

In my own experience of the war of liberation in Rhodesia back in 1979, a group of young combatants arrived at my parents' home and pressed me to address a political meeting in my local community, because others of my age were dying in the bush. I first protested using the excuse that my involvement in the war was through prayer and nothing else. Even though my mother was in the room, I was faced with a decision I had to make independently of my mother. I had only just turned 20 and was very young in the Lord. All I knew was how to testify to the world about how the Lord saved my soul, but I could not imagine myself addressing a political meeting. I had to quickly recall that I could have been one of the fighters in the bush if my cousins had not run away without me, thus appreciating the fact that I was privileged to have remained behind to be born-again. Others perished in the bush without knowing the Lord. Where much is given much is required.

I had to learn to be a politician at speed on our way to the community hall and they helped me recite answers to the possible questions the crowd would throw at me. I had to recite the reason Joshua Nkomo and ZIPRA were at war, their strategy for peace now that we were facing the upcoming elections, the first opportunity for a black person in Rhodesia to cast their vote. Nkomo trusted the wrong man. He failed to discern Mugabe's motives in good time. Spiritual discernment would have saved the nation of Zimbabwe and especially thousands of lives in Matabeleland from the Mugabe's 5 Brigade holocaust.

The parallel to the Holy War we are about to enter is that most of us will have to learn to evangelise in less than half an hour and to lay our hands on the sick and bring deliverance to the captives and the bound. There will be no one idle in this end time. There will be no time to listen to testimonies. Just as we read how Jesus went about doing good and how He never waited to be thanked or appreciated for His work, there will be no time to expect people to come to us and say thank-you. The work will be done at great speed. What God's evangelists and pastors, men and women of God have been doing all these years we will all learn to do in less than half an hour. We will develop the same compassion for the burden that evangelists have been carrying on their own. The wealth of the sinner will be supernaturally removed from the sinner's control to God's faithful stewards around the earth. Pastors and evangelists will not have to waste time appealing for financial help to do the work of God. The faithful stewards of this wealth will be distributing it towards the work of God. This is how the Gospel will be preached at great speed.

> *And I will shake all nations, and the desire of all nations shall come: and I will fill this house with glory, saith the Lord of hosts. The silver is mine, and the gold is mine saith the Lord of hosts.*
>
> *Haggai 2: 7–8*

> *And Joshua said unto the people, sanctify yourselves: for tomorrow the Lord will do wonders among you.*
>
> *Joshua 3: 5*

Therefore to qualify to be in the Army of God the following qualities must be urgently developed in every born-again Believer in Christ:

- Trust in God
- Holiness – meditation on the Word of God and obeying it
- A life of prayer and intercession
- Love, compassion, humility and always forgiving
- Sensitivity to the Holy Spirit for divine leading and direction
- Faithfulness to God and to the Body of Christ
- Integrity – being honest and trustworthy to the Body of Christ
- Longsuffering, patience and courage, not giving up
- Relentlessness and perseverance in prayer
- Focus on the purpose of the war and on Christ
- Praise and worship to God

In my vision, I heard a loud voice saying, "Worship! Your tool to departure as the world's economic system changes."

What is the significance of the word economy? Those who have studied economics know what the word involves in the world. However, I will explain as revealed to me the significance of the word and its relevance to the Church, the Bride of Christ today. The subject is one that most Christians hate. But Believers who love Christ love it and understand its function and its importance in the period we have entered.

If you have not been faithful and obedient to God in the area of tithing to the Kingdom of God according to Malachi 3: 10 and sowing or giving according to Luke 6: 38, you will not be able to reap a harvest from the forthcoming supernatural wealth transfer. This means, you will *not* have a Kingdom Account to withdraw from. 2 Chronicles 20: 20 states, "Believe in the Lord your God, so shall ye be established: believe in His prophets, so shall ye prosper." You will then live like a beggar, begging from those who have been sowing and tithing faithfully and obediently to God. To have food to eat, you might find yourself being a sell-out in the Kingdom like Robert Mugabe or Judas Iscariot. You will betray God's wealthy Saints just to get food for you and your family and friends. You will be vulnerable to the enemy that the Army of God is about to fight in unity worldwide. The enemy will target you as a disobedient one to God and use you against the Body of Christ.

You manipulated God just like you manipulated others in the House of God through gossip and caused them to be disobedient to the voice of God like you. You ate the tithe because you did not trust God to look after you. You will miss out because of your disobedience to God and to His servants who preached to you and you never cared to obey them according to 2 Chronicles 20: 20. So you will be full of jealousy and this will cause you to be a threat to the faithful and just to God. You will betray them to Satan's terrorists, the ones that are about to lose their wealth to the just. You have been hanging around with the just, so you know them very well. Therefore you will be able to identify them to their enemies just so you can get food.

However, for the rebellious believer, there is still an opportunity to qualify to the supernatural wealth transfer that is about to take place, but on one condition: You will have to sow double what you should have been sowing ever since you were first asked to sow (double for your disobedience in order to have an Account in the Kingdom which you can withdraw from). Your seed could have brought many souls into the Kingdom, but you deprived souls from being reached by the Gospel of the Lord Jesus Christ. Preachers and evangelists were dependent on the seeds that you could have sown in their ministries to enable them to do the work of God, but you were tight-fisted because you saw them as the beneficiaries of your money themselves, and you gossiped about them. You lied and blasphemed against the people of God. God be with you, because if you still fail to obey now you will be like Judas Iscariot in the Kingdom, a threat to the Saints of God.

Therefore we have a responsibility as the Saints of God to identify our friends from our enemies, the betrayers. We should separate ourselves from our enemies. Some enemies are anointed; God will reveal them to us. But do not forget that Saul was anointed when he visited the Witch of Endor. The Holy Spirit reveals all truth. He will show us who our true friends are and who our enemies are. It is for our own good if we are to win this battle that we humble ourselves before God always. Humility will enable us to identify the wolves among us. The wolves are selfish, full of envy, jealous and greedy, haters, liars, pretenders, gossipers, deceivers and they hate the truth.

> Blessed is the man that walketh not in the counsel of the ungodly, not standeth in the way of sinners, nor sitteth in the seat of the scornful. But his delight is in the law of the Lord; and in his law doth he meditate day and night. And he shall be like a tree planted by the rivers of water, that bringeth forth his fruit in his season; his leaf also shall not wither; and whatsoever he doeth shall prosper.
>
> *Psalm 1: 1–3*

God's Holy Angels are now positioned to remove the wealth from the sinner to the just. It can happen any minute, even while you are still pondering on it and dilly-dallying. The reason is that the suffering people of God have been waiting for too long for help: the orphans, the homeless, the poor and forsaken. Most of you might have seen or heard on television or on social media the Servants of God (His Preachers) constantly appealing for money to help the poor lives globally. This appeal was a set-up by God and it is still on-going. God is not short of money, He is simply giving many the opportunity to learn to be givers as HE is a Giver to us Himself. HE gave us Jesus, His only begotten Son, for the remission of our sin for our salvation from eternal damnation. Giving to the poor is an opportunity to participate in the burden of the Lord Jesus Christ in this end time, The poor are the burden of the Lord and learning to give is an important principle championed by God Himself. He also wants the poor reached with the gospel and saved. He wants them saved, healed, restored and empowered both spiritually and financially. He wants His lost delivered from the captivity of Satan and his demonic world of darkness. There are others still trapped in it that are still not yet reached with the Gospel. God wants justice for the hurting in the earth. His black people in the so-called Third World have been rejected and forgotten for too long. Even when they came to the West, the West remained blind to their cries, but oppressed them further. When they wanted help they were thrown into prison or sent back to Africa.

The justice system is about to change. The current justice system on the earth does not reflect heaven. The current justice in the earth is wicked and corrupt. God is now taking over complete control of the justice system on earth.

God's promises to His people who have been robbed and left hurt are very clearly stated in the Holy Bible:

And I will restore to you the years that the locust hath eaten, the cankerworm, and the caterpillar, and the palmerworm, my great army which I sent among you. And you shall eat in plenty and be satisfied, and praise the name of the Lord your God, that hath dealt wondrously with you: and my people shall never be ashamed.

Joel 2: 25–26

Whenever Jesus did a good deed, He was opposed and criticised by the Pharisees and the Sadducees. Even when he walked away from them, they would still follow Him just to see what He was up to. He maintained His focus in what He was supposed to do and therefore He could not be put off by His critics from doing what mattered to Him. He had tenacity. Even though people hurt Him, none would come back and say sorry. When He healed people they did not come back to Him to say thank-you either, except for one Samaritan who was among the ten lepers that cried to Jesus for help from a distance, who when he saw that he was healed, turned back and with a loud voice glorified God and fell down on his face at His feet giving Him thanks. And Jesus answering said:

> *Were there not ten cleansed? But where are the nine? There are not found that returned to give glory to God, save this stranger. And He said unto him, Arise, go thy way: thy faith hath made thee whole.*
>
> *Luke 17: 17–19*

God knows the names of every politician and every judge and everyone in authority. He is the Most High God who is the first cause of everything. "The earth is the Lord's and the fullness thereof, the world and they that dwell therein" (Psalm 24: 1).

To the married women in ministry

No one has a right to stop women from obeying the unction of the Holy Spirit. The traditions of men must never be allowed to hold God's women back from obeying God. When Mary was told that she would be filled with the Holy Ghost and conceive a baby, she did not say to the Angel of God, "Only if Joseph agrees." She quietly obeyed and accepted. While Joseph was still pondering on how to get rid of Mary from his life, the Angel of God appeared to him and summoned him to stick with her and to support her.

Matthew 1: 18–20 and 25 states:

Now the birth of Jesus Christ was on this wise: When as his mother Mary was espoused to Joseph, before they came together, she was found with child of the Holy Ghost. Then Joseph her husband, being a just man, and not willing to make a public example, was minded to put her away privily. But while he thought on these things, behold the Angel of the Lord appeared to him in a dream, saying Joseph thou son of David, fear not to take unto thee Mary thy wife: for that which is conceived in her is of the Holy Ghost. And she shall bring forth a son, and thou shall call his name Jesus: for he shall save his people from their sins. Now all this was done, that it might be fulfilled which was spoken of the Lord by the prophet, saying, Behold, a virgin shall be with child, and shall bring forth a son, and they shall call His name Emmanuel, which being interpreted is, God with us. Then Joseph being raised from sleep did as the Angel of the Lord had bidden him, and took unto him his wife:
And he knew her not till she had brought forth her firstborn son: and he called his name Jesus.

Traditionally and according to Deuteronomy 24: 1, Joseph had a right under the circumstances to break his engagement from Mary, but He had to obey the voice of God and still marry Mary and father Mary's baby. While the baby grew in Mary's womb, Joseph feared God in his heart and would not know Mary as his wife during that period of nine months. So from the example of Mary the mother of Jesus, married women in the ministry should fear God and put God first, and so should their husbands. No husband should compete against God. The work of God should not be adulterated.

If God has assigned a married woman to a special mission, she should be respected while she is on God's mission. The will of God should come first, before our own. This is giving God the Glory that He deserves. He created marriage. No man should behave as if they created marriage. So to come between his wife and God would be rebelliousness to God. Once the woman finishes doing what God has assigned her to do, she would know, as the Holy Spirit would confirm it with her. She can then resume her duties as a wife to her husband. No married woman in Ministry should feel intimidated by her husband when it comes to the work of God.

All men in the earth are born of a woman. Women are not lesser beings. We should be careful of those who despise women.

The traditions of man have been very oppressive to God's women. We must reject them otherwise we may miss the mark. Women are equally valuable to God as soldiers in His end time army against the satanic spirit of oppression and division. Women should not allow themselves to be affected by those the enemy uses to despise and undermine women in ministry. Women should press on towards the mark of the high calling that Paul encouraged himself to press for. Women are no lesser beings. God uses whom He chooses.

Intimacy with God

Now unto Him that is able to do exceeding abundantly above all that we ask or think, according to the power that worketh in us, unto Him be Glory in the Church by Christ Jesus, throughout all ages, world without end, Amen.

Quality time in worshipping God develops intimacy with him.

You will recall the vision I saw in October 2008, where the man hoped to engage the spouse but the spouse was throwing the ring away. Then there were brides dressed in red being dragged to the wedding because they did not want intimacy with the groom.

God sacrificed His Son for us to have eternal life. The blood of Jesus was shed for us. There is power in the blood of Jesus. We are washed by the blood of Jesus from all sin and made pure and worthy to be called God's children, sons and daughters. Jesus made us righteous and worthy to worship God. Therefore God wants His Church to be engaged in praise and worship and be intimate with Him. God wants to be loved back, praised and worshipped by His redeemed, the collective Body of Christ, as well as privately in our dwelling places. As we worship God, our love for Him will develop and hence our intimacy with our Groom, the Lord Jesus Christ. Worship and intimacy with the Groom will therefore enable us to win the War Against Division in the Church simply because we are up against Satan, the ex-worship leader.

We should not forget that Satan could have humbled himself before God and repented, but he was too proud and too jealous to repent. He wanted what God was getting from His creation; he wanted the worship to belong to him too. Theologians say he was the worship leader in heaven before his fall. Leading the worship made him feel so important that he forgot that the worship belonged to his Creator, the one who created him, the one he was worshipping. God had deposited so much creativity in Satan that he began to imagine himself above his Creator. Satan knows the power of worship. He even knows how important worship is to God and how it pleases Him to be worshipped. This is the very reason he does everything possible to bring division among brethren. He fears unity among the born-again Saints of God, and he fears worship.

This is exactly our strategy against him, to do what he fears most, to come before God collectively as His Body in repentance from the sins of the Church in unity and in worship. This is the plan that God revealed to me, as our weapon of mass destruction to the devil's camp. God inhabits the praises of His people. As we continue to worship we will attract a fresh fire of the Holy Spirit into our lives and into our church denominations. The Holy Sprit brings healing and restoration in our lives and in our relationships; and therefore unity will be born in the Church, the Body of Christ.

To achieve this, we need humility to be quick to judge ourselves and repent from our rebellious ways individually and collectively as His Body. We need His Love in our own hearts, so we can be able to love one another. We need His Grace to focus on unity as His Body in order to be able to accomplish His will on earth. We need His Understanding on why we should do what we should do. We need His Wisdom on how to do it and when to start doing it. The Holy Spirit reveals secret things to God's people. There are more things we need to accomplish as the Body of Christ before Christ comes. We need to move in speed because we do not know when Christ is coming. It would be a shame if Christ came while we were still debating the issue of unity in the His Body. We need the Grace of God.

Therefore may God give us His Grace to humble ourselves and repent from our stumbling ways, and furthermore to repent as the Body of Christ. May our spiritual eyes be opened to see the desperate need for holiness in the Church, without which we will delay the fullness of God's favour upon the Church. We cannot afford to open doors for the enemy to bring condemnation upon us as those who claim to be in Christ yet are divided. Satan knows that lack of unity caused a lot of pain to Jesus while he walked this earth. It was the religious Jews, his own people, who opposed Jesus the most because they hated the truth that He spoke; they also hated the good that He did among the poor and the needy. He enjoyed this division among the Jews and he still uses the same spirit to divide families and the Church.

Therefore we need to seek the Grace of God for holiness in our daily walk. "The steps of a good man are ordered by the Lord: he delighteth in his way" (Ps 37: 23). The desire and quest for holiness in the Body of Christ will enable the Holy Spirit to transform our hearts. Then, we will be transformed through the Word of God, meditating on the Word and using the Word as our weapon against wrong thoughts that lead to sin; rebuking Satan with Jesus' authority that we have, and using the Word of God as we do so; binding his strongholds of division – witchcraft, lies, jealousy, criticism, rebelliousness, hatefulness, racism, tribalism, idolatry, competition among believers, based on Matthew 16: 19 and Matthew 18: 19; and pulling down these strongholds from the atmosphere into the pits of hell in Jesus' Mighty Name. We will soon be experiencing the fullness of God's favour.

I believe that unity will bring healing and deliverance on a large scale. The poor and unreachable will be reached and assisted and the gospel will be reaching them as we help them. The favour of God will bring supernatural provision into manifestation to enable the Church to do His work with speed throughout the earth.

And I will shake all nations, and the desire of all nations shall come and I will fill this house with glory, saith the Lord of Hosts. The silver is mine, and the gold is mine, saith the Lord of Hosts.

Haggai 2: 7–8

If we are quick to hear and obedient to the voice of God, He will not put us to shame. Ask of me, and I shall give thee the heathen for thine inheritance, and the uttermost parts of the earth for thy possession.

Psalm 2: 8–9

As this battle against division in the Church is a spiritual one, it requires no bullets but God's Love in our hearts. Only the Holy Spirit will transform us from within, as we humbly desire to truthfully repent and as we worship Him in Spirit and in Truth.

The following is from a great man of God:

Let's talk spiritual. Today we have millions of people sitting in our churches who have been "Bible taught" without being "Spirit taught". Many know everything about the book and nothing about the Author. The truth is: You can have Bible doctrines, Bible facts, isms and zisms stored in your head for a lifetime and never have a positive effect on your moral character, your feelings for others, or real peace of mind. However, spiritual truth is creative, warm, soul saving and transforming. Believe me, there is a vast difference between information and transformation! Amen? We are not saved by what we know... but who we know!

Paul the Apostle at one stage in his life was a brilliant religionist. He knew the law from A to Z, could translate Greek Hieroglyphics, read Babylonian cuneiform, and speak several different languages, he was a master of Theology, but didn't know a thing about God! Like many today, an unsaved religionist.

Remember this: the Devil is a better Theologian than any of us... But, he is still the devil! Just knowing the "Written Word" without knowing the "Living Word" will never satisfy the hungry heart. No, no! God's Revelation can only be received by spiritual minded people. "As many as are led by the Spirit are the children of God." We need to understand that truth consists not in correct doctrine alone but in correct doctrine plus the inward enlightening of the Holy Ghost.

To find our way out of darkness we need more than light... we also need sight! The beginning of knowledge is like the rising of the sun; the sunrise means nothing to the unseeing eye... the blind. Between light and sight there is a wide difference. One man may have light without sight; he is blind. Another may have sight without light, he is temporarily blind. The Gospel is the light, but only the Holy Ghost can give sight!

Consider the woman at the well, John Chapter 4. In verse 4 it says, "Jesus needed to go to Samaria." We never think of Jesus having a need. Do we? But a trained surgeon is not a surgeon without a patient. The fisherman needs a boat, the pilot is useless without a plane... a healer must have someone to heal... a saviour must have someone to save. So Jesus needed this woman at the well. She's very religious, she knows where to worship but not who to worship. Here is this woman who is very troubled, a sinner, with a broken past, a confused present, and a bleak future. But Jesus never looks at who you are or what you've done. He only sees what you can become!

Jesus opens the lines of communication by simply asking for a drink of water. And by doing this He opens Himself to humiliation. I often wondered, if He knew this woman's heart, and He did, then He knew in advance she would refuse Him. Then why allow this woman to put Him down? You see, the truth is: Jesus knew the traditional prejudice that was in her heart, she didn't. Sometimes you are not aware of the hidden feelings that are buried deep in your heart until the right circumstances bring them to the surface. The Holy Spirit knows just how to bring these feelings to the surface so you can deal with them.

Then Jesus very discreetly shifts the subject from religion to "Living Water" Spiritual! Here is a woman, deeply troubled searching for some answers. She had been married five times.

"The Spirit of Truth" supersedes everything. It breaks through all barriers. Racial, Denominational, Cultural, Social, and Financial. And God says, "By one Spirit I will baptize you all into one body, one church, *and one people." Just being in a "Big Church" doesn't make you a "big Christian". And signing the church card, shaking the preacher's hand and being baptised doesn't make you a child of God... As far as I'm concerned, you may as well write your name on the barn door, shake a mule's tail and jump in the pond. What makes you a child of God and sets you free is "having the love of God shed abroad in your heart and knowing the Holy Ghost truth!" Jesus shook this lady and then she shook Samaria..."*

So if after reading this story you feel shaken by the love of Jesus like the woman in Samaria, it makes two of us. As the Holy Spirit feels us afresh with God's love, then we shall become the salt of the earth and thus bring taste and flavour where there is none. Setting the captives free, healing the sick and bringing hope to the hopeless on a large scale as a United Church, the Bride of Christ.

The burden of Christ: The poor

In one of the visions God has given me concerning the poor and the injustice on the earth, I was put on a balcony in the early hours of the morning to observe a moving object far below. When I ran downstairs to see what it was, I discovered in horror that while I had had a good night's sleep, my disabled eldest daughter was crawling outside in the early hours of the morning with swollen eyes and the side of her face, looking very exhausted like she had never slept at all and trying to find somewhere hidden to sleep under the building where I was. I have also been personally put on the street for the night as a homeless person and I cannot adequately describe the loneliness, the pain, the desperation, the shame and the vulnerability associated with being homeless.

But the vision I was shown on 1st November 2009 of my upper body exposed in public and the ridicule I got from men in the vicinity was something else. I was very relieved to wake up and find that I was actually in my bed in my home and had not actually exposed myself, but God instantly reminded me that there were women going through what I had just experienced and that for them it was not a dream, it was their reality. Where much is given, much is required.

If God had not removed me from Zimbabwe at the time He did, where would I have got all the items required to enable me to care for my physically disabled daughter today? Disabled people crawl everywhere in the streets and into dirty public toilets where they touch other people's filth with their hands and use the same hands to beg for food and eat from the same dirty hands. We may avoid facing reality by turning our heads aside as we pass them by, but Jesus does not. He loves them as much as He loves us all. He died for everybody to have an abundant fruitful life.

This is the burden of the Lord Jesus Christ for the poor. He wants men and women who are not prejudiced to feel His pain and do something about it. As the Head of the Church, Jesus Christ sits on the right-hand side of His Father. He paid the price for His Body on earth to take the dominion that He suffered for. Where is the compassion in the Body of Christ? For how long are these things to continue being given a blind eye? How long are the cries of the captives supposed to last for before they can be heard? If the politicians are in charge and the Body of Christ on earth is quiet, whom is the Lord Jesus Christ supposed to entrust with His voice to speak on behalf of His suffering people? "Behold I come quickly" (Revelations 22: 7).

That is why every Believer needs to get intimate with Jesus and stop using church buildings as places of gossip and casting witchcraft spells on each other, especially God's black people. There is too much division by way of witchcraft in African families and communities. People you love and miss are so full of evil that you just have to keep them at arm's length. They are in covenant with Satan who drives them to be terrible oppressors of their own. Even some fallen born-again believers in Christ get trapped in witchcraft.

In view of this, God spoke to the Prophet Ezekiel:

Likewise, thou son of man, set thy face against the daughters of thy people; which prophesy out of their own heart; and prophesy thou against them, And say, Thus saith the Lord God; Woe to the women that sew pillows to all armholes, and make kerchiefs upon the head of every stature to hunt souls! Will you hunt the souls of my people, and will ye save the souls alive that come to you? And will ye pollute me among my people for handfuls of barley and for pieces of bread, to slay the souls that should not die, and to save the souls alive that should not live, by your lying to my people that hear your lies? Wherefore thus saith the Lord God; Behold, I am against your pillows, wherewith ye there hunt the souls to make them fly, and I will tear them from your arms, and will let the souls go that you hunt to make them fly. Your kerchiefs also will I tear, and deliver my people out of your hand, and they shall be no more in your hand to be hunted; and ye shall know that I am the Lord. Because with lies ye have made the heart of the righteous sad, who I have not made sad; and strengthened the hands of the wicked, that he should not return from his wicked way, by promising him life: Therefore ye shall see no more vanity, nor divine divinations: for I will deliver my people out of your hand: and ye shall know that I am the Lord.

Ezekiel 13: 17–23

Witches are bloodthirsty. They thrive on the blood of the innocent. Witchcraft is a result of a jealous and envious heart. James states:

But if ye have bitter envying and strife in your hearts, glory not, and lie not against the truth. This wisdom descendeth not from above, but is earthly, sensual, and devilish. For where envying and strife is, there is confusion and every evil work. But the wisdom that is from above is first pure, then peaceable, gentle, and easy to be entreated, full of mercy and good fruits, without partiality, and without hypocrisy. And the fruit of righteousness is sown in peace of them that make peace.

James 3: 14–18

African People, especially Zimbabweans, must repent from this evil that has caused so many innocent souls to suffer and to perish. They must stop being used by Satan like that because at the end Satan will dump them like a hot potato. Among witches there is always suspicion and division and hatred. When they gather together pretending to love each other, it is because they are planning to destroy the life of the innocent. There is no heaven for witches. Witches must seriously consider breaking the agreements and the covenants that they made with Satan before it's too late for them. Hell is a permanent place of destiny for the lost soul.

There is witchcraft among other nations as well, but I am addressing black people because their long suffering has moved God, although His compassion does not alter His expectations. He is Holy and He only moves for the humble, those who are ready to acknowledge their sin and to repent of their sinful ways. He vindicates the weak, the hurting innocent, and recompenses them. He rewards holiness and integrity. God will not force anyone to leave their rebellious ways. He already bought us with the price of the precious blood of His Son, Jesus. He gave us free will to choose.

How can His divided body worship Him?

A friend sent me a forwarded email, which read, "When you were born you were crying and everyone around you was smiling". I thought hard about it and I realised that it was out of order and should never be so for a newborn baby. The spirit inside a new-born baby came from God in Heaven, a place of worship. Once it got into the womb of its mother it figured out that something had gone wrong around it: the worship had suddenly ceased. It was not used to any other sound except that of music, the sound of worship. As the baby developed its spirit strove and longed for the sound of music, those voices of worship like the ones it was used to. The silence would cause the baby to kick and kick inside its mother's womb, but there was hardly any music or worship, although it began to hear other voices. At last, it was time to come out and hear worship once again, but the day of its birth was even worse, there was chaos all around. There were screaming voices similar to those of people who were condemned to death in hell. What was going on? It is a shock indeed to come out to this cold, unwelcoming place where there is no worship, no music. The baby wonders where is my Father, what happened to all the worshippers and what place is this? Why should a newborn baby not cry?

So if unity in the Body of Christ is absent, how can we worship Him as a Church, His Bride? A broken body is in casualty; it cannot function properly unless it is delivered, healed and restored. As the worship begins around the earth, healing and restoration in the Body of Christ will also begin. The love of God will then be imparted in us for unity. Yes, Jesus will be glorified by His united Body. The enemy will be put to shame as we unite in the love of God. With men it is impossible, but not with God, for with God all things are Possible.

Whoso offereth praise glorifieth me: and to him that ordereth his conversation aright will I shew the salvation of God.

Psalm 50: 23

Let us therefore glorify Christ in love and unity. Unity in the Body of Christ will enable us to bring change in our communities and transform the unjust systems of this earth. In this book I have highlighted a lot of injustice on the poor, the fatherless, the widows and black people in the systems and services that are available to the public. The united Body of Christ has the responsibility to ensure that earthly systems operate in line with God's principles, because He is a God of order. God will not come down and do this for us. Complaining and whining about injustice while we do not all participate in bringing change to pass will not help.

In Matthew 6 Jesus said:

After this manner therefore pray ye: Our Father which Art in heaven, Hallowed be Thy Name. Thy kingdom come. Thy will be done in earth, as it is in heaven. Give us this day our daily bread. And forgive us our debts, as we forgive our debtors. And lead us not into temptation, but deliver us from evil: For thine is the kingdom, and the power, and the glory. Forever. Amen.

Matthew 6: 9–14

God wants to see His united Body planning for change on a larger scale based on the creativity He has given us individually. Remembering that it is He who gives us power to get wealth, that His covenant of blessings that He promised to our fathers Abraham, Isaac and Jacob may be fulfilled in the earth. It is time to repossess the wealth that the enemy stole from us due to our rebelliousness to God. It is time to take back our dominion in the earth and reach the uttermost parts with His Gospel of love and unity; to reach the unreachable and to touch the untouchable with His Gospel of love in order to build the kingdom of God in preparation for the coming of His Son, the risen Christ, Jesus our Lord and Saviour, for His Bride, the Church.

> *He brought me up also out of an horrible pit, out of the miry clay, and set my feet upon a rock, and established my goings. And He hath put a new song in my mouth, even praise unto our God: many shall see it, and fear, and shall trust in the Lord.*
>
> *Psalm 40: 2–3*

Satan brought division in the Church, but we cannot afford to remain silent about it. Now is the time to declare the War Against Division in the Church!

In my vision, I saw a huge group of black men being trained in how to worship God, hours of worship on their knees. It was a place in Africa. I was attracted to get closer and as I got closer I heard a loud voice saying, "Worship: Your tool to departure, as the world economy system changes!"

2025 - Conclusion

The title of this book was given by God to me, fifteen years ago. Many readers who did not understand it before, I am sure now do. At the time of reproducing this book in 2025, I noted that insights and revelations that were given to me by God have been proven to be precise. There are many unfolding events happening around the world that are aimed at changing the status quo; these events were not happening when I first published this book in 2010. These events only prove that God is not a man that He should lie. (Numbers 23: 19)

We are witnessing events like third world countries that are currently grappling to take control of their own resources and economy.

Politicians are still fighting for the control of the economy. Many critical decisions are still being made outside God. Policies that are rebellious and dangerous like "Assisted Dying for the terminally ill and legalising abortion laws that threaten unborn babies from conception to full term in birth, are currently being debated in parliament in the United Kingdom. These are policies that are threatening the lives of those who cannot speak for themselves and meanwhile God, the Creator of heaven and earth, is still not being consulted through His Church.

Billions in money are being spent in weapons of war whilst there is no consideration for the poor. In some countries, pensioners are being threatened with poverty through the taxation of their pension, meanwhile the legal age of retirement is being rapidly increased by those in power, in order to delay paying out pensioners. Long life is a blessing from God but those in power see it as an economic burden upon them and an opportunity for their political budgets to benefit from pensioners' money. In some third world countries where there is lawlessness, pensions are raided so they only benefit those in institutions that are entrusted to manage them and are withheld from the authorised beneficiaries.

God owns us His creation; He owns the earth and the fullness thereof and that includes the world's economy, see Psalm 24: 1 and Haggai 2: 8.

As Jesus spoke of signs preceding His return in Matthew 24:12, the evidence of this is everywhere before our eyes. Sin is basically on the increase. There is lawlessness and wickedness in high places of authority. There is no justice for the vulnerable, the poor and the oppressed. God Himself is bringing justice in the earth because the earth is His. He will judge the living and the dead, see (Acts 10:42, Timothy 4:1, 1 Peter 4:5 and Revelation 20: 11-12)

Simply put, "The wealth of the sinner is laid up for the just" (Proverbs 13.22) This is the portion of a wicked man with God and the heritage of oppressors, which they shall receive of the Almighty. Though he heaps up silver as the dust and prepares raiment as the clay; he may prepare it, but the just shall put it on and the innocent shall divide the silver. (Job 27: 13,16 -17)

"Both riches and honour come of thee, and thou reignest over all; and in thine hand is power and might; and in thine hand it is to make great, and to give strength unto all." (1 Chronicles 29:4)

"He that is unjust, let him be unjust still; and he which is filthy, let him be filthy still; and he that is righteous, let him be righteous still; and he that is holy, let him be holy still." (Revelation 22:11)

"And behold, I come quickly and my reward is with me, to give every man according as his work shall be." (Revelation 22: 12)

There is no question on the power of worship. Worship has been happening on an unprecedented level globally. People are coming to the Lord globally like never before, through Worship. Intimacy with the Lord Jesus Christ has been happening globally as His people begin to worship Him with a hunger for Him and in sincerity. In Africa the UNITY of the Body of Christ is happening through WORSHIP! Miracles are happening in individual lives at home and in the collective Body of Christ. Friend, do not be left behind, worship Him! JESUS IS COMING SOON!

My Gratitudes

First, to my three daughters, Kholi, Sisa and Joy, you are a great blessing in my life. Thank you for teaching me how to be a mother and how to care. May God be glorified in your lives! I love you all very much and I am so blessed to be your mother. You're the best! To Kholi: "The Lord upholdeth all that fall, and raiseth up all those that be bowed down" (Psalm 145: 14). "Then shall thou walk in thy way safely, and thy foot shall not stumble" (Proverbs 3: 23).

I give Glory to God for divinely connecting me with my man of God, an uncommon mentor and His prophet, who has taught me and encouraged me since April 2005 to see myself only as God sees me, to trust God, to obey God and how to meditate on His Word always and never to allow Satan to make me focus on my weaknesses, as God is my source of strength. Thank you prophet of God for believing in me even when I did not understand what was happening, and for your patience and persistent prayers that move God on my behalf. God is your vindicator. Thank you for your continued prayers, encouragement and support in difficult times. Thank you from the bottom of my heart and may God richly bless you and all your loved ones. I love you very much and I wish you all a long, healthy, wealthy, peaceful and joyful life! Thanks to Dr Mike Murdock's $58 seed principle that divinely connected me with an uncommon mentor. God bless him.

The proceeds from the book sales are for the completion of my father Rev. John Mhlabi's projects for the needy, the completion of his SIYABONGA ORPHANAGE AND OLD PEOPLE'S HOME in Matabeleland, Zimbabwe. God gave him this burden following his own suffering from the beatings he received from President Robert Mugabe's

North Korean-trained army, the Fife Brigade aka Gukurahundi, and the holocaust of thousands of his Ndebele/Zulu people from 1982–1990. The extermination and oppression of the Ndebele people never stopped to this day. They languish in prisons for no reason and hence the neglect of the region's orphans and the elderly that has continued to this day while the perpetrators remain in power. Thank you for your valuable purchase. God bless you.

Bibliography

Activist Cont Mhlanga: Cont Mhlanga,Byo Zimbabwe

Haggard, Rider Henry (1885) *King Solomon's Mines,* www.statemaster.com/encyclopedia/king_solomon's_mines.

Intouch.org

JohnPerkins.org

Maathai, Wangari (2009) *The Challenge for Africa.* London: William Heinemann.

Nkomo, Joshua M. (2001) *Nkomo: The Story of My Life.* Harare: Sapes Books.

Roden, John (1999) *Northward from Cape Town: The Anglican Railway Mission in Southern Africa.* York: Sacram Publishing.

Smith, Ian (1997) *The Great Betrayal.* London: Blake Publishing.

Stiff, Peter (2000) *Cry Zimbabwe: Independence – Twenty Years On.* Johannesburg: Galago Publishing.

WisdomOnline.com

"Winning Ways" by Pastor Peter Popoff

About the Author

T he Author is a wife, a mother and a mother-in-law. Born in Rhodesia (now Zimbabwe) she is the 7th of 10 children to the late Rev J J Mhlabi and Mrs D Mhlabi. Married to Ian Mumford in Bulawayo, Zimbabwe she then relocated with her family to the United Kingdom where she studied Mental Health Nursing but left soon after completing her course at the Call of God to do His work. The Author's passion is to encourage Christians to praise and worship God through thick and thin, because He created Man for His pleasure, to worship Him (Rev 4:11) and to focus on HIM not on their circumstances or challenges; to praise and worship the Lord in good times or bad times because HE deserves it. HE redeemed us through Christ.

www.ingramcontent.com/pod-product-compliance
Lightning Source LLC
Chambersburg PA
CBHW032051020426
42335CB00011B/284